Opera Encore

Collected Essays on the Grand Art

Joseph A. Kestner

The Calliope Group

ISBN: 979-8-9866015-0-2 Trade Paperback
ISBN 979-8-9866015-1-9 eBook

Library of Congress Control Number: 2022942826

All essays originally appeared in *Opera News*, except the following:

"East is East," *Opera Cues*. Houston Grand Opera.

"Elektra as Nightmare," *The Washington Opera*.

"Exotic Seas," *The Washingotn Opera*.

"Fatal Man," *The Washington Opera*.

"Nineteenth Century Gamble," *Opera Cues*.

"Patience." Unpublished Lecture.

"The Combat of Sexuality," *The Washington Opera*.

"The German Carmen," *The Washington Opera*.

"The Impossible Dream." *The Dallas Opera Magazine*.

"The Scandal of *Hernani*," *The Dallas Opera Magazine*.

Other Books by Joseph A. Kestner

Jane Austen: Spatial Structure of Thematic Variations
The Spatiality of the Novel
Protest and Reform: The British Social Novel by Women
*Mythology and Misogyny: The Social Discourse of Nineteenth-Century
        British Painting*
Masculinities in Victorian Painting
Sherlock's Men: Conan Doyle, Masculinity and Cultural History
The Edwardian Detective
Sherlock's Sisters
Masculinities in British Adventure Fiction, 1880-1915

Cover Art: *L'escalier de l'Opéra* (1877), Louis Béroud

Table of Contents

Introduction

Joseph Kestner fell in love with opera when he was a graduate student at Columbia University. As a faculty member at Princeton and then the City University of New York, he continued to avidly attend Metropolitan Opera performances.

An English professor, he was in the habit of researching and writing, and in 1977 submitted an unsolicited piece on *Il Tabarro* to *Opera News*, the magazine of the Metropolitan Opera Guild. There was no response. Undaunted, he sent in another article, this one discussing *La Bohème*. Several months later he received a letter from Robert Jacobson, Editor of the magazine, stating he "enjoyed the writing enormously" and planned to use the *Bohéme* article in the March Broadcast Issue. Thus began Joseph Kestner's long and fruitful relationship with *Opera News*. He wrote years later:

> It has been one of the most rewarding aspects of my life as a writer to write for *Opera News*. I consider it a privilege to be included. There are, after all, only 17 or 18 issues a year. When people asked me what it is like to write for the magazine, I reply—very tough, very rigorous, and very demanding. In ten pages I must condense a mass of material, for the novice and the specialist. It must cater to the new people in the audience as well as the regulars and the diehards. As an example, I recently spent two days at the Folger Shakespeare Library in Washington researching the idea of Romeo and Juliet for an essay

on Gounod's opera, *Roméo et Juliette.* I now have the challenge of digesting, condensing, and wrenching that material into an essay that meets the standards of *Opera News.* The style is extremely difficult to achieve: at once engaging, popular, and substantive.

I did not know how lucky I was to be in the magazine until one day I visited the *Opera News* offices and glanced at a huge pile on a side-table. Immediately I knew what that was—the notorious "slush pile" dreaded by every writer—all the unsolicited manuscripts sent in by eager people. I didn't say a word. I was just glad my work had survived that competition.

The essays collected here show the breadth of Kestner's work and his ability to engage the varied readership he mentioned. His insights remain as timeless as the operas he wrote about and offer everyone, from the newest fan to the lifetime devotee, information to deepen their understanding of the genre.

In addition to *Opera News*, Kestner wrote for other publications, most notably for the Houston and Washington, D.C. operas. He continued to write about opera until the early 2000s when his academic commitments and interests at the University of Tulsa turned to film studies and cinema. He died suddenly on August 24, 2015, while preparing for a trip to research a book on Ingmar Bergman, a fellow opera lover.

OPERA AND THE VISUAL ARTS

As you will discover reading this collection, the visual arts were an important element and influence on the creation of many of the operas discussed. To enhance your reading and to reference the artwork mentioned, we have created a QR code below to access online images of the pieces. We hope that viewing them while reading will deepen your experience and enjoyment of the essays and the operas.

You can also discover the resources by visiting:
www.thecalliopegroup.com/opera-encore-resources/

East is East:
Verdi and *Aïda*

In the nineteenth century, "the Orient" designated the Middle East, including Egypt, Morocco, Algeria, Tunisia, the Holy Land, Syria, Lebanon, Turkey, Persia and sometimes India. Orientalism comprised the perception by the West of the East.

This construction was indelibly caught by Rudyard Kipling (born in India) in two memorable statements. Kipling declared, "Once you have heard the call of the East, you will never hear anything else." At the same time, he wrote: "East is East and West is West, and never the twain shall meet."

At a time when the Western world was fascinated by the East, Verdi apparently did not share the general enthusiasm. When his friend Camille du Locle, who was to play a major role in the evolution of *Aïda*, returned from a voyage to Egypt, Verdi commented that Egypt was "a land which once possessed a grandeur and a civilization that I could never bring myself to admire." In fact, Verdi never visited Egypt, not even for the premiere of *Aïda* on December 24, 1871, at the Cairo Opera House.

Orientalism in Europe was prompted by imperial conquest, traveling, archaeology, photography, literature, the visual arts and previous operas. Three events sparked these attitudes: In 1798, Napoleon landed his forces at Alexandria, preparing to conquer Egypt. In 1799, French soldiers discovered the Rosetta stone, with its texts in Greek, Egytian demotic, and hieroglyphic. Deciphered by Champollion in 1822, it unlocked Egypt.

There was much else that called the world's attention to Egypt. In 1833, an obelisk from the Temple of Luxor was removed to the Place de la Concorde in Paris. The Prince of Wales visited Egypt in 1862. In 1869, the Suez Canal was opened; the Cairo Opera House was inaugurated with a performance of Verdi's *Rigoletto* on November first of the same year. By that time, Thomas Cook, who founded the first modern travel agency, had established tours to Egypt and the Holy Land so his patrons could travel in comfort. England received its own obelisk in 1878, when Cleopatra's Needle from Alexandria was erected on the Thames Embankment in London, and in 1879 a similar obelisk was brought to Central Park in New York City—like the ones in Paris and London, it was a gift of the Khedive (viceroy) of Egypt. In September 1882, the British took control of Egypt after the Battle of Tel-el-Kebir to secure the Suez Canal, their lifeline to India.

Literary texts fired curiosity about the East. Among the most prominent were Byron's "Turkish" tales such as *The Giaour* (1813), *The Corsair* (1814), and *Sardanapalus* (1821), replete with pirates, slaughter and seraglios. In 1859, Edward FitzGerald translated *The Rubáiyát of Omar Khayyám*, and readers devoured its ecstatic yet brooding quatrains.

Ballet and painting did not lag behind. One thinks of *La Bayadère* (1877), set in India; *Le Corsaire* (1856), set in the Mediterranean; and *Schèhèrazade* (1910), evoking *The Thousand and One Nights*. About the last, Gothic novelist Horace Walpole declared, "I do not think the Sultaness' narratives very natural or very probable, but there is a wildness in them that captivates!" Artists from Eugène Delacroix in France to Lord Frederic Leighton in England were obsessed with the Middle East. The Arab Hall stuns any visitor to Leighton's London residence, which is now open to the public as an art gallery and museum.

Burning down the house brought down the house. A series of operas appeared that contained Orientalist elements ranging from forbidden sex to spectacular immolations; before *Aïda*. These included Bizet's *Les Pêcheurs de perles* (1863) and Meyerbeer's *L'Africaine* (1865); after *Aïda* came Saint-Saëns' *Samson et Dalila* (1877), Delibes' (1883), and Massenet's *Hérodiade* (1891) and *Thaïs* (1894), with Strauss's *Salome* providing a coda in 1905. By this time, opera attendees could hear works evoking exotic lands and then see the real thing, as the Orient Express began in 1883 to carry passengers between Paris and Istanbul.

In his books *Orientalism* (1978) and *Culture and Imperialism* (1993), the late Edward Said, raised in Cairo, detailed the West's construction of the East as a systematic domination of the region through militarism, economics, political coercion, and oppression. Strongly relevant to Verdi's *Aïda* is Said's thesis about the Cairo Opera House. To Said, Cairo is divided into two cities: the Eastern part, considered native and pre-industrial; and the Western section, colonial and steam-powered. The Cairo Opera (destroyed by fire in 1971, restored and reopened in 1988) was symbolic in its location at the center of the north-south axis of the city, facing its European part. Interestingly, the audience at the premiere of *Aïda* was predominantly European.

Aïda is an opera about two African nations at war. Let's ask a key question. When does it happen? Answer: no one knows beyond the libretto's description, "the epoch of the Pharaohs, in Memphis and Thebes." Owen Rachleff (*Opera News*, December 15, 1962) believed that the time of the New Kingdom (1573-712 BCE) fit the opera's scenario well.

Rachleff pinpoints the era to a series of wars fought between Egypt and Ethiopia, recorded in the first book of Chronicles in the Bible, around 930 BCE. From 1100 to 800 BCE, the priests held supreme power in Egypt, with the Pharaoh a figurehead; this appears to be the case in *Aïda,* with Ramfis controlling the state. Yet, no dates or specifics are given in the work itself. This enables *Aïda* to be the stuff of legend, ready made for an Orientalist project.

The synopsis of the story was by Auguste Mariette, a famous French Egyptologist. Camille du Locle wrote a prose scenario in French. The versified libretto was by Antonio Ghislanzoni, with whom Verdi corresponded intensely during the creation of the opera. But Egyptology is not Egypt, as Edward Said noted. In spite of Mariette's involvement and Verdi's research of ancient Egyptian culture, invalid elements remain in *Aïda*. In the original costume sketches by Auguste Mariette, the Ethiopians are black while the Egyptians appear Caucasian. (The same is the case in the famous 1953 film version of *Aïda* directed by Clemente Fracassi and starring Sophia Loren. Renata Tebaldi provided her singing voice.) Furthermore, no captain of the guard would have commanded the Egyptian army as Radames does in the opera; the Pharaohs led their armies. There were no triumphal arches in Egypt—these were a Roman invention. There would have been no Temple of Vulcan, where Radames was condemned to die, because the Egyptians knew nothing of this Roman god. The punishment of death for traitors was sometimes live burial, but another more likely method would have been being burned alive. It is understood that such inaccuracies are part of the poetic license artists take when they create a work of fiction, and while they do not disturb audiences, some of them do demonstrate Orientalism. But, then, Verdi never pretended absolute adherence to historical and cultural truth, once writing, "To copy reality can be a good thing, but to invent reality is better."

"I've never traveled, but I dare say you can't judge Egypt by *Aïda*," declares a character in Ronald Firbank's 1926 novel, *Concerning the Eccentricities of Cardinal Pirelli*. Nor can one judge Ethiopia by Orientalist attitudes that prevailed during the era of the opera's premiere. On March 1, 1896, Italy invaded Ethiopia with disastrous consequences. One hundred thousand Ethiopians decimated the Italians at the Battle of Aduwa. Had Italy bought into the stereotypes of the East as passive, feminine, chaotic and emotional and the West as active, masculine, ordered, rational?

Where is Egypt? What is it? Verdi wanted the final duet of the lovers "O terra, addio" (Act IV, scene ii) to be "ethereal" or "vaporous." It may be, but *Aïda* is as enduring as stone.

A Lyre at the Scaffold:
Giordano and *Andrea Chénier*

On July 25, 1794, the French poet André Chénier was conveyed from the Conciergerie prison to the Place du Trone Renverse (now the Place de la Nation), having been tried earlier that day before the Revolutionary Tribunal as an *ennemi du peuple*. With him was his fellow writer Jean-Antoine Roucher, who at the sight of the guillotine collapsed. Chénier is reported to have said, "Courage, ami, d'autres rivages!" (Courage, my friend, other shores!) When Roucher lamented the loss of his wife and daughters, Chénier responded, "C'est un reve qui finit!" (That's a dream which has ended!) Chénier's final gesture was to strike his forehead and exclaim, "I have done nothing for posterity, but I had something here." Three days later the architect of the Terror hmself, Maximilien Robespierre, was guillotined.

Had Chénier lived two days longer, he might have evolved into a greater poet but never into the martyr of legend. That legend has been immortalized in the opera *Andrea Chénier*, premiered at La Scala on March 28, 1896, by Umberto Giordano (1867-1948)—the fifth, along with Puccini, Cilea, Mascagni and Leoncavallo, of the most prominent Italian verismo composers. The French Revolution has produced a quartet of famous operas, including Massenet's *Thérèse* (1907), Poulenc's *Dialogues des Carmélites* (1957) and Einem's *Dantons Tod* (1947), and while the Poulenc recently has gained a place in the repertory, only *Andrea Chénier* has survived the ruthless test of time, thanks to a superb libretto by Luigi Illica (librettist of *La Bohème*), three extraordinary tenor arias and a Liebestod climactic duet.

The ultimate reason for the survival of *Chénier*, however, lies deeper—in a psychodynamic identification of composer and revolutionary poet. Both were on the brink, at a certain stage of their lives: Chénier was slaughtered, Giordano triumphed. This breathtaking existential challenge—was it fate? God? luck? plan? genius?—is the soul of *Andrea Chénier*.

In 1888, the Italian publisher Edoardo Sonzogno sponsored a competition for three new one-act operas. Among the aspirants was the young Giordano, who submitted *Marina*, based on a poor libretto by Enrico Golisciani. Of the seventy-three candidates who submitted works, Giordano was one of the six finalists. In the end, his opera was ranked sixth, and the prize went to Pietro Mascagni for *Cavalleria Rusticana*, which received its stupendous premiere in 1890. Sonzogno did not forget Giordano, however, and when he asked to hear *Marina* in December 1890, he told Giordano, "I will not take the work, because I do not like the libretto. But I will engage you to write a new opera." This was to become *Mala Vita*, premiered to considerable acclaim in 1892. When *Mala Vita* was performed in Vienna, Eduard Hanslick felt it was "vividly interesting . . . new and bold." Giordano had arrived.

Giordano's connection with the new school of Italian veristic composers is reflected in his letters following the premiere of *Mala Vita*. Visiting Venice in September, he wrote home, "Last night, after dining with Sonzogno, Mascagni, Cilèa, Leoncavallo and various other artists, we took a gondola along the Grand Canal . . . There was shouting and laughing all the way, beginning with Sonzogno, who is so proud at seeing a new generation of artists around him that he makes you think of a valiant captain at the head of his army."

Several days later, Giordano heard *Lohengrin* and was deeply moved: "Last night I went to the opera to listen to *Lohengrin*. I thank God, who has given me the ability to experience deep emotion that the majority of human beings must be unable to feel. I had never heard *Lohengrin* on the stage, although I have known the work by heart since I was a child. What in the world could give me such happiness? Only music."

This happiness was not to last. Like Chénier, Giordano found himself on a precipice. When his next effort, *Regina Diaz* (1894), failed, Sonzogno cut him: "I realize that, in spite of *Mala Vita*, you are completely lacking in musical talent. Art is not for you. I am withdrawing my support." When the composer Alberto Franchetti promised to give Giordano the libretto being prepared for him on the life of Chénier, Sonzogno relented to this extent: "I shall let you have the 300 lire a month for another year. But after that I won't listen to anyone, not even Franchetti. This is your last chance." To be near his librettist, Illica, Giordano moved from Naples to Milan, living in squalor. When Illica expressed compassion, Giordano was stoic: "Don't worry about it. Give me good verses and leave the rest to me."

Knowing literally that his musical life was at stake, Giordano kept in constant communication with Illica during 1895. A combination of praise and subtle criticism spurred Illica's muse. "It was a marvelous idea to put the 'Tribunal' into the third act. Thus the fourth act remains with just a single love duet, since the situation is so interesting. I am at work. The chorus of *cocottes* in the second act is very finely wrought; it is even more beautiful than the chorus of shepherdesses [in Act I]. I also have rewritten the prelude of the first act. So I am awaiting your revisions to complete the first act, which I can't wait to have."

On another occasion Giordano wrote, "Yesterday I completed the beginning of the second act up to the passing of the tumbril. I assure you this is beautiful stuff, because I've written it with enthusiasm. I'm very much in love with this Act II . . . Ah, if *Chénier* goes well!" Toward the premiere, however, Giordano's doubts vanished: "You will see that it will be a revelation. I have written a very beautiful opera, and I assure you I will have an enormous success."

Illica fashioned his libretto from a number of sources, including editorial remarks of Henri de Latouche, the first editor of Chénier's poetry in 1819; Arsène Houssaye's *Gallery of the Eighteenth Century*; Jules Barbier's drama *André Chénier* (1849); Joseph Méry's novel *André Chénier* (1856); and the Goncourt brothers' *History of French Society during the Revolution* (1854). Latouche inspired the trial in Act III and Houssaye the general atmosphere of the final act, although Illica failed to incorporate the eyewitness testimony of Chénier's execution, preferring fictitiously that Chénier die with Maddalena. Méry's novel incorporates a trial scene, a countess and her servant, and an exchange of letters, all of which suggested incidents for the drama *André Chénier*. The fact that Maddalena changes identities with the prisoner Idia Legray is inspired by Sidney Carton's assuming the identity of Charles Darnay in Dickens' *A Tale of Two Cities*.

Giordano's awareness of the historical Chénier was perhaps greater than Illica's. Originally Illica had Maddalena and Andrea sing only a duet in the first act, but Giordano wanted to present Chénier more sharply delineated as a poet; the result was the splendid *Improvviso* ("Un dì all'azzuro spazio"). Part of its success, however, is the fact that some of the aria is derived from Chénier's own poetry, the famous "Hymn to Justice" of 1787. This vein of authenticity contributes to the survival of *Chénier*.

The opera incorporates many of the literary modes in which Chénier expressed himself, including pastoral, satiric *iambes* and prose political invective. Chénier outlined his idea of poetry in "L'Invention" of 1787, arguing that writers must recognize the examples of their ancient predecessors without slavishly imitating them:

From their ancient flowers let us make honey;
To depict our ideas let us borrow their colors;
Let us light our torches at their poetic fires;
Let us write ancient verses with new thoughts.

Chénier's Greek mother had taught him a reverence for the classics, which he felt must act as models, even as writers infuse contemporary ideas into epic or lyric forms. In his *Elegies*, begun in 1787, Chénier evokes the spirit of Horace (No. 16), Propertius (No. 10), Tibullus (No. 8) and Ovid (No. 7), to specific types such as the *paraklausithyron* or lament of the lover outside the mistress' door. Even in such erotic poems, however, Chénier addresses liberty, which while connoting freedom from a mistress' cruelty also can carry a tinge of political awareness:

My dear liberty, my only inheritance,
Treasure unacknowledged while we use it,
So sweet when lost, alas!, and so soon regretted,
Do you await me on those shores, dear liberty?

The final two *Elegies*, Nos. 24 and 25, are arresting in their despairing, eerie premonitions of an early death:

> Often, disgusted with being enslaved and drinking
> The bitter cup called life to the dregs . . .
> I gaze at my tomb, longed-for sanctuary;
> I smile at death. (No. 24)

. . .

> I die. Before the night I will end my day's journey.
> My rose has faded before it scarcely opened. (No. 25)

This unifying of eroticism, poetry, death and liberty, so evident in the *Elegies*, provided Illica and Giordano with the essence of Chénier's nature. When the Revolution broke out in 1789, Chénier was in London as a secretary in the French embassy. When he returned to Paris around May 1790, he became a convinced constitutional monarchist. He began his political journalism in August with his "Advice to the French People on Its True Enemies," in which he praised "moderate enthusiasm" and noted that "the wicked are never powerful except from the ignorance of those who hearken to them." In the 1791 "Observations of the Spirit of Party," Chénier denounced the hypocrisy that "sows such seeds of hatred . . . that the most preposterous accusations . . . do not astonish anyone." Chénier's virulent opposition to the Jacobins was soon to endanger him, even as he began writing poetry extremely political in nature.

After the disintegration of the constitutional party in August 1792, Chénier withdrew to Versailles, where he wrote his famous "Ode to Versailles" the following month. Chénier asks that Versailles nourish "the flickering flame of my pale torch, if I am destined to live," noting that the palace has been "witness to the success of evil." One of the most political of his poems was the "Ode to Charlotte Corday," executed on July 18, 1793, for having slain Jean-Paul Marat, an outspoken Terrorist, whose death was immortalized by Jacques Louis David. Refusing to denounce her, but rather regarding her as a defender of freedom, Chénier wrote:

> Truth is silent! In its numbed mouth its tongue,
> Constrained by chains of fear,
> Refuses the just homage to such glorious deeds!
> No, no, I will not honor you in silence,

You who by your death tried to resurrect France . . .
Your sweet nature, your simple and kind words,
Showed the government that however powerful crime may be,
One who renounces his life is more powerful than evil.

He concluded about Corday: "Only you were a man, who avenged the human race."

Four of Chénier's poems, however, have a direct bearing on the configuration of the narrative of Giordano's *Andrea Chénier*. *The Improvviso*, which Giordano demanded to delineate Chénier's character as poet, prompted Illica to turn to Chénier's "Hymn to Justice" of 1787 for part of its language. Set at the Château de Coigny in 1789, the soiree already has witnessed a pastoral entertainment when Chénier is asked to improvise a poem. The "love" he praises is the love of one's fatherland, "patria mia," which for him subsumes, on a top B-flat, all other forms. The operatic Chénier, like his historical counterpart, sees the country corrupted by the clergy and aristocracy, who care nothing for the sufferings of the poor, the priest who does not help a beggar.

In the "Hymn" Chénier records:
I have witnessed lamentable misery in villages,
Ghastly begging and harsh sorrow. I have seen you in your chattels,
  indigent laborer,
Cursing the severity of a greedy and merciless treasury,
Pouring forth useless tears at the feet of the great,
Everything soaked in sweat, barren for yourself,
Discouraged from living, full of a righteous dismay;
Forced labor, duties, corroding debts, heavy taxes,
A source of oppression and various scourges.
Twenty brigands, invested with the holy name of prince,
Unite to destroy a sad province.

Illica and Giordano omit from this poem the praise of England, which observes laws, and the utopian retreat with which the poem concludes. However, the number of repeated notes in the vocal line reinforces that this is supposed to be a poet reciting.

In its essence, the *Improvviso* captures the spirit of Chénier's apostrophe to Justice, where love is communal, fraternal, equal. In fact, in the triangle of Chénier/Gérard/Maddalena one may see symbolized the three revolutionary ideals of Liberty/Equality/Fraternity. Chénier's awareness of the inequities of French society in the poem proved all too prophetic. Echoing this insight, the opera then proceeds with the gavotte, interrupted by the incursion of beggars into the château.

The remaining acts of the opera are set during the Terror, 1794. The scene of the tribunal of July 24, 1794, in Act III contains Chénier's defense of himself "Sì, fui soldato"—a historical misconstruction, since Chénier was only briefly in the military during 1782-83. In its nautical imagery, with the poet compared to a ship, the aria echoes the marine images of Chénier's *Elegies* No. 17 and No. 18, in the latter of which he imagines sailing to Byzantium. More closely linked to Chénier's poetry is "Come un bel dì di maggio" of Act IV, derived from the immortal *Iambes* No. 9, "Comme un dernier rayon!" and reputed to have been written only days before Chénier's execution. Chénier had been arrested on March 7, 1794, and incarcerated at Saint-Lazare Prison, where he penned his virulent *Iambes*, denouncing the slaughters of the Terror: at one point, 1,285 people were guillotined within forty-six days.

Chénier's verse begins with sharp cognizance of his perilous situation:
> Like the last ray, like the final breeze which
> Animates the end of a beautiful day,
> At the foot of the scaffold I take up my lyre.
> Perhaps it soon will be my turn.

Chénier imagines the emissary of the tribunal taking him from prison; then, at line 25, he appears to begin to accept death, even welcoming it as a mode of deliverance. Beginning around line 40, however, Chénier longs instead to live, so that through his writing he may expose the villainy of his political enemies.

"I suffer, but I live," he declares; he describes his heart as "full of hatred, starved for justice," declaring, "You, virtue, weep if I die." In the opera, although the first lines of his aria echo the opening of *Iambes* No. 9, Chénier regards his imminent death as the highest point of his existence, asking only for one supreme moment of expression before his execution.

Rather than going to his death with a fellow poet, as did the historical Chénier, the opera's Chénier goes with Maddalena, who exchanges places with another prisoner to die with her lover. The inspiration for this episode is Chénier's famous ode to "a young female prisoner," dedicated to Aimée de Coigny, Duchesse de Fleury, whom Chénier met when both were imprisoned in Saint-Lazare and who escaped the guillotine to die in 1820. In the poem, Chénier imagines himself overhearing the lament of the prisoner:

> My beautiful journey is still far from its end!
> I am leaving, and of the elms which border my path
> I have scarcely passed the first.
> My lips have only a moment pressed
> The cup still full in my hands.
> I am only at my spring. I wish to see the harvest,
> And like the sun, from one season to the next,
> I wish to finish my year.
> I have seen only the fires of morning,
> I want to reach the end of my day.
> I do not want to die yet.

From this dedication of the ode to the Duchesse, Illica fashioned the meeting of Maddalena and Chénier, who, rather than regretting their deaths, embrace the guillotine in an ecstatic Liebestod: "Our death is the triumph of love! . . . Long live death—together!"

To enhance the mood of the Terrorist period, Giordano incorporated revolutionary songs into the 1794 acts of Chénier, including "Ca ira" and the Marseillaise. Mathieu, the sans-culotte, hums the Carmagnole while illuminating a bust of Marat. (In Act I, the shepherdesses and gavotte had encapsulated the *ancien régime*.) The inclusions of the Spy as an *incroyable* (dandy) and of Bersi as a *merveilleuse* (prostitute)—types actually part of the post-Terror *jeunesse dorée*—sustain the authenticity of a libretto invested with the language of Chénier. On the other hand, departures from accuracy, such as the imprisonment of Chénier for several days rather than four months, the death at dawn rather than sunset, and with his beloved rather than with fellow writer Roucher, increase the dramatic thrust of the opera.

The triumphant progress of *Chénier* was not an accident. The Risorgimento of the 1860s was a living memory; in 1893 the Worker's

Party became the Italian Socialist Party; and in May 1897 King Umberto I survived yet another assassination attempt. Illica subtitled the libretto for Chénier "dramma di ambiente storico" (drama of historical period), and Giordano's insistence on authenticity assured the immortality of the poet executed on the scaffold in 1794, in essence reborn in 1896. This fervid commitment by the composer—linked with Illica's brilliant libretto—granted *Chénier* its enduring force. As a colleague recalled, "Giordano neither trembled before *Chénier* nor doubted after it. He felt, rather, a profound inner conviction and certainty."

Wondrous Transformation:
Strauss and *Ariadne auf Naxos*

In March 1911 Hugo von Hofmannsthal wrote Richard Strauss about their continuing collaboration as librettist and composer, already established with *Elektra* (1909) and *Der Rosenkavalier* (1911): "If we were to work together once more on something (and by this I mean something important, not the thirty-minute opera for small chamber orchestra which is as good as complete in my head; it is called *Ariadne auf Naxos* and is made up of a combination of heroic mythological figures in eighteenth-century costume with hoopskirts and ostrich feathers and, interwoven in it, characters from the commedia dell'arte; harlequins and scaramouches representing the buffo element which is throughout interwoven with the heroic); well now, if we were to work together once more . . . it would have to possess colorful and clear-cut action." At this stage, *Ariadne auf Naxos* appeared to be a diversion. Little did Hofmannsthal know!

By July, however, he told Strauss that *Ariadne* was "at least equally as good" as *Der Rosenkavalier*. By 1913 he was confident that "this work of beauty will last." From being a detour on the road to *Die Frau ohne Schatten*, *Ariadne auf Naxos* gradually became central to the evolution of librettist and composer. Even before its premiere, Strauss confided to Hofmannsthal, "My score is a real masterpiece." It had to be—nearly fifty operas have competed for attention on the subject of Ariadne, her abandonment by Theseus and her rescue by Bacchus.

Like its mythological princess Ariadne, *Ariadne auf Naxos* is a work distinguished by transformation. First performed at Stuttgart in October 1912, where it was well received despite interminable intermissions, the opera was conceived as an "operatic divertissement" to follow a German version of Molière's *Le Bourgeois Gentillhomme*, a substitution for the excised Turkish ceremony of the drama. The revised version, first given in October 1916 in Vienna, was separated from the Molière altogether. For the revision, Strauss created the prologue, with its idealistic Composer.

Hofmannsthal's description of the work as "a spirited paraphrase of the old heroic style, interspersed with buffo ingredients" indicates the fundamental strategy of *Ariadne auf Naxos*—a system of contrasting polarities: mortal/immortal, *opera buffa/opera seria*, unfaithful sex/faithful love, terrestrial/transcendental, female/male, Eros (Desire)/Thanatos (Death). For Hofmannsthal, "Ariadne and Zerbinetta represent diametrical contrasts in female character." The greatness of *Ariadne*, however, emerges because these polarities coexist and interpenetrate. Hofmannsthal wrote Strauss in June 1911, "I build on contrasts to discover, above these contrasts, the harmony of the whole."

During early discussions about *Ariadne*, the librettist outlined his theme:

> What it is about is one of the straightforward and stupendous problems of life: fidelity; whether to hold fast to that which is lost, to cling to it even unto death—or to live, to live on, to get over it, to transform oneself, to sacrifice the integrity of the soul and yet in this transmutation to preserve one's essence, to remain a human being and not to sink to the level of the beast, which is without recollection . . . the heroic voice against the human. In the present case we have the group of heroes, demigods, gods—Ariadne, Bacchus (Theseus)—facing the human, the merely human group consisting of the frivolous Zerbinetta and her companions, all of them base figures in life's masquerade. Zerbinetta is in her element drifting out of the arms of one man into the arms of another: Ariadne could be the wife or mistress of *one* man only, just as she can be only *one* man's widow, can be forsaken only by *one* man. One thing, however, is still left even for her—the miracle, the god. To him she gives herself, for she believes him to be Death: he is both Death and Life at once; he it is . . .

18

who makes her an enchantress, the sorceress who herself transforms the poor little Ariadne . . . who preserves her for us and at the same time transforms her.

The function of Zerbinetta was to serve as foil to Ariadne, "the juxtaposition of the woman who loves only once and the woman who gives herself to many." Hofmannsthal continued, "But what to divine souls is a real miracle is to the earthbound nature of Zerbinetta just an everyday love affair. She sees in Ariadne's experience the only thing she can see—the exchange of an old lover for a new one. And so these two spiritual worlds are in the end ironically brought together in the only way in which they can be brought together, in noncomprehension." Strauss, however, was always partial to Zerbinetta, insisting on her reappearance during the transformation of Ariadne at the end of the opera. There is perhaps more comprehension on Zerbinetta's part than Hofmannsthal intended.

Hofmannsthal emphasized this transformation from a lower to a higher existence in Ariadne by replicating it in the figure of Bacchus:

> Bacchus represents no mere deus ex machina . . . His first affair was typical, with a woman of easy virtue, you may say, or you may call her Circe . . . Confronted with the enormity of erotic experience, all is laid bare to him in a flash—the assimilation with the animal, the transformation, his own divinity. So he escapes from Circe's embraces still unchanged, but not without a wound, a longing, not without knowledge. The impact on him now of this meeting with a being whom he can love, who is mistaken about him but is enabled by this very mistake to give herself to him wholly and to reveal herself to him in all her loveliness, who entrusts herself to him completely, exactly as one entrusts oneself to Death, this impact I need not expound further.

For Hofmannsthal this transcendence of the lower self by the higher constitutes the mystical essence of existence. In the opera, Ariadne and Bacchus—the one wounded by Theseus, the other by Circe—attain this ennobling consciousness. Hofmannsthal's brilliant decision to have the opera-buffa harlequinade of Zerbinetta and her lovers presented simultaneously with the opera-seria legend of Bacchus and Ariadne indicates the continuum of existence, the transcendental being a transformation of the lower but essential earthly experience, the metamorphosis from sensuality to spirituality. As Hofmannsthal recognized, "The conclusion rose more and more to a higher spiritual plane from something that was meant merely to amuse."

For Hofmannsthal, this transformation was distinguished by *das allomatische Element*, the "allomatic" or mutual transformation of one person by another. Having suffered at the hands of Theseus and Circe, respectively, Ariadne and Bacchus achieve a mystical transformation of each other. Ariadne asks Bacchus, "Wie schaffst du die Verwandlung?" (How will you transform me?). Later she hails him as "Verwandler" (transformer), and finally she can exclaim "Wie wunder, wunderbar verwandelst du!" (How miraculously, wonderfully you transform!). From its origin as a divertissement, the achieved *Ariadne auf Naxos* became a profound existential allegory.

Ariadne auf Naxos, however, is greater than even its explicit philosophical conception suggests. During its initial genesis in 1911, Strauss had suggested that the work "could become a companion piece to *Meistersinger*: fifty years after." *Ariadne* therefore is not only theater or opera, it is meta-opera and meta-theater—that is to say, opera about opera, theater about theater. It is an artwork about life, but it is also an artwork about art.

Thinking of writing the prologue for the *Ariadne* opera, Hofmannsthal wrote Strauss in 1913, "More strongly than ever before the focal point will be the musician's destiny, exemplified by the young Composer . . . as a man in love, fooled, as guest, child, victor and vanquished in this world." For him, the Composer's "outburst 'Music!' [is] a kind of little Prize Song— indeed the whole *Ariadne* with the prologue possesses a remote, purely conceptual affinity with *Meistersinger*." The revised figure of the Composer, as Hofmannsthal realized, is "tragic and comic at the same time, like the musician's lot in the world; the two fundamental Ariadne motifs, anchored or rooted as they are in the heart of the musician, all this I believe is poetic and has substance—it can last." The Composer, that is, unites in himself the tension of terrestrial with transcendental that will be resolved in the *Ariadne* opera he has created. His life has not yet achieved the higher, transforming consciousness his art proclaims. Deceived by the patron, the Major-domo, the Music Master and Zerbinetta, he awaits in life the regeneration that Ariadne and Bacchus achieve in art.

The prologue, therefore, comprises far more than a glimpse backstage. The Composer's idea in his final declamation, that the world of art is separate from life, is untransformed, immature and simplistic. The complexity of existence cannot be reduced to crudely separate spheres. Art for art's sake becomes mere self-indulgence. At this point *Ariadne* reveals itself as meta--theater, for the saving figure of Bacchus is also the Dionysus who was the presiding deity of Greek theater. The god of theater becomes the catalyst of the transformation of life—art for life's sake, not for art's sake.

As the Greeks realized, and as Hofmannsthal and Strauss emphasize, art exists to transform life, to elevate consciousness, to improve existence. Dionysus transmutes the Ariadne who in life suffers from the infidelity of Theseus. It is from the chaotic life of the theater of the prologue (intrigue, jealousy, revision, incomprehension, intolerance, haste) that the transcendental regeneration by art takes its origin. *Ariadne auf Naxos*, in its constituent parts of prologue and opera, is the paradigm of the inter penetration of life and art, embodied in the transformation of the god of the theater himself, Dionysus. Though immortal, he suffers mortal despair with Circe (the chaos of life) to demonstrate that art can elucidate life, not by evading but by confronting it.

To achieve his objectives of meta-theater as philosophy, Hofmannsthal drew on a range of European sources for his adaptation of the legend of Ariadne and Bacchus. The earliest reference to Dionysus and Ariadne appears in Hesiod's *Theogony*, written in the eighth century B.C. The poet records that "golden Dionysus took to wife/The fair haired Ariadne, Minos' child; /The son of Kronos saved her from death and age." As early as this account, Dionysus is the one who transforms Ariadne to immortality.

The most famous account of Ariadne's encounter with Theseus, lamented by her in the opera, is the epyllion ("little epic") by the Roman poet Catullus (c. 84-54 B.C.). Recounting the marriage feast of Peleus and Thetis (the parents of Achilles), Catullus describes the tapestry that covers their marriage bed; it is a famous *ekphrasis* or verbal description of a work of art, like Keats' "Ode on a Grecian Urn." Ariadne, a princess of Crete, is depicted as abandoned on the island of Dia (Naxos), lamenting

21

her abandonment by Theseus, to whom she had given the thread that allowed him to invade the Labyrinth and slay the Minotaur. She stands on the shoreline like a bacchant, a worshipper of Dionysus, mad with grief. Catullus summarizes the manner in which she aided the faithless Theseus. Ariadne's monologues in the opera, "Ein Schönes war" and "Es gibt ein Reich," reveal the trauma she has endured as a result of Theseus' infidelity: she longs for Hermes in his role as Hermes Psychopompos, or "Guide of Souls," to remove her to Hades, land of the dead.

Hofmannsthal's Ariadne does not ask for vengeance on Theseus, as does the heroine in Catullus' poem, who beseeches Zeus to make Theseus suffer. Her prayers are answered when Theseus forgets to hoist the white sail of victory to his father, who, believing him dead, commits suicide. In both Hofmannsthal and Catullus, however, Ariadne longs for death. Catullus records the appearance of Bacchus at the end of his description of the marriage bed, suggesting the solace Ariadne will find in his arms.

An important representation of Ariadne exists in the work of the Roman poet Ovid (43 B.C.-A.D. 18). In the *Ars Amatoria*, his treatise on the art of love, Ovid describes Ariadne abandoned by the shore. Soon bands of satyrs and bacchants herald the approach of Bacchus, who tells her, "I am here for you, a lover more faithful/ . . . You shall be mine, you will be adored as a star in the heaven/And your diadem guide sailors in trouble at sea." Ovid alludes to the legend that Ariadne's wedding wreath, given her by Dionysus, became the constellation Corona (crown). In the *Heroides*, Ovid writes a letter purporting to be from Ariadne to Theseus. She describes her abandonment, begging Theseus to return and save her from infamy. While there is no suggestion of her rescue by Bacchus in this letter, in the *Metamorphoses* Ovid records the apotheosis of Ariadne when she ascends to the skies with Bacchus: "And then, to make her shine among the stars,/[Bacchus] gave her a crown as she rose up to heaven./When she ascended through pale vaults of ether,/The jeweled tiara flamed with dancing fires." From the perspective of Strauss and Hofmannsthal, this jeweled crown symbolizes Ariadne's transformation.

Two other sources were undoubtedly known to Hofmannsthal. The Greek biographer Plutarch (A.D. c. 46-120) recorded several versions of

Ariadne's fate in his *Life of Theseus*, including one in which Ariadne dies bearing Theseus' child. A final significant literary source exists in Milton's *Comus* (1634), which served Hofmannsthal as the origin of the encounter of Bacchus with Circe, who bore his son Comus. From the coalescence of Hesiod, Catullus, Ovid and Milton, Hofmannsthal created the classical characters of *Ariadne auf Naxos*. Particularly significant for Hofmannsthal's system of contrasts is the fact that Ariadne's name was originally "Ariagne," meaning "holy" or "pure." The alternative name for Naxos—Dia, meaning "divine"—suggests her apotheosis through Dionysus.

Strauss and Hofmannsthal in *Ariadne auf Naxos* therefore are working in an extensive tradition involving Bacchus and Ariadne. Nineteenth-century Europeans associated Ariadne with the frail female, awaiting rescue by the heroic, dominant male. Hofmannsthal's contrasting of Zerbinetta with Ariadne parallels a standard period division of women into the whore and the virgin, the one faithless, the other faithful. Mythographers regarded the legend as the renewal of earth after winter (Ariadne) by the revivifying spring (Bacchus), a cosmological rendering of the rescue motif. The English novelist George Eliot particularly emphasized the Bacchus/Ariadne substructure in her novels. In *Romola* (1863), the deceitful Tito Melema conceives of Romola as an Ariadne awaiting himself as Dionysus to initiate her into a passionate existence. In *Middlemarch* (1871-72), Will Ladislaw is the Bacchus who rescues Dorothea Brooke, an Ariadne forsaken after her disastrous first marriage.

Middlemarch deploys a crucial source of the mythic story for Hofmannsthal and Strauss, the artistic representation of the mythological characters of *Ariadne auf Naxos*. In Eliot's novel, Ladislaw first sees Dorothea as she contemplates the marble *Ariadne* in the Belvedere Court of the Vatican. The Vatican *Ariadne*, probably from the first century A.D., shows Ariadne sleeping on Naxos, unaware of Theseus' departure. Titian's *Bacchus and Ariadne* (1523) shows the god accompanied by bacchants and satyrs, descending from his chariot to rescue Ariadne. He shows her the constellation that will mark her apotheosis. Tintoretto's *Bacchus and Ariadne* (1578) depicts Ariadne being crowned as Bacchus approaches her. In a ceiling fresco of 1597-1601 for the Palazzo Farnese in Rome, Annibale

Carracci portrays *The Triumph of Bacchus and Ariadne*, with the latter receiving the crown. John Henry Fuseli completed his dramatic *Theseus Taking the Thread from Ariadne* in 1788.

During the nineteenth century, artists exhibited a renewed interest in the figure of Ariadne. The future president of the Royal Academy, Frederic Leighton, depicted *Ariadne Abandoned by Theseus* in 1868, with the heroine prostrate on a promontory of Naxos. In 1877, Evelyn De Morgan showed the abandoned Ariadne by silhouetting her against the barren coast line of the island in *Ariadne in Naxos*. In his *Ariadne on Naxos* of 1875, George Frederic Watts selects a moment filled with dramatic tension: Ariadne has just awakened to discover Theseus' treachery, while her attendant points to the imminent arrival of Bacchus, whose leopards have already appeared. Like Leighton's Ariadne, Watts' figure reveals the influence of the Elgin Marbles; the design of the painting recalls that of Titian, especially with the sky on the left and the pose of the attendant. In 1891, Leighton exhibited *The Return of Persephone*, showing Hermes as Hermes Psychopompos, whom Strauss' Ariadne invokes in "Es gibt ein Reich." In 1913, the year after the premiere of the first *Ariadne*, Giorgio Di Chirico completed the best known twentieth-century depiction of Ariadne, possibly influenced by the opera.

The collaboration of Strauss and Hofmannsthal was to endure after *Ariadne auf Naxos* in *Die Frau ohne Schatten* (1919), *Die Ägyptische Helena* (1928) and *Arabella* (1933). In 1911 Hofmannsthal described himself and Strauss as "two artists who, with imagination and delicacy, are seeking new ways of expression." A few months before the premiere of the second *Ariadne*, Hofmannsthal declared: "You must guide me, I must guide you: perhaps in this way we shall one day reach wholly new and unexplored regions." Through the legend of Bacchus and Ariadne, Strauss and Hofmannsthal not only sighted new "regions" but attained them—by their own mutual transformation.

The Cruelest Story:
Bizet and *Carmen*

During the wars of the Empire, while husbands and brothers were in Germany, uneasy mothers had given birth to an ardent, nervous generation. They asked where their fathers were. But they received for answer that the war was ended, that Caesar was dead. Then a moody youth sat down on a world in ruins. They had dreamt for fifteen years of the snows of Moscow, and the sun of the pyramids. They had a whole world in their heads . . . Napoleon being dead, the divine and human powers were indeed restored in fact; but belief in them no longer existed. Condemned to repose by the sovereigns of the world, these gladiators felt an unbearable wretchedness in the depths of their souls . . . It was like a denying of all things of heaven and earth, which one may call disenchantment, or if one wishes, despair . . . Men doubted everything: young men denied everything.

These words, the prelude to Alfred de Musset's *Confession d'un Enfant du Siècle* (1836), encapsulate the consciousness of the era into which the creator of *Carmen*, Prosper Mérimée (1803-70), was born. The origin of Mérimée's famous *nouvelle* of 1845 and of Georges Bizet's opera of 1875 exists in the profound disillusionment of the generation that came to maturity in post Napoleonic France. Mérimée and Musset had another element in common—a woman, the writer George Sand, who had been Mussel's lover and had spent a night with Mérimée. Her verdict on their single encounter: "I had Mérimée last night; it wasn't much." There can be little doubt that this fleeting rendezvous of April 1833 remained in Mérimée's mind when he created Carmen, who symbolizes for both writer and composer the contingency of existence itself—all is relative, fated, inexplicable, determined. Mérimée's motto, "Memneso apistein" (Remember to be on your guard), is echoed by Bizet's heroine in her habanera—"Prends garde a toi." It is the cry of the age.

One scarcely can be surprised that the representation of such a character at the Opéra Comique encountered resistance. One of the directors of the theater, Adolphe de Leuven, said to Ludovic Halévy (co-librettist with Henri Meilhac), "Please try not to have her die. Death on the stage of the Opéra Comique—such a thing has never been seen, never! Don't make her die, I beg of you, my dear boy—don't."

But resistance to the opera cannot be explained only by the presence of Roma or the death of the heroine. It is rather what Carmen herself represents that was so disturbing. As a Roma, her alien status reflects the human existential condition—all mankind is born in exile. Her stark acknowledgment of death recognizes that mankind is condemned to death, albeit for unknown crimes, and is therefore guilty a priori. The Carmen of Mérimée and Bizet unnerves José and everybody else because she not only knows this truth but *is* it. José wants victory; Carmen settles for survival, the only course in an unpredictable universe. If everything is fated, then everything is inconsequential. Confronted with this paradox, one should indeed be on guard. Life becomes a *corrida de toros*.

It is the idea of existence as a bullfight, with everything disposed by chance as the agent of fate, that undoubtedly attracted Bizet to the writings of Mérimée. The fate motif heard in the prelude to *Carmen* is reiterated at crucial moments—when Carmen hurls the flower at José in Act I, before the card reading of Act III, in the final moments when José views his lifeless "Carmen adorée." In this emphasis, Bizet was following a line of thought that permeates the writings of Mérimée. From his earliest tales to his triumphant novellas *Colomba* (1840) and *Carmen*, ideas of chance and fate etch an insidious motif of post-Napoleonic despair that verges on nihilism.

As instruments of this fate, the characters in Mérimée often make disastrous choices. In *Mateo Falcone* (1829), the Corsican Falcone executes his son Fortunato for betraying the outlaw Gianetto Sanpiero to the police, thus betraying family honor: the boy's name ("lucky") refers ironically to Mérimée's worldview. A few months later. Mérimée published *Tamango*, a tale built on a series of coups de théâtre. Tamango, a Black warrior who sells other Blacks to slave dealers, is himself taken as a slave. After leading a revolt on the slave ship, he dies a drunken outcast at Kingston. In *L'Enlèvement de la Redoute* (The Storming of the Fort, 1829), an account of the capture of Chevardino near Moscow in September 1812, a young lieutenant witnesses the death of his captain, who believed he would die in the siege—and does. As in *Carmen*, life is a lottery.

Caught in this vise, men and women find the boudoir as dangerous as the battlefield. In *Le Vase Étrusque* (1830), Auguste Saint-Clair, trusting a rumor that his mistress the Comtesse Mathilde de Coursy had an affair with a rival, is forced to fight a fatal duel even though he learns the falsity of the tale; he is ruined by his own suspicions. The story is famous for its description of the hero, presumed to be a self-portrait of Mérimée as a sensitive individual forced to dissimulate to survive.

Mérimée had learned to conceal his emotions after a childhood incident when, punished by being sent out of the room, he begged forgiveness from his mother, who laughed at him. He rebuked her by saying, "If you are going to make fun of me, I will never ask your pardon again." Auguste Saint-Clair in his jealousy is a prototype for the José of *Carmen*. In *La Partie de Trictrac* (The Game of Backgammon), a man who cheated at cards attempts to recover his honor; this emphasis on *le point d'honneur* anticipates the José of *Carmen*, while the failure of two persons to comprehend one another in *La Double Méprise* (The Double Misunderstanding, 1833) suggests, as does *Carmen*, the futility of commitment between men and women. The epigraph to the tale veers toward nihilism: "Young girl, fairer than the flowers with your blond hair and green eyes, if you abandon yourself to love, lose well, or you will indeed be lost."

These themes of violence, chance, jealousy, misunderstanding and vengeance coalesce in the two novellas that secure Mérimée's place in French literature, *Carmen* and *Colomba*, alike in having fiercely powerful women as protagonists who became the agents of a remorseless fate. At the invitation of Orso Carabelli in 1839, Mérimée made an excursion to Corsica, where he encountered Orso's sister Colomba Bartoli, who had been engaged in a bitter feud with the Durazzo family. Based on this history, *Colomba* concerns the force Colomba della Rebbia exerts on her brother Orso to avenge their father's death by slaying the surviving members of the Barricini family. Defending her father like the Greek Elektra, Colomba pursues her revenge, though others consider her a devil, witch and sorceress. The power of this story was not lost on opera composers. Inspired by Bizet's success with *Carmen* a few years earlier, Axel Grandjean, Alexander Mackenzie, and Vittorio Radeglia produced versions of *Colomba* during the 1880s.

The origin of *Carmen* dates from Mérimée's first excursion to Spain, in 1830, during which he met Don Cipriano de Montijo, Count of Teba, whose daughter Eugenia would later become Empress of the French during the Second Empire. From Doña Manuela de Montijo, Mérimée heard the tale that contained the kernel of *Carmen*, as he admitted in a letter of May 1845: "I have just spent a week shut up writing . . . a story you told me fifteen years ago . . . It was published in 1831, about a *jaque* [braggart] of Malaga who had killed his mistress for devoting herself exclusively to the public." Mérimée based his Basque José Navarro on this man, Carmen on his mistress, adding lore about Roma from George Barrow's *The Bible in Spain* (1843) and *The Zincali* (1841). The tale of Carmen, recounted by Don José himself prior to his execution, is introduced by a brief chapter on the history of Andalusia, and in 1847 Mérimée added a postscript on Roma customs and language. The introduction and postscript frame the tale of José Navarro and Carmen to give it authenticity, making it appear like an anthropological report.

This journey to Spain yielded other documents crucial to *Carmen*, such as the *Lettres d'Espagne* Mérimée wrote to the editor of the *Revue de Paris*. The subjects of four of these provided key details for the novella. The first, "Les Courses de Taureaux," is a famous essay on bullfighting, the prototype of Hemingway's *Death in the Afternoon*. From this source Mérimée created the picador Lucas in *Carmen* on the model of his friend Francisco Sevilla. Bizet undoubtedly conceived Escamillo and his *couplets* from the essay. The second recorded the execution of a *majo* for murdering a soldier and a bailiff. The letter on thievery included an account of the brigand José-Maria, called El Tempranillo or "Early Riser." For *Carmen*, however, the most interesting was the letter entitled *Les Sorcières Espagnoles*, published in 1833. Written during Mérimée's time in Valencia, it recounts a trip during which Mérimée stopped at an inn and was waited on by a girl named Carmencita. His guide Vincente informs him after they depart that the girl and her mother are witches, according to the Spanish proverb "Prima puta, luego alchaueta, pues bruja" (First a whore, then a procuress, then a witch). The *Lettres d'Espagne* therefore, foreshadow elements that reappear in *Carmen*: smuggling, the bullfight, the bewitching woman, the murderer.

Transforming Mérimée's tale into a libretto, Halévy and Meilhac made numerous changes, some of which moderate the violence of Mérimée's narrative. They introduce the character of Micaela to appease the bourgeois audience of the Opéra Comique, based on a suggestion by Mérimée of Basque girls with blue skirts and plaited hair. The picador Lucas is transformed into the matador Escamillo, since the picador's lowly status does not accord with the grandiloquent emphasis of opera. In the novella, José kills García, Carmen's *rom*, whereas in the opera she has no common law husband. The dialogue of the Opéra Comique version retains the fact that José killed an opponent in a game before joining the dragoons. Lilias Pastia has his smugglers' den in the Triana, a low part of Seville, where Carmen drinks the Andalusian white wine manzanilla. Mérimée's characters El Dancairo and El Remendado are retained in the opera, perhaps for their exotic names, which mean "gambler" and "patched." Zuniga, however, killed in Mérimée, is only tied up in the opera.

Like her counterpart in Bizet, the Carmen of Mérimée prizes her freedom. She tells José, "What I want is to be free and do as I please." Conceiving the end, she declares, "You know, my boy, I do believe I love you a little. But it cannot last. Dog and wolf never get on well together for long . . . You have met the Devil—yes, the Devil. He isn't always black, and he hasn't wrung your neck. I am dressed in wool, but I am no lamb." Knowing she speaks the truth, Don José nevertheless confesses, "I was so weak in the face of that creature that I obeyed her every whim." Irresistible love, like death, is a form of inexplicable fate.

In Mérimée, José kills Carmen not during the corrida at Cordoba but after it, not outside the Plaza de Toros but in a desolate gorge. She is undaunted: "You're going to kill me, I can see that clearly . . . It's written, but you will not make me yield . . . I don't love you anymore . . . I could easily go on lying to you, but I don't want to take the trouble . . . Carmen will always be free. *Calli* [Roma] she was born, *calli* she will die . . . Now I love nothing anymore, and I hate myself for ever having loved you." When she throws the ring at him, José stabs and buries her, damning the Roma for having ruined her. The stark Greek epigraph for the tale reads, "A woman is like gall. Only two times is she any good—on her bed and at her death."

Bizet's *Carmen* retains much of the consistent presence of Mérimée, particularly in several of its most famous musical numbers. For the habanera, which Bizet re-wrote thirteen times, he supplied his own text when he was dissatisfied with that of Halévy, the music modeled on the song "El Arreglito" by Sebastián Yradier. Bizet's text emphasizes love as a form of fate: one cannot summon it, no threat or prayer avails against it, it knows no law. Bizet's text reflects the Mérimée not only of *Carmen* but of *Colomba* and the shorter stories. The seguidilla reiterates the idea: Carmen throws out one lover, has many offers and likes none of them, but when the weekend comes, "You got here at the right moment." Bizet includes no conventional love scene between José and Carmen. Nothing is predictable: the two meet by pure chance, at a point where she is receptive.

After this fated universe has been limned in Act I with the habanera and seguidilla, Act III reinforces the anarchy of existence by the frenzy of Carmen's opening *chanson bohème*. This piece is the prelude to Escamillo's toreador song, about which Bizet is reported to have said, "If they want trash, they'll get it." The hazards of the corrida that it describes, however, perfectly suit the unpredictable nature of Escamillo's, Carmen's, and (though he does not know it) José's existence. The term *toreador*, a French corruption of *torero* (bullfighter), is archaic and inappropriate, since the term can apply to all men involved in the corrida—banderilleros, picadors, matadors. The matador, as his name implies, is a "killer," and as such he becomes the emblem of the human condition: himself condemned to

30

death, he attempts to avoid it. He tries to be "en garde," yet he never knows victory, only survival—and ultimately he will die. In the card scene, Bizet's and Mérimée's Carmen are one: "But if you have to die, if the awful word is written by fate, the pitiless card will repeat, death!"

Bizet's coup de théâtre in *Carmen* is to have the slaying take place outside the Plaza de Toros. Nothing could emphasize more the hazardous nature of an existence dominated by chance. The non-Mérimée, Gounodesque accretions to the operatic *Carmen*, such as José's "La fleur que tu m'avais jetée" of Act II or Micaela's "Je dis que rien ne m'épouvante" of Act III, are exposed by the relentless jealousy, vengeance, fate and danger that engulf them. While these may have placated the management of the Opéra Comique, Bizet through Mérimée had the last word: all mankind is part of Escamillo's *cuadrilla*. The elimination of the original spoken dialogue, much of it from Mérimée, in favor of the recitatives by Ernest Guiraud for the grand opera *Carmen* obscured Bizet's fidelity to Mérimée, which infiltrates the habanera, seguidilla card scene, and Escamillo's swagger.

During the nineteenth century, the image of Spain became enormously attractive to artists, who saw in the country the actuality of fated existence. Goya, who professed to be a bullfighter as a young man, began recording scenes of the corrida after a trip to Seville in 1793. A particularly interesting painting, dating from around 1810, shows two bullfights in a split arena. On the left, a matador prepares his *estoque* to deliver the *eslocada* that kills the bull; on the right, a picador confronts a charging bull. An artist particularly fond of Spanish scenes was the Scottish painter John Phillip, who first traveled to Spain in 1851, settling in Seville. In such canvases as *The Gypsy Sisters of Seville* (1854), *The Dying Contrabandista* (1858), *Gypsy Musicians of Spain* (1855), *The Gyspy Queen of Seville* (1852), and *La Bomba* (1863), Phillip recorded terrain known to Mérimée.

Gustave Doré completed a number of designs of Spanish scenes, including depictions of the tobacco factory at Seville, a running of the bull, smugglers, Spanish dancing and *majas* with their lovers. Édouard Manet is famous for his representations of Spanish life. *Young Woman Reclining in Spanish Costume* (1862), *Young Man in the Costume of a Majo* (1863), *Matador Saluting* (1867), *The Bullfight* (1866) and *The Dead*

Toreador (1865) attest to this fascination. John Singer Sargent painted a famous dancer in *La Carmencita* in 1890, while Émile Wauters painted a lost *Carmen* (1892) based on Bizet, a sultry woman holding a cigarette. Narcisse-Virgile Díaz' *Bohemians Going to a Fete*, completed the year before Mérimée's *Carmen*, shows an exotic band of Roma and others traversing a forest path. Two years before the premiere of *Carmen*, Mary Cassatt painted her *Torero and Young Girl*. Artists such as Théobald Chartran were attracted to famous singers, as in his 1894 *Emma Calvé as Carmen*. The Spain of *Carmen* resonated through the century.

Analysts have noted the disturbing ambiguity of Mérimée's motto "Memneso apistein": on guard against what? Others, oneself, a malign universe? *Carmen* and his other works depict mankind suffering from a fundamental anxiety about existence, its inability to be explained, challenged, even defied. Carmen for José, the corrida for Escamillo, represent this uncertain nature of destiny, an awareness Bizet embodied in *Carmen*. (Nietzsche described the music as "evil, cunning, fatalistic.") Writing in 1890, Walter Pater said of Mérimée, "That sense of negation, of theoretic insecurity, was in the air, and conspiring with what was of like tendency in himself made of him a central type of disillusion." Mérimée's style has "the polish of the stiletto" to convey his truths: "Pity and terror, we know, go to the making of the essential tragic sense. In Mérimée, certainly, we have all its terror, but without the pity . . . You seem to find your hand on a serpent, in reading him." Pater's summation of Mateo Falcone is just as apt for Mérimée's and Bizet's *Carmen*, with their horrifyingly inexplicable universe: "the cruelest story in the world."

Out of the Tinder Box:
Mascagni and *Cavalleria Rusticana*

On May 19, 1890, a young man in Rome wrote to his father, "I feel as though I'm losing my mind. It was really overwhelming." The young man was Pietro Mascagni. Two nights before, at the Teatro Costanzi, he had started a revolution. Though Italy had endured a major political upheaval, the Risorgimento, during the nineteenth century under Garibaldi and Mazzini, it took the first performance of *Cavalleria Rusticana* to revolutionize opera. Mascagni's sixty curtain calls would echo, damningly for him, the remainder of his life. Verismo had arrived.

Where did it begin?

In 1880, through the genius of Giovanni Verga, another young man entered the world, Turiddu Macca, in the story "Cavalleria Rusticana," included in a history-making volume, *Vita dei Campi* (Life in the Fields). In nineteenth-century Italian literature, two figures dominate, at the beginning Alessandro Manzoni (*I Promessi Sposi*, 1825, opera by Ponchielli, 1856) and toward the end of the century Verga (1840-1922). For Mascagni, Verga's literary revolution provoked his own that May night in 1890, for with Verga, French *naturalisme* became Italian verismo.

Verga had begun his literary career by leaving Sicily and going to the mainland (or "the Continent," as the Sicilians called Italy), especially to Florence in 1865 and Milan in 1870. There he enjoyed success as the author of *Eva* (1873), *Tigre Reale* (1873) and *Eros* (1875), novels analyzing the decadent aristocratic world. In 1874 his short story *Nedda* indicated the path by which he would make Italian literary history and influence world opera. This account of a poor girl, with a dying mother and a dead lover, opened to Verga the potential of literature dealing with the peasantry of his native Sicily. In his two collections *Vita dei Campi* (1880) and *Novelle Rusticane* (1883), and in his great novels *I Malavoglia* (1881) and *Mastro Don Gesualdo* (1888), Verga probed what he called "i vinti," the vanquished—human beings whose lives vanish unnoticed by literature. Since his plan derived from Emile Zola's series of naturalistic novels *Les Rougon-Macquart*, it is actually in France that the genesis of *Cavalleria Rusticana* lies.

In Paris in 1865, as preface to their *Germinie Lacerteux*, Edmond and Jules de Goncourt wrote a brief notice, the quiet origin of a literary explosion:

> We must ask the public's pardon for giving it this book, and warn it as to what it will find there.
>
> The public loves false novels; this is a true one.
>
> It loves books that pretend to move in polite society; this book comes from the streets.
>
> In the present day, when the novel has undertaken the studies and obligations of science, it can demand the liberties of science. Let it seek Art and Truth; let it show to the happy people of Paris misery that should not be forgotten, human suffering, immediate and alive; let the novel have that religion to which the past century gave that encompassing name *Humanity*. Such a consciousness will suffice it. Its right lies there.

This account of the wretched life of a servant greatly influenced Zola. By coincidence, *Germinie Lacerteux* appeared in the same year as Claude Bernard's *Introduction to the Study of Experimental Medicine*, developing a theory of scientific observation, which Zola welded to the influence of the Brothers Goncourt. For the word "doctor" in Bernard's treatise, Zola admitted, one had only to substitute the word "novelist" to grasp the doctrines of naturalism—that environment and heredity determine human motivation, and that the novelist's duty is to record the "truth." In his preface to the first of the Rougon-Macquart novels in 1871, Zola observed, "Heredity has its laws, like weight."

In his manifesto *The Experimental Novel* (1880), Zola became fervid in the belief that "Man is not alone; he lives in a society." Man must be analyzed in the context of his social milieu; literature, Zola argued, "must itself become a science, a general inquiry into nature and man. Thus we apply the experimental method." Zola's novels, like *L'Assommoir* (1877), the story of a laundress; *Nana* (1880), the study of a courtesan; *Germinal* (1885), an analysis of miners' lives; and *La Terre* (1887), a brutal story of peasant life, were powerful influences on Verga, contributing directly to verismo opera. When Zola visited Italy, both Puccini and Mascagni were guests at a banquet in his honor.

Several of Verga's own statements show how extensive was this influence. In a preface to "Gramigna's Mistress," another of the stories in *Vita dei Campi*, Verga observed:

> I believe the novel will attain its triumph when the sincerity of its realism will be so evident, and its method so inevitable, that the hand of the artist will remain absolutely unseen, and the novel will have the character of an actual event, and the work of art will seem to have made itself, to have arisen and matured spontaneously, as if it were a natural phenomenon.

When composing *Cavalleria Rusticana*, Mascagni took these statements to heart. Verga stated in *I Malavoglia*, "The observer of life has no right to judge it: the best he can do is to study it dispassionately and to render it clearly, with its true colors, to represent reality as it has actually existed, or would seem to have existed." So great was the influence of *Vita dei Campi* that Puccini, while working on *La Bohème*, contemplated an opera based on another of its stories, "La Lupa" (The She-Wolf).

The relation of Verga to Mascagni is complex. Originally intending it as part of *I Malavoglia*, Verga excised "Cavalleria Rusticana" from the final version of his novel to include it as a short story in *Vita dei Campi*. In 1884, Verga rewrote "Cavalleria Rusticana" as a one-act play. The libretto devised by Giovanni Targioni-Tozzetti and Guido Menasci is based on this dramatic version, in its day a great vehicle for Eleanora Duse as Santuzza, recognized even by George Bernard Shaw. The movement from story to drama to opera, however, is a key to the meaning of verismo to Mascagni.

Verga's drama, by including a host of minor characters to depict the small Sicilian town, definitely diffuses the brutal, lightning intensity of his short story. Mascagni therefore had a dual aim: to realize the metier of the stage play but to achieve the intensity of the original work of fiction.

The first paragraph of Verga's story gave Mascagni the method for achieving this union:

> When Turiddu Macca, Nunzia's son, came back from the service, he used to strut in the square on Sundays in his *bersagliere* uniform with the red cap that looked like the one worn by the fortuneteller who sets up a bench with a cage of canaries. The girls, on the way to Mass, their noses in their mantillas, eyed him longingly, and the urchins buzzed around him like flies. He had also brought a pipe with a carving of the king on horseback that seemed alive, and he lit matches on the rear of his pants, lifting his leg as if giving a kick.

Learning that Lola was marrying Alfio, Turiddu "vented his rage by singing all the scornful songs he knew under the girl's window. He walked behind the girl, swaying while the tassel of his cap danced here and there on his shoulders." Unmistakably, Verga establishes the sexual allure of Turiddu by repeated phallic images—the red cap, the pipe, the matches, the swinging tassel. In Verga's drama the first scene is occupied with village gossip. Instinctively, with Turiddu's immortal *siciliana*, Mascagni returned to the story rather than to the drama of Verga.

Of particular importance is Verga's tendency to eliminate transitions between paragraphs and incidents, simulating the abruptness, spontaneity and inexplicability of life itself. The *coup de théâtre* of Turiddu's *siciliana* ("O Lola ch'ai di latti la cammisa") Mascagni at first hesitated to use, despite precedents by Rossini and Meyerbeer, who had used voices in their preludes. However, when Mascagni played the *siciliana* for the judges of the Sonzogno competition in 1890, they were in wonder. With its spontaneous intrusion into the music, its emphasis on the solo voice and naked emotion, and its seeming inevitability, this *siciliana* has become the signature of verismo opera. "I would like to stay very close to the original drama," Mascagni told Targioni-Tozzetti; for the most part he did, but the *siciliana* was a momentous reversion to the story. The use of such an intrusion is also exceptional in Lola's stornello ("Fior di giaggiolo"), when she disrupts the impassioned confrontation between Turiddu and Santuzza. Mascagni hesitated about using a Tuscan form of song but found it psychologically valid when he realized Turiddu had returned from the mainland and could have taught it to Lola. This stornello, in both content and form, has complete psychological validity.

This use of the *siciliana* and the necessity of having the stornello motivated demonstrate to what extent Mascagni wished to reinforce Verga's realism. The lowered curtain during the prelude suggests that the listeners will eventually get "behind the scenes" not only of the stage but of life—an effect enhanced by the statement "Time, the Present" and by the restriction of the action to a single day. The authenticity of dialect is particularly evident in Turiddu's name, deriving from Salvatore, which in its diminutive becomes Salvatorillo ("little Salvatore"), then Torillo, and finally, with "o" and "l" blunted, Turiddu. In the *siciliana*, the customary "Paradiso" becomes "Paradisu." When Mascagni submitted *Cavalleria Rusticana* to the Sonzogno competition, he wrote under its title, "With the consent of Verga."

It is no accident that Turiddu's complete name is Salvatore ("rescuer," "savior"), since the story, the drama and the opera emphasize Easter, for specific veristic purposes. Easter is the initial theme of the opera, followed by that of Santuzza's love and then the *siciliana*, a sequence of great realism. Since Easter required the "Easter duty," the confession of one's sins, the music moves inexorably from the moral law to the sinner to the cause of the sin. Easter also explains why Alfio returns—to be with his wife for the holiday. An even stronger realistic element about Easter in Sicily is noted in Verga's story "The Gentry."

He observes that when men went to a spiritual retreat during the days preceding Easter, there was a rampage of adultery between their wives and the younger men of the village, who cared nothing for religion. In several of Verga's stories, especially "The Mystery Play," personal vendettas are carried out during Easter. Turiddu's brindisi ("Viva il vino spumeggiante"), his name, and his concern for his mother and Santuzza have, in fact, an unmistakable quality of the Christ *manqué*. In the world of the Sicilian *paesani*, Mascagni and Verga show man bereft of God: the brutality of

Turiddu's death will be remembered every Easter by Santuzza, Mamma Lucia, even Lola and the village, as a time not of resurrection but of death.

Mascagni's *Cavalleria*, despite its harsh vision, tends to ennoble its characters over those in Verga's story. For example, Santuzza betrays Turiddu to Alfio only after he rejects her to trail Lola into church, whereas in the story this episode originates out of pure revenge, with no impression of Santuzza's remorse. In the opera one is not aware that in fact Alfio kills Turiddu only by blinding him with dust. The title "Cavalleria Rusticana" is an irony in itself, since "chivalry" would be associated with aristocratic, not "rustic," honor. With Turiddu's willingness to admit his wrong, both Mascagni and Verga ennoble peasant honor. On a sociological level, Verga in fact indicates why such "chivalry" existed at all: "Law is made for those who've got money to spend," he writes in "Don Licciu Papa." Such brutal peasant life receives no stronger explanation than in Verga's story "Black Bread," where one character notes, "The trouble is, we aren't rich enough always to like one another." Mascagni recorded that the final words "Hanno ammazzato compare Turiddu!" ("They've killed neighbor Turiddu!") rang in his ears until he found the seventh chords to close the opera. "Thus I began my opera at the end," he declared, at the root question of "chivalry."

While *Cavalleria Rusticana* was enjoying its unprecedented success, another struggling Italian composer was in great frustration. Ruggiero Leoncavallo, commissioned to compose a trilogy on the Italian Renaissance by the publisher Ricardi, produced *I Medici*, only to have it rejected by Ricardi as too costly for performance. Irritated at Ricardi and inspired by the fact that Ricordi's rival Sonzogno had sponsored *Cavalleria Rusticana*, Leoncavallo in four months composed *Pagliacci*, which Sonzogno accepted. It was mounted in triumph on May 21, 1892, at the Teatro dal Verme, Milan, conducted by Toscanini.

Corresponding to the statements by the Goncourts, Zola and Verga, Leoncavallo gave verismo opera its manifesto in the prologue to *Pagliacci*, following the suggestion of the first Tonio, Victor Maurel. Much influenced by Wagner, in the prelude Leoncavallo establishes four themes—those of the players, of Canio's despair, of love and of suspicion—before Tonio emerges from behind the curtain to address the audience. One recognizes immediately how similar and yet how different are Mascagni and Leoncavallo: the *siciliana* in *Cavalleria Rusticana* is sung with the curtain down; in *Pagliacci* the prologue breaches the space between audience and stage, a daring strategy, to enforce the idea that life and art are identical. Leoncavallo titles his opera *Pagliacci* to provide a documentary universal reference, that all mankind are "players." Mascagni, on the other hand, with the title *Cavalleria Rusticana*, describes and interprets rather than documents the action of his opera. Both the prologue and the *siciliana*, nevertheless, have the veristic spontaneity of Verga, intruding into their preludes. This spontaneity is reinforced by confining the action to two holidays, Easter in *Cavalleria* and the Assumption of the Virgin, August 15, in *Pagliacci*.

Costumed as Taddeo for the forthcoming commedia dell'arte, Tonio in the prologue declares, "The author has taken a slice of life . . . The artist is a man and writes for men—and he tells the truth." Several words recurring in the prologue, particularly "spasimi" (griefs), "vedrete" (you'll see) and "uomini" (mankind), stress Tonio's—and Leoncavallo's—idea that the stage and life are not separate. The music, he declares, originated "un giorno" (one day), an expression connoting the spontaneous nature of life, the occurrence of the opera on a single day, and especially, the fact that such events happen every day. That life and the stage are one is emphasized by Leoncavallo's brilliant idea of having Nedda's lover, Silvio, be not a part of the troupe but one of the village spectators.

Leoncavallo had not only the illusion of reality but actuality itself on his side when he composed *Pagliacci*. After the performance of *Pagliacci*, Catulle Mendes charged that Leoncavallo had plagiarized from his drama *La Femme de Tabarin* (1887), involving a murder by a man playing a role on the stage. In 1874, however, Paul Ferrier had produced his own *Tabarin*. Leoncavallo noted, in a response to these charges in 1894, that the idea of a man in stage character committing murder was quite old, dating as far back as *Drama Nuevo* by the Spanish writer Estabenez earlier in the century. In this same letter to Sonzogno, furthermore, Leoncavallo revealed, "In my childhood, while my father was a judge at Montalto in Calabria [the scene of the opera], a jealous player killed his wife after the performance." At the trial, presided over by his father, young Leoncavallo had heard the enraged husband declare, "I repent nothing! If I had to do it over again, I'd do it again!" Those words he never forgot. The murderer in fact offered to defend Leoncavallo if Mendes pressed his accusation. Verga's story "The Mystery Play," moreover, recounts how Nanni killed Venera's lover Cola, with whom she fell in love while he was performing in a play during Easter. The fact that Leoncavallo knew of one actual murder gave him the impetus to compose the prologue to *Pagliacci*.

It is from the prologue that the tension of *Pagliacci* emerges. In his address to the villagers ("Un tal gioco"), Canio declares, "The stage and life are not the same thing." This assertion, clearly made in ignorance, shows how far Canio is from the brutal truth revealed in the prologue. His "Vesti la giubba," therefore, has unbearable power, because a masker, an actor, has been unmasked—about life. Leoncavallo makes this particularly evident in Canio's repetition of words from the prologue, "uom," "singhiozzo" (sob) and "spasimo." His confused identity from "Tu se' Pagliaccio" to "No, Pagliaccio non son" exposes the terrifying similarity between the stage and life. The original score and Leoncavallo's widow attest that the final line of *Pagliacci*, "La commedia e finita!," was to be sung, not spoken, by Tonio, ending the opera as he began it. When uttered by Canio, however, its bitter truth is revealed. In fact *Pagliacci* uses the ancient comedic characters of the *alazon* (braggart, Canio) and the eiron (ironist, Tonio) to subvert comedy itself: life is not what it seems.

The contrasts between *Cavalleria Rusticana* and *Pagliacci* indicate that the term verismo is relative and arbitrary. Veristic operas ultimately are a created, not a representational, truth. Puccini, even in *Il Tabarro*, never used street or regional language and was never attracted to genuine *paesani*. Mascagni rarely dealt with Italian subjects, and few verismo operas ever had their setting in Italy or among the lower classes. It is true that verismo cornerstones like *La Bohème*, *Tosca*, *Adriana Lecouvreur* and *Andrea Chénier* depict artist figures ruined by sordid life, but their contexts scarcely correspond to the *paesanismo* of *Cavalleria* or *Pagliacci*.

"I found your successor in your predecessor, Verdi," Hans von Billow once remarked to Mascagni. From the perspective of the twentieth century, one realizes that the revolution inspired by *Cavalleria Rusticana* and *Pagliacci* had marked antecedents. From *Rigoletto* came the idea of the "jester jested" in *Pagliacci*; atmospheric music and a romanticized "low life" appear in *Carmen*; *Cavalleria Rusticana* with its impassioned passages recalls *Il Trovatore* and in its local color even Aida. Opera in modern dress had already taken place with *La Traviata*, while the exchanges between Canio and Tonio in *Pagliacci* parallel in *Otello*.

"It is a pity I wrote *Cavalleria* first. I was crowned before I became king." So confessed Mascagni later in life. But the revolution he initiated remains one landmark of the transition from the nineteenth to the twentieth century, with *La Bohème*, *II Tabarro*, *Andrea Chénier*, *Tiefland*, *Louise*, even *Wozzeck* and *Katya Kabanova*, revealing its significance. In his story "Ieli" Verga wrote, "Anybody who knows how to write is one who keeps words in a tinderbox." Like Mt. Etna brooding over Sicily, such explosions occur— as did *Pagliacci* and *Cavalleria Rusticana*.

The Combat of Sexuality: Mozart and *Così fan Tutte*

In August 1789, a distraught young man wrote his wife: "I am glad indeed when you have some fun—of course I am—but I do wish that you would sometimes not make yourself so cheap . . . A woman must always make herself respected, or else people will begin to talk about her. My love! Forgive me for being so frank, but my peace of mind demands it as well as our mutual happiness."

The writer was Wolfgang Amadeus Mozart, the possibly erring woman his wife Constanze. So concerned was Mozart about the potential for infidelity that he added in the letter: "Remember that you yourself once admitted to me that you are inclined to *comply too easily*. You know the consequences of that."

Indeed, both Mozart and Constanze knew the consequences. The proof is one of the world's greatest exposés of sexuality, *Così fan tutte*, which Mozart composed during the autumn of 1789, at the time of his tormented letter to his wife. Premiered on January 26, 1790, at the Burgtheater in Vienna, *Così fan tutte* definitely was *not* a *jeu d'esprit* on the composer's part.

Instead, it was—and is—a searing inquiry into the natures of men and women, the deception inherent in human sexuality, and the delusions lovers have about one another. The subtitle of the opera, *La scuola degli amanti* or "The School for Lovers," indicates its philosophical intention.

An intimate friend of Casanova, the librettist Lorenzo da Ponte (who also supplied Mozart the texts of *Le nozze di Figaro* [1786] and *Don Giovanni* [1787]), always referred to this work by its subtitle.

It was Mozart who labeled the opera *Così fan tutte* ("All women are like that"), based on the anxieties underscored in his letter. The cultural question, however, is: Who is to blame? Mozart's answer hovers in the title of his opera, but this response is complicated by the subtitle, which suggests that *both* men and women are responsible. In fact, should the title be *Così fan tutti* ("All men are like that") rather than *Così fan tutte*? Full of complexity, paradox and conflict, the evidence of the opera, as the subtitle argues, is yes.

Mozart intends to make the situation complicated. In an opera famous for its symmetrical construction, Mozart focuses not on a single couple but two pairs, comprised of the sisters Fiordiligi and Dorabella and the two "brother" officers Guglielmo and Ferrando. Despite this pattern, however, the contrasts beneath the parallels signal the challenges of the issue: Fiordiligi, soprano, is less pliable and more strong willed than her mezzo soprano sister Dorabella; similarly, Ferrando, tenor, is more idealistic and romantic than his aggressive and pragmatic comrade, the baritone Guglielmo. The differences in voices demarcate differences in temperament, which Mozart will underscore as the opera advances. In the third number of the opera, a trio, Mozart gives Ferrando a dignified cantilena ascending to G as he states he will spend the wager money on a serenade; Guglielmo, on the other hand, will spend it on a banquet.

There is a similar complication in the presentation of Don Alfonso, the older male/counselor/advisor who inaugurates the wager about women's fidelity: Is he a cynic? a philosopher? a skeptic? a devil? a jealous ex-libertine? an objective seeker after truth? In his manipulation of Fiordiligi and Guglielmo and of Dorabella and Ferrando, he suggests a product of the 18th-century Enlightenment, the initiator of a speculative disputation about the nature of love and sexuality. The opera's philosophical drift is reinforced by being set in Naples, the locus of the Italian Enlightenment.

The intricacy of Mozart's response is inscribed in Don Alfonso's declaration "Tutte accusan le donne" before the Act II finale. Declaring that he excuses women for their frailties, he claims this is "a necessity of the heart," an inherent element of female sexuality. Then, he states that a disappointed lover should blame himself for his erroneous judgment. If this attitude appears even-handed, one has only to look at the concluding phrases of his remarks, where he announces "Così fan tutte" and compels Ferrando and Guglielmo to utter the same. This contradiction exposes the discord between the opera's title *Così fan tutte* and its subtitle *La scuola degli amanti*. Are women alone culpable, or are men as well? The opera, obviously, is as much about the deceptive behaviors of men as the susceptibility of women.

This conflict originates in the ultimate sources of *Così fan tutte*, beginning with the legend of Cephalus and Procris from Ovid's *Metamorphoses* (Book 7). A young man, Cephalus, is abducted by the goddess Aurora whom he subsequently rejects, claiming he loves only his wife Procris. Beset by doubts implanted by Aurora, Cephalus, his appearance altered by the goddess, tempts Procris. When he thinks she is yielding, he accuses her of infidelity. After a reconciliation, she overhears Cephalus invoking "aura" (the breeze) but thinks he is wooing a nymph. Procris, spying on Cephalus. is slain by him when he mistakes her for a deer while hunting. That Mozart had this tale in mind is evident from Ferrando's Act I aria "Un'aura amorosa." Ovid's account censures the male for harboring doubts about female fidelity: Cephalus indicts "the error of my fancy" as he holds his dying wife. The legend became a play in 1487; a German poet esteemed by Mozart, Christoph Wieland, published a poem *Cephalus and Procris* in 1768; and artists as great as Poussin painted scenes about it.

A key source of *Così fan tutte* is Ariosto's *Orlando furioso* (1516). In canto 27, a landlord compares a faithful wife to a phoenix: "Just as the phoenix is unique . . . so of a faithful wife let no one speak." This is the origin of Don Alfonso's remark in the second trio of Act I that "woman's faithfulness is like the Arabian phoenix. Everyone says it exists, where it is . . . no one knows." In a later canto (43) of the same poem, Ariosto includes the tale of a knight who pretends to depart, only to return in disguise as a former suitor to test his wife's fidelity; when she yields, he rebukes her. So angry is she with him that she becomes the lover of the former suitor.

Hearing this story, the hero Rinaldo does not reprove the wife but rather the knight: "You looked for what was better left unknown . . . You of the two were more at fault. You would yourself have shown no greater strength" (stanzas 47, 49). In *Orlando furioso* it is males who initiate the conflict about women's fidelity. Ariosto's poem also contributed the names of characters to *Così fan tutte*: Doralice, Fiordispina and Fiordiligi. Both Ovid and Ariosto indict men, not women, for originating marital strife.

Central to *Così fan tutte* is the motif of the wager about a woman's fidelity. Here, two precedents are important. In Boccaccio's *Decameron* (1348-53), a merchant, Bernabo, makes such a bet with Ambrogiuolo, who fails to seduce the wife, whereupon the husband and wife are reconciled. In Shakespeare's *Cymbeline* (1609-10), the husband Posthumus is forced into a wager about his wife Imogen with the crafty Iachimo.

The wager and disguise theme are united in a tale, *La novele del curioso impertiente* ("The tale of one who was too curious") interpolated into the first part of Cervantes' *Don Quixote* (1605-15, in which Anselmo, married to Camila, compels his friend Lotario to test the virtue of his wife. At the end of this grim story, Anselmo writes in a note before dying: "A foolish and ill-advised desire has robbed me of my life . . . I was the creator of my own dishonor."

Thus, in the models for the wager, testing and disguise elements of *Così fan tutte*, it is men—not women—whom European culture condemns for their suspicion, mistrust and plotting. For Mozart's audience, familiar with these antecedents, the title of the opera was therefore ironic—it *should* have been *Così fan tutti*. That the two couples—Fiordiligi/Guglielmo and Dorabella/Ferrando—are affianced rather than married compounds the irony.

This complexity of *Così fan tutte* is reinforced by its amalgamation of disparate elements. Primary among these is that the scenario contains *opera buffa* elements while parodying the conventions of *opera seria*. Of the former, one notes the impertinent and conniving maid in the figure of Despina; the emphasis on ensemble singing (especially in Act I); the contemporary dress; the resort to diguise by Despina, Ferrando and Guglielmo; the fake suicide of the "Albanians"; and the feigned marriages.

While these elements stress the lighter aspect of the wager theme, at the same time Mozart inscribes the passions of *opera seria* characters in several arias, especially in Act I the "Smanie implacabile" of Dorabella and the "Come scoglio" of Fiordiligi, the latter (with opening line from Virgil's *Aeneid*) replete with vocal histrionics.

It is this very conjunction of *opera buffa* and *opera seria* elements that makes the work so stirring, as Richard Strauss noted about *Così* in 1910 when he stressed its "careful evolution of a purely psychological plot . . . the exaggerated, almost comic, but quite genuine pathos of the two ladies." In 1944, Strauss commended the "detached irony" of the opera, which is achieved by the juxtaposition of *opera buffa* with *opera seria*.

Throughout the nineteenth century, the subject of *Così fan tutte* was regarded as immoral, especially the behavior of its women. Its harsh irony was camouflaged. The opera was presented with a new libretto at Copenhagen in 1826. In Paris in 1863, *Così* was presented as *Les Peines d'amour perdues* ("The trials of lost love"), with a text derived from Shakespeare's *Love's Labours Lost*. In 1909 at Dresden, it became *Die Dame Kobold*, with a story from a drama by Calderon. Each of these misguided efforts sought to avoid the stark revelations of the genuine *Così*, which, although *buffa* in substance, is unavoidably *seria* in its sober, pensive, painful, potentially tragic effect.

Many factors contribute to this result. Consider the stress on the "unity" of time: all the action occurs within twenty-four hours; the deceptions are practiced and exposed with ruthless rapidity. In addition, the second act accents the aria as the first had the ensemble, with harrowing implications. Despina's "Una donna a quindici anni" advises that women *must* learn to deceive in order to confront the practices of men. Fiordiligi's rondo "Per pietà" condemns her own inconstancy; Dorabella's "È amore un ladroncello" blazons her capitulation; Ferrando's cavatina "Tradito, schernito" betrays his enslavement to Dorabella; and Guglielmo in "Donne mie" persists in blaming women for his own foibles.

The opera is indeed *Così fan tutte* ("Everyone behaves like this"). The effect of these self-exposures is that the action constitutes a "school for lovers" implicating all four principals, not just or even primarily the women. The precedents of Ovid, Shakespeare, Ariosto and Cervantes indicate it is men who provoke their own despair by their jealousy and suspicion, however much they construct women as "unfaithful." After these caustic revelations, no one can return to the self-delusion of Act I. Ultimately Mozart never signals who returns to whom at the conclusion. Thus the tragic element exists not because the individuals betray each other but because each betrays the self. Mozart prefers to ignore symmetry for what Strauss cited as Mozar's "deepest penetration of artistic fancy and of the subconscious . . . Plato's Eros"—that is, the very essence of sexual response. Well might Mozart write his wife in 1789: "You ought to love me all the more because I make so much of honor."

The Scaffold of Honor:
Poulenc and *Dialogues des Carmelítes*

"I am never to be torn from that eternal place chosen for me—I remain the prisoner of His Agony in the Garden." Thus does the young Cure d'Ambricourt ponder the nature of honor in Georges Bernanos' novel *Journal d'un Curé de Campagne* (1936). Writing between World Wars, with shattering memories of the First and unutterable premonitions of the Second, Bernanos (1888-1948) discovered that the experience of Christ at Gethsemane is the mystical core of existence. The injustice and fear so brutally demonstrated in World War I converged on Gethsemane, "without which there can be no inner life." Therefore in Bernanos' last work, *Dialogues des Carmélites*, published posthumously in 1949, the heroine becomes Sister Blanche of the Agony of Christ.

The challenge for Francis Poulenc (1899-1963) was to embody in music this mystical concept of honor. After the premiere of the opera in 1957, Bernanos' confessor, the Abbé Daniel Pézeril, wrote to the composer, "Bernanos would say thank you for having understood in music the meaning of his words, and for having invented in another way the same mystery of Blanche's ascent. Right from the beginning you found the way into the heart of the *Dialogues* . . . a meeting of souls if ever there was one." So intense was Poulenc's dialogue with the author that Albert Béguin, editor of Bernanos' *Dialogues*, commented, "You have, it seems to me, accomplished a true tour de force in adapting his text of *Dialogues des Carmélites* to the demands of music, remaining faithful to its spirit. I rediscover *all* of Bernanos in your presentation." Poulenc's dialogue with Bernanos is the history of an opera and summit of a spiritual quest.

Poulenc found in Bernanos not only a man but a movement, for *Dialogues des Carmélites* encompasses centuries of French thought. To form the philosophical system of *Dialogues*, Bernanos drew on his political experiences, well known to Poulenc. For example, since he came from a strongly nationalist and royalist family, Bernanos made several of the nuns in *Carmélites*, including Madame de Croissy, Sister Constance, Mother Marie and Blanche de la Force, persons of noble blood. Having been enrolled in 1898 at the Collège de Vaugirard, which the young Charles de Gaulle also attended, in 1904 Bernanos went to the Collège Sainte-Marie, where his political ideas were shaped by the writings of the right-wing thinker Edouard Drumont (1844-1917). Bernanos became an enthusiastic supporter of the monarchist Action Française, and by 1906 he had been involved in political agitations.

While at the Sorbonne he joined the street-fighting *camelots du roi* in 1908. Incarcerated in Santé prison in 1909, he wrote his first political publication from his cell, denouncing moral laxity in romantic writers and exhibiting the influence of Charles Maurras (1868-1952), one of the leaders of Action Francaise. If from Drumont he inherited the doctrines of the Catholic-monarchist cause, from Maurras he derived the distinction between the *pays réel*, the France of historical tradition, and the *pays légal*, the artificial bourgeois society of republicanism. In 1917, when he married Jeanne Talbert d'Arc, a direct descendant of the brother of Jeanne d'Arc, Bernanos' contact with the French past was solemnized.

Over and above its historical resonances from the past, *Dialogues des Carmélites* cannot be separated from political events in France during the twentieth century. In *Les Grands Cimetières sous la Lune* (1938) Bernanos violently attacked both Franco and Mussolini, comparing Spain to France during the Terror, while the following year, in *Scandale de la Vérité*, he denounced the Munich Pact. Of France between the wars Bernanos wrote in 1944, "The temperature was that of a bordello, the franc fallen below zero, and the newspapers were discovering a genius every day. On the boulevards one could smell the extermination camps that were to open." For Poulenc and Bernanos, the appalling similarity of these wars to the Terror during the Revolution made their *Dialogues* a political as well as a religious manifesto.

Bernanos' first encounter with the subject of *Dialogues* is integrally bound with politics. With the shadow of Hitler looming over Europe, Bernanos was living at Toulon in February 1938 when his friend the Reverend Raymond-Leopold Bruckberger lent him a French translation, *La Dernière à l'Échafaud*, of the novel *Die Letzte am Schafott* by Gertrud von le Fort (1876-1971). Disgusted with the French, Bernanos sailed in July for South America, settling in Brazil, from where he wrote polemical tracts against Nazism and the Vichy regime. At the end of the war, Bernanos returned to France at the behest of De Gaulle but soon became disillusioned with the Fourth Republic, with its technocracy and materialistic democracy. On May 30, 1947, Bruckberger wrote Bernanos asking if he would write the dialogue for a cinema script based on a scenario that he and Philippe Agostini had created from Gertrud von le Fort's novel. In January 1948 Bruckberger visited Bernanos and heard sections of the work, which Bernanos completed April 8, 1948, after working eight to ten hours a day. Between Bruckberger and Bernanos there existed a friendship cemented by their dual political and religious allegiances, for Bruckberger had been chaplain general to the Resistance and had welcomed De Gaulle at Notre Dame in 1944 at the Liberation. Poulenc inherited a text composed in three stages—the novel in 1931, the scenario in 1947, the play Bernanos completed in 1948.

Though Bernanos had read the novel in 1938, during the composition of his drama he had with him only the scenario by Bruckberger and Agostini. Bruckberger recalled in 1957, "It was I who gave Bernanos the novel, which he had not known. When he composed the dialogue, he no longer had the book. It was taken from the scenario alone." In 1949, when Gertrud von le Fort read Bernanos' text for the first time, she wrote, "For the film—if it is ever realized—I wish it would follow my novel more strictly. It is very regrettable that Bernanos composed his dialogue without my book. I do not understand why Reverend Bruckberger did not give him a sample.

I would myself have given him a section for this purpose." Furthermore, Bernanos avoided historical sources, telling his secretary he "did not intend to write a historical work," and with a certain humor he added he did not work on "documents." Even when Bruckberger gave him a file of papers relating to the Carmélites, Bernanos returned it unopened. In 1950, when Bernanos' editor, Béguin, proposed making the script into a play, Gertrud von le Fort endorsed the project, declaring the text "too lofty and rich for a film," but by 1951 she was again insisting on the dependence of the Bernanos script on her novel. At its publication in 1949, it was Béguin who gave it the title *Dialogues des Carmélites*, possibly invoking Bernanos' story about a writer and an unbeliever, *Dialogue d'Ombres* (1928).

Bernanos, Bruckberger and Gertrud von le Fort all had similar political ideas. In 1947, when Bruckberger founded the short-lived journal *Le Cheval de Troie*, both other writers appeared in its pages. Bruckberger and Bernanos were critical of democracy. Bruckberger wrote in 1948, "To me it seems certain that dictatorship is inherent in the internal logic of a radical social democracy, from the moment it is admitted that authority resides only in the multitude. It cannot be denied that Hitler was the delegate of the multitude. So is Stalin." Recording the origin of her novel, Gertrud von le Fort likewise associated it with Nazism:

> The point of departure for my creation was not primarily the destiny of the sixteen Carmélites of Compiegne but the figure of the young Blanche. In a historic sense she never lived, but she received the breath of life from my internal spirit, and she can not be detached from this origin, which is hers. Born in the profound horror of a time darkened by the signs of destiny, this figure arose before me in some way as the embodiment of the mortal agony of an era going totally to its ruin.

When Bernanos died in 1948, Bruckberger wrote in his diary:

> Georges Bernanos is dead. He knew that he was going to die. He felt that his foot was already caught in the stirrup.
>
> I have never known a Christian so constantly obsessed with the idea of divine justice and what seems divine injustice, and by the holy agony of Christ. Now he has finished his exile. Honor, to him, was Christian honor. To Bernanos, the fatherland was France, the chosen land of Christian honor, illustrious by our saints and our chevaliers;

land of freedom because it was the land of sacrifice.

For Poulenc, who composed one of the most famous songs—"C"—of the Resistance, these writers of the *Cheval de Troie* were spiritual adherents.

While the character of Blanche de la Force is the creation of Gertrud von le Fort, the incident of the sixteen nuns from the Carmelite convent at Compiègne executed on July 17, 1794, became the historical grid for the Bernanos/Poulenc *Dialogues*. The Marquis de la Force alludes to Blanche's birth in 1770 during the fireworks celebrating the marriage of the Dauphin to Marie-Antoinette. The actual Madame Lidoine was elected prioress in 1786 and reelected in 1789. The revolutionary tribunal prohibited the taking of vows provisionally on October 29 and definitively on February 13, 1790. On August 4 the commission first visited the convent to take inventory of its possessions, returning the next day to interrogate the sisters. A year later, August 15, 1791, the wearing of religious garb was forbidden. Between June and September 1792, Madame Lidoine proposed a vow of atonement. September 1792 brought the greatest changes to the convent: on the 12th the Carmelite convent of Compiègne was pillaged; on the 17th the sisters were dispersed into four groups. Louis XVI was executed on January 21, 1793. In April of the year following, Marie de l'Incarnation went to Paris, so she was not taken when the Carmelites were arrested on June 22, 1794. They were transferred to the Conciergerie prison on July 12-13, tried. condemned and executed on July 17. Ten days later, the Terror ended with the fall of Robespierre.

Gertrud von le Fort and Bernanos/Poulenc, however, made changes in the history. Since Blanche enters the convent at sixteen, the novel compresses the years 1786-89. In the novel and opera there are two vows; the first initiated by Marie de l'Incarnation in 1792, the second by Madame Lidoine. The second vow in Bernanos/Poulenc, however, is taken to stunning effect in the Conciergerie. In the novel the Carmelites are condemned and executed a day earlier than in reality, dying on July 16, the feast of Notre Dame du Mont Carmel.

Bernanos and Poulenc were likewise drawing on history in characterizing the nuns. Madame de Croissy was Prioress of Carmel from 1779 to 1786; from that date until her execution she was Mistress of Novices, a role that is shared in the novel and opera by Madame Lidoine and Mother Marie. Poulenc, Bernanos and Gertrud von le Fort alter history by having her die early in the story rather than on the scaffold. Sister Constance is modeled on Marie-Geneviève Meunier (1766-94), who was invested in 1788 and pronounced her vows in December 1789. One of her brothers attempted to persuade her to leave Carmel, an incident that prompted Bruckberger and Agostini to create the Chevalier de la Force, who does not appear in the original novel. In all Poulenc's sources the actual Marie Meunier is divided into both Constance and Blanche. To Bernanos and Poulenc they partake of the youth and chivalresque honor of the revered Jeanne d'Arc.

The contrast between Mother Marie and Madame Lidoine is pivotal in Bernanos and in Poulenc. The actual Marie de l'Incarnation (Francoise-Genevieve Philippe), the illegitimate child of a royal prince, entered the Carmélites in 1786, having been miraculously healed in her youth at the tomb of Madame Acarie, who under the name Marie de l'Incarnation had introduced the Carmelite order into France. Mother Marie survived all her sisters to write the *Relation*, published after her death in 1836 as *Histoire des Religieuses Carmélites de Compiègne*. In contrast to these nuns, all aristocratic by birth, is the peasant origin of the actual Madame Marie-Madeleine Lidoine, the new prioress. Gertrud von le Fort enhanced the role of Mother Marie (e.g., initiating the first vow of martyrdom) to present starkly the two "pillars" of France, the noble military (Mother Marie) and the strong peasantry (Madame Lidoine). Each woman interprets the Agony of Christ at Gethsemane as her class would dictate: to Mother Marie it is *agonia* or conflict, to Madame Lidoine its meaning is *passio* or suffering.

The differences between novel and scenario very much influenced Bernanos and Poulenc. In the novel the entire story is narrated by Monsieur de Villeroi, eliminated in Bruckberger's scenario. In addition to introducing the Chevalier, Bruckberger and Agostini developed the great episode of the agony of the Prioress Croissy, barely alluded to in Gertrud von le Fort. Whereas the novel has nothing about the Carmélites in prison, Bruckberger developed this element as well as concluded the scenario with the execution rather than with Mother Marie's despair, as in the novel. Working with the Bruckberger scenario and retaining his memory of the novel, Bernanos made subtle alterations. In accordance with his monarchist views, he makes the Marquis de la Force, almost Voltairean in the novel, less rationalistic. Throughout his drama Bernanos intensifies the spiritual significance of the scenario. For example, when Blanche and Constant are discussing the illness of the prioress, Bernanos has Constance propose that they offer their lives for the prioress; he adds as well Constance's premonition that she and Blanche will die together. In effect, Bernanos used the novel as an outline and the scenario as a reduction, but such mystical themes as the Agony or the exchange of deaths between Madame de Croissy and Blanche remain his own.

When Poulenc was asked by Guido Valcarenghi of Ricordi in 1953 to compose an opera, he took Valcarenghi's suggestion of the *Dialogues*, having read the work and seen it as a play. Though Poulenc remained faithful to Bernanos in general, he cut some passages of considerable significance. In the first scene, for instance, he excised Blanche's protest to the Marquis: "What chance do we have to prove ourselves, we young women? To be worth something, one must know what one is worth." He eliminated from the same scene Blanche's belief that "There are several kinds of courage." In the first interview with the Prioress, Poulenc cut her references to Blanche's noble birth and her warning, a Bernanos paradox: "In wanting to descend too low, one risks overstepping the mark." Poulenc softened the confrontation between the dying Prioress and Mother Marie in his fourth scene. In Bernanos, in an exchange cut by Poulenc, Mother Marie calls her suffering "delirium" and advises the Prioress not to struggle against nature, to which Madame de Croissy angrily responds, "Delirium! Delirium! Have you ever seen this kind of delirium before? . . . Struggle against nature! Have I ever done anything else all my life?" Throughout the opera, many references to class distinctions among the sisters are muted or eliminated to subdue Bernanos' monarchism.

Both Poulenc's and Bernanos' *Dialogues* must be placed in two contexts—the religious history of France during the seventeenth and eighteenth centuries, and French religious drama during the twentieth. In French history, the expulsion of a group of nuns inevitably recalls the history of the convent of Port Royal. This community was a stronghold of

Jansenism, which emphasized the power of grace; as such, it was opposed by the Jesuits and their Molinism, which minimized the importance of grace. From 1656 to 1657, Blaise Pascal undertook the defense of Port Royal in his famous *Lettres Provinciales*. The dispute was stopped rather than settled when Pope Clement XI dissolved the convent in 1705 and ordered its destruction in 1710. Since grace, the validation of spiritual honor, is crucial to *Dialogues des Carmélites*, Poulenc and Bernanos cannot avoid this association; at the time of the execution, the spirit of Port Royal was still very much alive.

Also from the eighteenth century, the writings, especially the philosophical dialogues, of Denis Diderot express doctrines that *Dialogues des Carmélites* ethically opposes. Diderot's skepticism and rationalism emphasize progress, liberalism and anti-authoritarianism, paving the way for the French Revolution. It is no accident that Gertrud von le Fort alludes to Diderot's notorious anticlerical novel *La Religieuse* (The Nun) of 1760. This tale recounts the life of Suzanne Simonin, a girl placed in a convent to conceal her illegitimacy, based on the case of Marguerite Delamarre in 1758. The illegitimacy hints at the birth of Mother Marie, while Blanche's entry into Carmel at sixteen parallels Suzanne's experience. At the convent of Longchamp, the superior, Madame de Moni, resembles Madame de Croissy; there is even a change of prioresses, as in Bernanos/Poulenc. Though Blanche wishes to remain in the convent and Suzanne to leave it, one should regard *Dialogues des Carmélites* as a response to the anticlericalism of *La Religieuse* and its moral relativism. The Bernanos/Poulenc *Dialogues* evokes *La Religieuse* to refute it.

In addition to *La Religieuse*, Diderot's two great philosophical dialogues *Le Neveu de Rameau* (1762) and *Le Rêve de d'Alembert* (1769) are invoked by the title *Dialogues des Carmélites*, particularly the first work, where Diderot recounts a conversation with Jean-Francois Rameau, nephew of the composer. Belief in the natural goodness of man is pitted against the nephew's cynical, amoral determinism as he wonders "Is virtue made for everybody?" while spouting maxims like "I congratulate myself on my failings more often than I deplore them." In *Le Rêve de d'Alembert*, an imaginary dialogue among the mathematician d'Alembert, Mademoiselle de L'Espinasse and the physician Bordeu, conventional morality and the supernatural are demolished in favor of determinism and amorality. The insistent rationalism of Diderot's dialogues is the counter-argument to the Christian morality of *Dialogues des Carmélites*, revealing the two poles of eighteenth-century belief, determinism and divinity: thus Poulenc places the saraband and Carmagnole against the "Salve Regina" and the "Veni Creator."

If one part of the background of *Dialogues des Carmélites* is the eighteenth century, Port Royal and Diderot's dialogues, its other dialogue is with twentieth-century French religious drama, especially the work of François Mauriac, Paul Claudel, Jacques Copeau and Henri de Montherlant. Their plays invoke the great tradition of French religious drama, such as *Polyeucte* (1641) by Corneille, which involves Christian martyrdom, and *Esther* (1689) by Racine, who studied at Port Royal and wrote its history. Claudel's *L'Annonce Faite à Marie* (1912) bears several similarities to Bernanos/ Poulenc: it includes a mystical experience at Christmas (cf. the conclusion of Poulenc's Act II), the exchange of deaths and the intermingling of the natural and the supernatural. In Mauriac's *Asmodée* (1938), which bears striking resemblance to Bernanos' novel *Monsieur Ouine* (1943), a young girl, Emmanuele, decides against the religious life after the evil of her home is exposed. The persecution attending the founding of the Franciscans is the subject of Copeau's *Le Petit Pauvre* (1946). Of all these works, however, it is Montherlant's *Port-Royal* (1954, begun 1940) which the Bernanos/ Poulenc *Dialogues* most involves. In this drama, Montherlant deals with Jansenism in 1664. The prioress, Sister Angélique, who resembles Madame de Croissy, expresses ideas bearing on the Carmélites: "Monastic life," she declares, "was not established for us to sing well, but for us to die well to ourselves." At its end, twelve nuns are expelled and handed over to the Jesuits, but the issues of fear, doubt and justice are as stringent as in *Dialogues des Carmélites*.

By its incisive dialogue with French religious thought and literature, *Dialogues des Carmélites* evolves a rigorous philosophical system of its own. Central to Bemanos/Poulenc are three statements in both the drama and the opera: "We do not die for ourselves alone, but for each other. Or some times even instead of each other" (Constance, Act II, Scene 1); "What God wishes to test is not your strength but your weakness" (Madame de Croissy, Act I, Scene 2); and "You have to run the risk of fear, as you run the risk of death" (Chevalier, Act II, Scene 2). Constance's belief is the core of Bernanos/Poulenc's idea of the transmission of grace and the mystical exchange of deaths, founded on Christ's death for the sake of humanity.

Madame de Croissy's statement about the testing of weakness expresses a concept of honor, not heroism, revealing the reliance of the natural on the supernatural and the example of Christ in the Agony at Gethsemane. In Bernanos' drama, Madame Lidoine defines Carmelite honor in a passage cut by Poulenc: "Our vocation is in no way to oppose ourselves to injustice but simply to atone for it, to pay the ransom . . . we ourselves are that ransom. A Carmelite who desires martyrdom is as poor a Carmelite as a soldier who seeks death before having carried out the orders of his commander." "Prayer is a duty, martyrdom a reward" declares the prioress in Act II, Scene 2. Blanche early recognizes the true nature of honor (Act I, Scene 1) when she tells her father, "I abandon all! I renounce all! So that God may restore me to honor." In Bernanos/Poulenc there are four key episodes involving this mystical honor: Madame de Croissy endures a despairing death so that Blanche might die differently; Constance deliberately votes against the vow of martyrdom so that Blanche will have the courage to vote for it; Mother Marie, feeling "dishonored" when she cannot die with her sisters, must learn the more severe honor of giving up her own sacrifice; Blanche, by accepting her fear, becomes honored.

The idea of fear expressed by the Chevalier is a key to Bernanos' philosophy. One of the peculiarities of Poulenc's opera is his elimination of many of Bernanos' most crucial statements regarding fear. For example, in Act I, Scene 1, Blanche argues to the Marquis, "I do not despise the world. For me the world is simply an element in which I cannot live." The same passage in Bernanos is "I do not despise the world, it is scarcely true to say I fear it. For me the world is simply an element in which I cannot live." In Bernanos, Blanche seeks in Carmel not a refuge but a remedy for her fear. And this fear is not ordinary. It is the *agonie*, which in French refers solely to the anguish of death. Blanche's religious name, Soeur Blanche de l'Agonie du Christ, when joined to her secular name, Blanche de la Force, becomes for Bernanos the central paradox: *l'agonie* is *la force.*

For this reason, Madame Lidoine in Bernanos tells her community, "Remembering the Garden of Gethsemane, where in the heart of our Lord the whole of human anguish was made divine, the distinction between fear and courage seems to me of little import, and fear and courage seem like the trinkets of luxury." Poulenc's excision of this passage cannot be justified; it demystifies Blanche's fear. "What we call anguish, despair, are not states of the soul but the soul itself," declares the Curé d'Ambricourt in the *Journal.* When Albert Beguin edited *Dialogues des Carmélites* after Bernanos' death, he added the following passage from Bernanos' novel *Joie* (1929) as an epigraph: "In one way Fear is also God's daughter, redeemed on the night of Good Friday. She is not beautiful—no—ridiculed at times, at others cursed, disowned by everyone . . . and yet, make no mistake, she is present at every death agony—she is man's intercessor." The risk of fear, the reexperiencing of the Agony of Christ at Gethsemane, is the test of honor. "It is the fear of fear that shapes the face of a brave man," declares the Legionnaire Olivier in the *Journal.* He speaks for Blanche de la Force.

"I suffer but I live," wrote the French poet André Chénier, whose execution three days after the Carmelites' death is commemorated in Umberto Giordano's opera *Andrea Chénier.* Chenier's conviction applies to Blanche, for her suffering inaugurates rather than terminates life. As in that other great mystical opera, Wagner's *Parsifal, Dialogues des Carmélites* reveals that suffering by loss of self leads to self-realization. For Bernanos and Poulenc this loss of self is achieved through grace, so the dying curate of the *Journal* can exclaim, "Tout est grâce"—Everything is grace. In *Dialogues des Carmélites* this includes *agonie*, fear. When *agonie* and *force* merge, the dialogue of these *Dialogues* becomes resolved in Blanche's monologue at the scaffold invoking grace, "Veni Creator."

Fatal Man:
Mozart and *Don Giovanni*

Can there be a greater coincidence in the history of opera?

On October 29, 1787, a new opera was performed at the National Theater, Prague. Its title was *Il dissoluto punito ossia il Don Giovanni* by Wolfgang Amadeus Mozart. Just as stunning as the premiere was the presence of a man famous throughout Europe—Giacomo Girolamo Casanova.

Thus, one of the world's great seducers attended the opera now generally known simply as *Don Giovanni*. Although Casanova, who had met Mozart in 1787, and Don Giovanni are not identical, their amorous histories, actual and mythical, harmonized one night.

In 1787 alone there were three operas about Don Giovanni, although Mozart's has become the definitive presentation of this promiscuous rogue. Since the expression "a Don Juan" has endured as a description of hypersexual males, who or what does Giovanni represent?

A list of possible interpretations includes diverse identities: misogynist, narcissist, seducer, adolescent, sadist, egotist, rebel, skeptic, nihilist, allegorical Lust, blasphemer, adventurer, brigand, misanthrope, *esprit fort,* abstract power, *élan vital,* male sexuality, cynic, blind instinct, secret religionist, Enlightenment rationalist, atheist, rapist, libertine and/or, above all, the *homme fatal,* the man "mad, bad and dangerous to know."

Such multiplicity attests to one supreme element—the Don Juan idea is an inexhaustible myth of masculinity. Few legends have had such varied transformations as has this profligate *hidalgo*.

Don Juan makes his first appearance in the Spanish play *El Burlador de Sevilla y convidado de piedra* (The Deceiver of Seville and the Guest of Stone), written around 1616. Its author was a friar, Gabriel Telléz, who wrote under the *nom de plume* of Tirso de Molina. The drama conjoins the two key elements of the Don Juan story: the hero's sexual escapades and the invitation to the Stone Guest, the Commander whose hand leads the Don to Hell. Mozart's complete tide for his opera reflects this duality: *The Libertine Punished, or Don Giovanni.*

The drama by Tirso defines the enduring elements of the legend: the Andalusian cavalier Don Juan Tenorio, the Duchess Isabela, and Doña Ana (the prototypes of Mozart's Donna Anna), the Don's servant Catalinón (the future Leporello), the peasant Aminta (Zerlina) and her bridegroom Patricio (Masetto) and Don Gonzalo (Mozart's Commendatore). Don Juan's harrowing adventures include a shipwreck.

Don Juan boasts: "My greatest pleasure is to trick women, leaving them dishonored," threatening, "I'll kill whoever stops me." He defies the Stone Guest: "What! *Me* afraid? Were you both Hell and Death, I'd dare to give my hand." So universal is his notoriety that he can declare, "I am a man without a name" in the first scene—that is, a living legend. The Don's father, Don Diego Tenorio (not in Mozart) has a confrontation with his errant son, whom he curses: "May God reward you as your sins deserve." Don Juan's servant Catalinón (whose name means "coward") rebukes Don Juan: "I know you are the scourge of womankind." Thus, within the drama there is explicit rebuke of the hero's "sexploitation" of women.

Following Tirso, the Don is reincarnated in Molière's *Dom Juan ou Le Festin de Pierre* (Don Juan, or The Stone Guest) first performed in 1665 with Molière, himself labeled a *libertin*, in the role of che servant Sganarelle (Catalinón/Leporello). Molière's contribution to the legend is the creation of Elvire (Mozart's Elvira), who damns her seducer: "Heaven will punish you, you faithless villain." Sganarelle indicts his master: "A great gentleman who is really wicked is a terrible thing." Don Juan's father Don Louis denounces his dissolute son: "Birth is of no account unless accompanied by nobility of character. Virtue is the true title to nobility." At this the Don, a tough atheist, retorts: "Make haste and die." Don Juan declares that if he is a hypocrite, so is the rest of society: "Hypocrisy has become a fashionable vice." The Don is defiant to the end: "Nothing that was ever made can frighten me."

Although described by the librettist Lorenzo da Ponce as a *dramma giocoso* and by Mozart as an *opera buffa*, *Don Giovanni* unquestionably is a mixture of comic and tragic, with elements of *opera seria* (Donna Anna, the Commendatore, Don Ottavio) and *opera buffa* (Zerlina, Masetto, Leporello). Confining the action to twenty-four hours, from night to night, endows Giovanni with both mystery and intensity.

Mozart presents the seducer from several perspectives, the Don's own and those of others. In the "champagne aria" of Act I, "Finch'han dal vino," the five stanzas constitute a miniature agenda of a rake's progress: plan a party, round up some women, dance the night away, flirt with anyone, and seduce the lot. The suavity of Giovanni emerges in the duet with Zerlina from Act I "Là ci darem la mano." Leporello's "catalogue aria" in Act I enumerates 2,065 conquests by his master. Through the eighteenth century, Don Juan, Lust itself, is a fearless, careless, reckless, blasphemous, defiant, remorseless seducer.

In the nineteenth century, however, new theories began to emerge. In 1813, E.T.A. Hoffmann wrote his story "Don Juan: A Fantastical Occurrence," in which he argued that Don Juan was a virtual superman or *Übermensch*: "nature endows Juan with all that brings man close to Divinity. With a longing for the infinite, Juan was doomed to find earthly life shallow to the end. He was driven onward by a deep contempt for the common features of life, to which he felt superior. He was forced to rebel." Hoffmann's reinterpretation is central to any modern grasp of Mozart's protagonist.

The French novelist Stendhal in *De l'Amour* (1822) exonerated the Don: "Don Juan's desires are imperfectly satisfied by cold reality. He must be forgiven. He sees none but himself in the universe." To Hoffmann, Don Juan is a romantic rebel and idealist, to Stendhal a narcissist. Alfred de Musset in *Namouna* (1823) labeled the Don a "guileless corrupter" who pursued the ideal, a "magnificent symbol of man on earth." In Baudelaire's 1846 poem "Don Juan aux enfers" (Don Juan in Hell), the Don remains "calm while grasping his rapier," indomitable even in the Inferno.

In the famous Spanish drama of the era, *Don Juan Tenorio* (1844) by Jose Zorilla, the Don, after a life of seductions and crimes, repents at the last second for love of the convent novice Ines, whom he had abducted. Danish theologian Søren Kierkegaard devoted part of *Either/Or* (1843) to an analysis of Don Giovanni, believing he is not so much a seducer (which implies ethics and calculation) as the embodiment of "desire, the energy of sensuous desire and the absolute victory of this desire"—Giovanni is life force, power and energy, beyond morality. George Bernard Shaw, who remolded the Don into a misogynist in *Man and Superman* (1903), wrote "Don Giovanni Ex plains" in 1887, in which Giovanni claims to have been more the seduced than the seducer, exerting "an infernal fascination in spite of myself."

The landmark psychoanalytic interpretation of Don Juan remains *Die Don Juan Gestalt* (The Don Juan Legend) by Otto Rank (1924), prompted by a Viennese performance of the opera in November 1921. Rank contended that Giovanni manifested the Oedipus complex, desire for the mother and defiance of the father: "The many women whom he must always replace anew represent to him the *one* irreplaceable mother; and the rivals and adversaries whom he deceives, defrauds, struggles against and finally even kills represent the *one* unconquerable mortal enemy, the father." Leporello is the "ego ideal," since he "represents the inner criticism, the anxiety and the conscience of the hero." The fact that Mozart had a conflicted relationship with his father Leopold, who died in May, 1787, during the composition of *Don Giovanni*, validates for Rank these contentions. The Commendatore represents the guilt felt by the son for his incest and parricide.

Mozart's *Don Giovanni* by its greatness legitimates all these interpretations. Ultimately, the operatic Don Giovanni must be assimilated to the mythic Don Juan. No one recognized this fact more than philosopher Albert Camus, who in his *Mythe de Sisyphe* (Myth of Sisyphus) (1942) insisted: "Don Juan knows and does not hope. Hell for him is a thing to be provoked. He rejects regret, that other form of hope. He knows he is right and that there can be no question of punishment. A fate is not a punishment." *Don Giovanni* triumphs in the eighteenth century, as Juan/ Giovanni will triumph in the twenty-first.

The Impossible Dream:
Massenet and *Don Quichotte*

During the19th century, few operatic composers could resist the lure of Spain. Such attraction produced one masterpiece after another, in fact. Beethoven's *Fidelio* (1805), Rossini's *Il barbiere di Siviglia* (1816), Bizet's *Carmen* (1875) and Verdi's *Ernani* (1844), *Il trovatore* (1853), *La forza del destino* (1862) and *Don Carlo* (1867) are landmarks attesting to the century's Hispanism (or attraction to all things Spanish).

The French composer Jules Massenet (1842-1912) was no exception. In his grand opera *Le Cid* (1885), Massenet recounted the exploits of Spain's warrior Rodrigo Díaz de Vivar, who fought against the Moors in the 11th century and was the hero of Spain's national epic *Poema de Mio Cid* (c. 1140). In 1894, Massenet composed his veristic opera *La Navarraise*, concerning the Carlist Wars in Spain during the 1870s.

For Massenet, these two operas are preludes in their Hispanism to his final masterpiece *Don Quichotte*, which premiered at Monte Carlo on February 24, 1910, with the Russian bass Feodor Chaliapin as Don Quichotte and the contralto Lucy Arbell as La Belle Dulcinée. This is not to say that Massenet was the first to adapt the famous novel *Don Quixote* by Miguel de Cervantes (1547-1616), since more than 50 operas have derived from this quintessential Spanish masterpiece.

The Libretto by Henri Cain used Cervantes via the verse drama of a minor playwright, Jacques Le Lorrain, whose *Le Chevalier de la longue figure* was performed in 1904. Le Lorrain's Don Quixote is an idealist who espouses charity and justice, with echoes of the practice of Jesus Christ.

Massenet himself had need of some charity at this point in his life and identified with the trials of Jacques Le Lorrain, who had lived in poverty and died a few days after seeing his play performed. Massenet's previous opera *Bacchus* (1909) had been a failure. In *My Recollections* (1912), Massenet recalled: "Don Quichotte came into my life as a soothing balm. I had great need of it. Since the preceding September I had suffered acute rheumatic pains and I had passed much more of my existence in bed than out of it."

Massenet was particularly taken with the alteration by Le Lorrain of the character of Dulcinea from Cervantes' original: "What charmed me and decided me to write this work was Le Lorrain's stroke of genius in substituting for the coarse wench at the inn, Cervantes' Dulcinea del Tobosa, the original and picturesque La Belle Dulcinée. The most renowned French authors had not had that idea. It brought to our piece an element of deep beauty in the woman's role and a potent poetical touch to our Don Quichotte dying of love."

Two strokes of fortune enabled Massenet to be especially pleased with the premiere. He noted "the curious audacity of Lucy Arbell, our La Belle Dulcinée, in wanting to accompany herself on the guitar in the song in the fourth act. In a remarkably short time, she made herself a virtuoso on the instrument . . . Knowing her vocal abilities, I brightened the role with daring vocalizations." In addition, for the death of Don Quichotte in the fifth act, it was Raoul Gunsbourg, administrator of the Monte Carlo Opera, who suggested "A knight should die standing!" This advice assured the triumph of Chaliapin as Don Quichotte.

In his memoir *Pages from My life* (1927) Chaliapin observed about Massenet's *Don Quichotte* when he first heard the composer perform it: "When I left, I was still too much under the spell of this work, so touchingly, so immortally beautiful, played by Massenet himself, in the sanctity of his own home, to be able to talk very much. There are many composers, of course, that I could mention who have written more profound music than Jules Massenet, yet I must confess that I never remember being more intensely moved than by his interpretation of the score."

The Monte Carlo premiere was acclaimed, befitting a work that is Massenet's equivalent of Shakespeare's *Tempest* in its summing up of a lifetime of dedication to art, theater and music, signified by the fact that the composer and the librettist labelled the opera a "comédie héroïque."

Massenet's *Don Quichotte* stresses this heroic dimension, albeit it is critiqued in Cervantes' original. Published in two parts in 1605 and 1615, Cervantes' novel was written to sabotage the tales of chivalry which had obsessed European culture. The hero of the novel is a man from the village of La Mancha, one Quejana, a "lean and gaunt" individual "close on to 50," who "went completely out of his mind" so far as chivalry is concerned. Naming himself Don Quixote de La Mancha, he sets out on exploits, initially alone.

Intending to mock the Don's obsession, Cervantes simultaneously— even if inadvertently—aggrandize it. In Part I, chapter 7, of the novel, the Don acquires a "squire" in the figure of a peasant, Sancho Panza, who plays the role of realist to the Don's idealist.

This immortal pair permits Cervantes to explore every conceivable contrast: illusion vs. reality, idealism vs. materialism, fantasy vs. truth, belief vs. skepticism, faith vs. doubt. It is central that the Don is "mad" only when the *idée fixe* bout chivalry penetrates his mind; otherwise, he is sensible. The opposing attitudes toward life of the Don and Sancho Panza allow Cervantes to engage in debates as profound as those in any dialogue by Plato, in a comedic/mock-epical—but definitely *not* superficial—strategy.

Massenet's *Don Quichotte* sustains Cervantes' original debate while elevating its tone. For example, Dulcinea, a tavern wench in the novel, becomes a sensitive albeit mercurial courtesan in the opera, particularly in Act 4, when she shifts from the melancholy of her aria "Lorsque le temps d'amour a fui" ("When the time of love has flown") to the carefree song with guitar accompaniment a few moments later, "Ne pensons qu'au plaisir d'aimer" ("Think only of the pleasures of love"). In Act I, Sancho alludes to the Cid to focus the heroic dimension. In Act 3, Don Quichotte transforms the bandit Ténébrun and blesses him, recalling the deeds of Jesus, to whom the Don is explicitly compared by Sancho at the end of Act 4 when he denounces those who mock his master in "Vous commettez tous um acte épouvantable" ("All of you have done an appalling deed").

This heroic element is stressed in Act 3, when Don Quichotte states his credo to the bandit chief with "Je suis le chevalier errant" ("I am the knight-errant"). Throughout the opera, echoes of Cervantes remain. For instance, Sancho in Act 2 alludes to the flocks of sheep, which the Don believed were armies of enemies, from Part 1, chapter 18, of the novel. The famous charging of the windmills as if they were giants, from Cervantes' Part 1, chapter 8, constitutes the climax of Act 2 in *Don Quichotte*. Each of these occasions engages the debates about idealism/realism, delusion/sanity, and fantasy/reality.

Nothing encapsulates these issues so well as the Don's immortal serenade to Dulcinée "Quand apparaissent les étoiles" ("When the stars begin to shine") in Act I, sung to exquisite effect with the mandolin. The stars of night evoke Dulcinée's eyes, provoking the Don to a prayer of love. When the cynical rival Juan asks if the love song is sad or happy, Don Quichotte declares: "It can be either, equally well, for it is the song of a love." This acceptance of the ambiguous happiness of human existence is valiant.

"This will to be oneself is heroism" wrote José Ortega y Gasset in his *Meditations on Quixote* in 1914. Such bravery constitutes courage for a composer heading toward death—and for an era careening toward World War I. Massenet's *Don Quichotte* is a masterful distillation of the eternal existential dilemma whereby each person is lured to idealism but confronted by reality. To die standing, as does Don Quichotte, indeed *is* a heroic act!

Elektra as Nightmare:
Strauss and *Elektra*

"A huge volcano, spluttering forth a vast amount of dirt and muck, through which every now and then, when the fuming ceases and a breath of clear air blows away the smoke, we see the grand and strong original outlines of the mountain." So observed British critic Ernest Newman at the first performance of Richard Strauss' *Elektra* in London in 1910. *Elektra* has invited controversy ever since. Wrote Robert Donington in 1990: the opera was "not so much archetypal as pathological." Perhaps they are both right: Strauss' *Elektra* can be seen as a masterpiece of pathology—psychological, familial, cultural, musical and theatrical. It is a one-of-a-kind night at the opera.

The dazzling complexity of the work, first performed on January 25, 1909, at the Royal Opera in Dresden, was immediately apparent, since Strauss had composed a score requiring 115 instruments. At rehearsals he is reputed to have shouted "Louder!" to the conductor because he could still hear the voices of the singers. The first-night audience reeled.

The wild response originates in the Elektra legend itself. Elektra's father, King Agamemnon of Argos in ancient Greece, was slain by his wife Klytemnestra at his palace of Mycenae on his return from the Trojan Wars. Klytemnestra kills her husband for various reasons, according to the legend. He sacrificed her beloved daughter Iphigenia in order to sail to Greece (a fact noted in the legend but ignored in the opera). Agamemnon also brought back a concubine, the Trojan princess Cassandra, and paraded her in front of the populace, outraging his wife. Klytemnestra, however, had a few secrets of her own, above all that she had taken a lover, Aegisthus, during Agamemnon's ten-year absence at the siege of Troy.

After Klytemnestra murders Agamemnon, the palace of Argos is strafed by violence: Elektra, Agamemnon's other daughter, is reduced to slavery, although a princess; Klytemnestra rules with an iron hand while luxuriating in her sexual affair with her paramour, Aegisthus; and Klytemnestra exiles her son Orestes to prevent retaliation against herself and her lover. Elektra, obsessed with her father, determines that Klytemnestra and Aegisthus will die. It is a legend saturated with blood, revenge and hatred, all of which pulse through Strauss' opera.

Strauss' immediate source, however, was the one-act play by dramatist Hugo von Hofmannsthal, a condensed adaptation of the dramatic version by Sophocles. Hofmannsthal wrote the drama for the actress Gertrud Eysoldt, and the first performance, on October 30, 1903, in Berlin, was a shocker. The dramatist had written as early as June 1903 that "almost against my will, a strange *Oresteia* in two parts" had possessed his mind, "the first part *Orestes Elektra* with the matricide [of Klytemnestra]."

It was a legendary triumph. Hofmannsthal noted to his brother-in-law ten days after the premiere: "The success has happened. A long series of performances to be expected, 70 already scheduled for the current season. The play accepted by 22 theaters within four days after the premiere." Strauss saw the revival of the drama in 1906 and was staggered.

On March 11, he wrote Hofmannsthal, "I am as keen as ever on *Elektra* and have already cut it down a good deal for my own private use. The only question I have not finally decided is whether, immediately following *Salome* [his scandalous hit of 1905], I shall have the strength to handle a subject so similar to it in many respects with an entirely fresh mind." Hofmannsthal shot back, "I would be very glad if you could manage to stick to *Elektra* . . . the 'similarities' with the *Salome* plot do seem to me to dwindle to nothing" beyond the fact that both were one-act dramas, had a woman's name in the title, occurred in ancient Greece and were created by the same actress in Berlin.

It was the differences that were important, the dramatist argued: "the blend of color in the two subjects strikes me as quite different in all essentials: in *Salome* much is so to speak purple and violet, the atmosphere torrid; in *Elektra*, it is a mixture of night and light, or black and bright."

All doubts vanished. Strauss wrote two weeks later: "I am already busy with the first scene of *Elektra*." He did demand that Hofmannsthal supply three additional short but terrifying elements: Elektra's description of Orestes' pursuit of their mother ("Hinab die Treppen"); Elektra's gentle refusal to be embraced by Orestes ("Nein, du sollst mich nicht umarmen!"); and the final encounter between Elektra and Chrysochemis at the conclusion. Each underscores Elektra's profoundly conflicted consciousness.

Her conflicts arc at the heart of Strauss' and Hofmannsthal's sources, the four tragedies from ancient Greece that delineate Elektra's character: the *Choephori* (part of the trilogy the *Oresteia*) by Aeschylus, presented in 458 B.C.; the *Elektra* of Sophocles from about 4155 B.C.; and two dramas by Euripides, his *Elektra* of 413 B.C. and his *Orestes* of 408 B.C. All stress in varying degrees Elektra's hatred for her mother, her obsessive love for her father despite his crimes and infidelities, her passionate love for her brother and her brother's revulsion at his mother.

But there are striking differences between these plays as well, which reveal manifold ways of interpreting Strauss' opera. In Aeschylus, Orestes opens the play and Elektra, here reliant on males, disappears half-way through the drama; its most arresting moment is Orestes' narration of Klytemnestra's dream of giving birth to a snake (which Orestes concludes is about himself and his impending matricide). In Aeschylus there is no Elektra/Klytemnestra confrontation.

Sophocles reverses the order of the killings: Klytemnestra is murdered first, then Aegisthus. In Sophocles' conclusion, Elektra does not die in an ecstatic dance, as in Strauss, but rather lives, falling silent to leave in suspension the moral conflict. For Strauss, Sophocles' most significant addition is the introduction of Elektra's sister Chrysothemis, the counter-foil in the operatic *Elektra*.

Incredibly, the two dramas by Euripides outdo their precedents in horror. In his *Elektra*, Euripides injects an unmistakably incestuous attraction between Elektra and Orestes, has Elektra married to a farmer who has left her a virgin, and underscores Elektra's sexual jealousy of her mother, who is able to attract and retain a lover, Aegisthus. In his *Orestes*, Euripides depicts Orestes as intermittently mad as he and Elektra (here vicious and homicidal) await the verdict of the elders of Argos on their matricide. They are condemned to die, saved at the end by the *deus ex machina* appearance of the god Apollo, who had compelled Orestes to carry out the killing in the first place.

In the legend as progressively treated by the Greeks, Elektra and Orestes become more and more mad, vicious, deranged and perverse. And though Strauss followed Hofmannsthal's adaptation of Sophocles, it is the mood of Euripides that pervades the operatic *Elektra*.

Elements of all four dramas, however, become dazzlingly synthesized by Hofmannsthal and Strauss, who distill and explode in their *Elektra* every component of the myth: matricide, homicide, power, royalty, political tyranny, personal oppression and enslavement, incest, madness, sibling rivalry, hatred, savagery, horror, alienation, retribution and revenge.

No one recognized the shocking nature of this myth more than Carl Jung. In 1912, he formulated his idea of the Elektra complex: "A daughter develops a specific liking for the father, with a correspondingly jealous attitude towards the mother." It was the female version of Sigmund Freud's Oedipus complex for males.

Jung also suggests that males are prey not only to the Oedipus complex (violent resistance to the father, dependency on the mother), which is the *direct* result of their sexual conflict, but also to the possibility of an *indirect* result, an Orestes complex (in which the son exhibits submission to the father and antagonism to the mother). If "the libido remains...glued to the family," Jung stresses, both murder and incest loom. United in their loathing of Klytemnestra's sexuality, Elektra and Orestes in both tragedy and opera demonstrate this potential.

In 1942, Strauss reflected that in *Elektra* he wanted to "contrast this possessed Greece of the 6th century" with the tranquil Greece of eighteenth-century art historian Johann Winckelmann and the author Goethe. For Strauss, Greece was a Dionysian, unhinged world, not an Apollonian, rational one. He determined to "increase musical tension to the very end." Strauss felt he had achieved in *Elektra* the "uttermost limits of harmony [and] psychological polyphony."

It all hinged on one word—*Elektra*—which at its root [elektra] signaled "unmarried" or "unmated," a woman trapped by the culture, by her father Agamemnon, by her brother Orestes, by her mother Klytemnestra, by her own neurosis. Strauss' staggering masterpiece is as haunting as a nightmare—and as profound. He emphasized in 1928: "Let us write mythological opera, the truest of all art forms!"

From Cynicism to Compassion:
Tchaikovsky and *Eugene Onegin*

"Pushkin died in the full bloom of his creative power, and no doubt he carried with him into his grave some great secret. And now we, with him no longer among us, are endeavoring to solve it."

In 1880 Fyodor Dostoevsky, one year after the premiere of Tchaikovsky's *Eugene Onegin,* grasped the enigmatic nature of the opera's inspiration, Alexander Pushkin's verse novel *Eugene Onegin* (1833). Peter Ilyich Tchaikovsky, like the generation before him, had come under the spell of the great secret. In 1877, while he was searching for a new subject for an opera, the singer Yelizaveta Lavrovskaya had said, "What about *Eugene Onegin?*" Tchaikovsky reacted:

> The idea struck me as wild, and I didn't answer. Later, while dining alone in a restaurant, I recalled her words, and on second thought the idea did not seem at all preposterous. I quickly made up my mind and at once set off to find Pushkin's works. I found them with some difficulty. I was enchanted when I read the work. I couldn't sleep that night. Result—a sketch of a delightful opera based on the Pushkin text.

For Tchaikovsky, the opera was to be his declaration of independence:

> You have no idea how mad I am about this subject. How grateful I am to avoid the banal pharaohs, Ethiopian princesses, poisoned cups and the rest of those tales of automatons! What a wealth of poetry is in *Onegin*! I am not unaware of its faults. I know full well that it gives small scope for treatment and will be poor in stage effects. But

the wealth of poetry, the human quality and simplicity of the subject. expressed in Pushkin's inspired lines. will make up for whatever it lacks in other ways.

"I am in love with the image of Tatyana. I am under the spell of Pushkin's poetry and am compelled to compose the music as if by irresistible attraction. I am lost in the composition of the opera," he wrote to his brother Modest in June. The irresistible secret of Pushkin drove Tchaikovsky to include verbatim entire sections of the poem in his libretto. Ivan Turgenev wrote to Leo Tolstoy, "Undoubtedly notable music. The lyrical, melodic passages are particularly good. But what a libretto!" About the text he could not have been more wrong, for Tchaikovsky had been stirred.

By the time Alexander Pushkin began the composition of *Eugene Onegin*, in 1823, he had already led an amazing life. Born in 1799, Pushkin began writing poetry as early as 1814. When he completed his college studies, he became an attaché at the Ministry of Foreign Affairs, publishing his *Ruslan and Ludmila* in 1820. Banished for libertarian writings to southern Russia, he traveled to the Caucasus and wrote in 1820 *The Prisoner of the Caucasus* and in 1822 *The Fountain of Bakhchisarai*, two early Byronic poems. On moving to Odessa in 1823, Pushkin, already notorious, began *Onegin*. His nature during this time is revealed in a landmark letter of youthful cynicism that he wrote to his brother in 1822:

> You will have to deal with men with whom you are not yet acquainted. Always commence by thinking of them all the evil imaginable: then you will not have to lower your opinion very much.
>
> Be cold with everybody: familiarity always harms; but especially guard against letting yourself go with your superiors, no matter how they may lead you on. They can always put you in your place very quickly.
>
> What I have to say to you about women would be completely useless. I will point out to you only that the less one loves a woman, the surer one is of possessing her.
>
> I am indebted to sad experience for the principles which I am proposing to you. May you adopt them without ever being forced to. One day you will hear my confession.

Eugene Onegin became part of that confession.

Pushkin's correspondence during the long composition of *Eugene Onegin*

(1823-31) reveals the intensity that engrossed Tchaikovsky, for during this period the poem was to be the chronicle not only of its protagonists' lives but of Pushkin's own. To his friend Peter Vyazemsky the poet wrote, "As for what I am doing, I am writing not a novel but a novel in verse—a devil of a difference. It's in the genre of [Byron's] *Don Juan*. There's no use even to think of publishing. I am writing the way I feel like writing." A few days later from Odessa he wrote Anton Delvig, "I am now writing a new poem, in which I chatter to the limit," adding, "Is it true that Rossini and the Italian opera are coming where you are? My God! They are representatives of heavenly paradise. I shall die of yearning and envy." This linking of opera and *Onegin* was not accidental. By January 1824 he could say of *Onegin*, "It is my best work." Despite his worries about censorship, the first chapter was passed for publication in December 1824. It was just in time, for Pushkin's patience was running out: "I need money." The work appeared in parts from February 1825 through January 1832, with a complete edition in March 1833.

Pushkin's *Eugene Onegin* is as complex as its author. When finally published, the work contained eight chapters, to which Pushkin originally gave titles: Chapter 1, "Hypochondria," St. Petersburg, 1819-20, introducing Onegin, age twenty four; Chapter II, "The Poet," June 1820, dealing with Lenski (eighteen) and the Larin family, Olga (sixteen) and Tatyana (seventeen); Chapter III, "The Damsel," summer 1820, including Tatyana's letter; Chapter IV, "The Countryside," containing Onegin's reply; Chapter V, "The Name Day," January 12, 1821, including Tatyana's dream, the celebration and the challenge; Chapter VI, "The Duel," January 14, 1821; Chapter VII, "Moscow," concerning spring 1821, Tatyana's visit to Onegin's deserted house during the summer and her removal to the Moscow marriage market in the autumn; and Chapter VIII, "The Grand Monde," involving Tatyana's marriage, 1822, Onegin's letter to her in October 1824, his seclusion during the winter and his final interview with her in April 1825.

Pushkin originally projected a chapter, "The Wandering," concerning Onegin's travels after the duel, of which only fragments survive, and also another chapter involving Onegin in the Decembrist revolt of 1825. For

Eugene Onegin Pushkin created the famous "Onegin stanza" of fourteen iambic tetrameter lines rhyming a-b-a-b-c-c-d-d-e-f-f-e-g-g, which may have had some precedent in La Fontaine and the minor Russian poet Dmitriev. The *ottava rima* stanza of Byron's *Don Juan* (a-b-a-b-a-b-c-c) may have induced Pushkin to use the couplet conclusion for *Onegin*. The *Onegin* stanza provides endless diversity, with the opportunity for a proposition (a-b-a-b), a development (c-c-d-d-e-f-f-e) and a stinging conclusion (g-g), a musical theme and variation. Pushkin did not love Rossini for nothing.

What did Pushkin himself think of *Onegin*? When his friend Raevsky objected to it, Pushkin declared in 1824, "He expected romanticism from me and thought he found satire and cynicism. But he did not get a really good whiff." Far from being romantic, *Eugene Onegin* is anti-romantic in its indictment of self-indulgent individualism, critical not only of Onegin but also of Lenski and Tatyana. Though Pushkin at first declared his work to be modeled after Byron, in 1825 he wrote Alexander Bestuzhev:

> You compare the first chapter with *Don Juan*. Nobody esteems *Don Juan* more than I do, but there is nothing in common with *Onegin* in it. You talk of the Englishman Byron's satire and compare it with mine, and demand of me the same thing! No, my dear fellow, you want too much. Where do I have *satire*? There is not even a hint of it in *Eugene Onegin*.

While there are some superficial resemblances between the two works (self conscious narrators, numbered stanzas with rapier couplets, digressions), Byron's political satire could not exist in *Onegin* because of czarist censorship. Pushkin had already exhausted the purely Byronic strain in *The Prisoner of the Caucasus* and *The Fountain of Bakhchisarai*. Pushkin called Onegin a *nélzhudim*, declaring in 1824, "A *nélzhudim* is not a misanthrope, i.e., one who hates people, but one who flees from people. Onegin is a *nélzhudim* for his country neighbors." In his *Weltschmerz* Onegin is totally unlike Byron's haplessly heroic Juan. As an epigraph to the entire work, Pushkin gave this clue about Onegin: "Infected with vanity, he suffered even more from that kind of conceit that makes one display with the same indifference both one's good and evil actions—the result of a feeling of perhaps imaginary superiority." Onegin's mystery is not his hostility but his indifference, for the indifferent are the genuine radicals.

The key letter about Tchaikovsky's relationship to Pushkin is also the one recording his disastrous intention to marry. Writing to his patroness Nadezhda von Meck on July 15, 1877, Tchaikovsky recounts receiving in May an impassioned letter from Antonina Milyukova. On May 30, she not only declared her love but threatened, "I can't go on without you, and so it may be that I'll soon put an end to my life." Her persistence did not abate when he told her of his homosexuality. The letter of July 15 unites this episode to composing *Eugene Onegin*:

> In June I wrote the main part of the opera *Eugene Onegin*. I should have written much more had I not been so disturbed in spirit. I do not regret the choice of subject . . . Pushkin . . . by the power of his genius very often breaks out of the narrow sphere of poetry into the infinite space of music. His words are more than mere words. Over and above his literal meaning, the verse itself possesses something that pierces to the depths of one's soul. And that something is music.

Not only does Tchaikovsky link *Onegin* to his wretched marriage, he also discovers the secret of Pushkin's poem—that it is music. However, this is not the complete reason for Tchaikovsky's reaction to Pushkin's poem. Pushkin once jested in 1824 about being "a prophet in my own country," but for Tchaikovsky this became both a triumphant and a bitter truth: Tchaikovsky turned Pushkin's text into life itself in dealing with Antonina, transforming her into a Tatyana but catastrophically deciding not to react like Onegin. He would rescue Pushkin's heroine.

Amid all this turmoil, so thoroughly did Tchaikovsky undertake the opera that in August 1877 he worked on it at Kamenka, where Pushkin had frequently visited the Decembrist Basil Davidov. The following month, Tchaikovsky formulated ideas explaining the transition from Pushkin's cynicism to his own compassion:

> Now that my first ardor has passed and I am able to look at this composition objectively, it seems to me destined to failure and lack of public response. The contents are completely artless, there are no scenic effects, the music lacks brilliance and noisy, scintillating effects. Those, however, capable of seeking in an opera musical recreation of everyday, simple emotions, common to all humanity and far removed from tragedy and theatrical effects—they (I hope) will be content with my opera. In a word, it is written in all sincerity,

and on that sincerity I rest all my hopes.

By the following January, he clarified his intention: "I composed this opera because one beautiful day an inexpressibly strong desire to set to music all that in *Onegin* cries out for music overwhelmed me. I don't give a fig for effects! I need people, not puppets. I don't want kings and queens, popular uprisings, battles, marches—in a word, anything that is an attribute of grand opera. I am looking for an intimate but forceful drama." Confronting the eight chapters of Pushkin's poem, Tchaikovsky searched for the "forceful drama," eliminating Chapters I and VII as well as Tatyana's nightmare from Chapter V. These excisions reveal how Tchaikovsky's reading of Pushkin intersected with his relationship with the woman who was determined to marry him.

The elimination of Chapter I from the opera removed Pushkin's unusual narrator, who sometimes passes as an associate of Onegin (1.45-48), a narrator conscious of *Onegin* as both a parody of conventions and a new form simultaneously. This narrator, for instance, postpones the invocation to the Muse until the seventh chapter, remarking, "I've paid my due to classic art:/it may be late, but it's a start" (all quotations are from Charles Johnston's translation, Viking 1977). He digresses on ladies' feet, country life, kinship, albums, critics, even on digressions: "Let no more such digressions lurk/in this fifth chapter of my work." He is preoccupied with literature, rejecting Byronic self-consciousness, detailing plans for his novel, probing Tatyana's reading, contrasting sentimental and romantic literature and the French and Russian languages, taunting the inquisitive reader: "All in good time, on each point/I will give you a complete reply." His most cavalier statement is the final line: the narrator calls blessed the person who "early/has wished [life] an abrupt goodbye—/and, with my Eugene, so have I." He devastates with couplets:

> My tongue kept drawing from the heart—
> But now I've rather lost the art.
> I need to rest from all this rhyme:
> I'll end my tale some other time.

Without sparing the world in general, he applies his stinging lash to Lenski's German idealism or future fate, Olga's ordinariness, Onegin's posturing or Tatyana's dreaming. Tchaikovsky, though excising this narrator, often adapts his language into direct discourse for his characters, unconsciously forming an ironic subtext to his ardent score. Lost, however, is the symmetry of Pushkin's text, which begins and ends in St. Petersburg.

Two other excisions involving Tatyana, however, are scarcely defensible. Tchaikovsky cut entirely Tatyana's dream of being seized by a bear before her name day fête on January 12. This nightmare functions to suggest motifs of the forthcoming party: taken by the bear to a banquet of monsters, Tatyana finds Onegin among the guests. He grabs her, then attacks Lenski, who opposes him, with a knife. The animal (as in *Little Red Riding Hood* or *Goldilocks*) represents her repressed sexuality and her fearful attraction to Onegin, whose behavior at the party is less surprising in Pushkin than in Tchaikovsky. The composer, wishing to believe even in the subconscious innocence of his Tatyana (and of his Antonina), suppresses the sexuality of Pushkin's Tatyana dreaming of Onegin's phallic supremacy (the knife) over Lenski.

Tchaikovsky's decision to cut Chapter VII eliminated an excursion Tatyana makes to Onegin's abandoned estate during the summer of 1821 before her removal to Moscow to find a husband. With this episode Pushkin's attitude to Tatyana changed, and it is in Chapters VII and VIII that Tchaikovsky's attitude toward Tatyana is found. Given permission to see Onegin's house, she finds a sado-masochistic whip as well as Byron's portrait on the wall. Most crucially, however, she discovers Onegin's library with books "where a sharp nail has made a dent." Perusing his reading, she learns the truth:

> And so at last, feature by feature,
> Tanya begins to understand
> more thoroughly, thank God, the creature
> for whom her passion has been planned
> by fate's decree: this freakish stranger,
> who walks with sorrow, and with danger,
> whether from heaven or from hell,
> this angel, this proud devil, tell,
> what is he? Just an apparition,
> a shadow, null and meaningless,

> a Muscovite in Harold's dress,
> a modish second-hand edition,
> a glossary of smart argot . . . a parodistic raree-show?

She learns that Onegin is a facsimile of Byron's self-torturing, self-exiled Childe Harold. Realizing he is a poseur, a re-creation of fictional creations, she goes to Moscow and marries a general. In the opera, an awareness of this scene would have added depth to her rejection of Onegin in Act III, which stems not only from duty to Prince Gremin but from her knowledge of Onegin's many disguises; she can never believe him.

"I have suffered all my life from my incapacity to grasp form in general," Tchaikovsky declared. Nevertheless, Pushkin's key structure of three central character revelations (Tatyana's letter, Lenski's farewell poem, Onegin's letter) supplied a paradigm of a pivotal revelation in the second scene of each act of *Eugene Onegin*—Tatyana's letter scene, Lenski's aria and Onegin's self-defense in Act III. Pushkin's second chapter became Act I, Scene 1, with the quartet drawn from stanzas 30-34 about Larina's marriage, where the Nurse's and Larina's words follow Pushkin. Olga's aria, contrasting her nature with Tatyana's dreamy essence, is Tchaikovsky's own creation, but the subsequent passages about Tatyana's reading amalgamate Pushkin (2.29 and 3.9.10) while eliminating the satiric mockery of the narrator. This same union of the second and third chapters occurs in the second quartet with astonishing effect. From the third chapter, the first genuine dialogue in Pushkin's poem, Tchaikovsky extracts Onegin's preference for Tatyana (3.5). He unites this to the narrator's fire/ice analogy of Lenski and Onegin's friendship (2.13), turning the narrator's observation into Lenski's direct speech: such condensation brings the two men's attitudes into the sharpest opposition.

This same intricacy characterizes Tchaikovsky's fashioning of Lenski's declaration of love to Olga in this first scene. From Pushkin's Chapter II he splits Stanza 20 into two parts, using it up to Lenski's recollection of boyhood, then incorporating Stanza 21, then reverting to the twentieth stanza, turning these narrated stanzas into an aria. To give Lenski the advantage, he lessens the force of the cliches of Stanza 20 by dividing the stanza in the aria, while eliminating satiric observations like the following:

"He sang of lifetime's yellowed page—when not quite eighteen years of age." By such astute wrestling with Pushkin's narrator, Tchaikovsky elevates Lenski's stature.

Tatyana's letter scene originates in Chapter III of Pushkin, with Tchaikovsky incorporating Tatyana's sleeplessness, the nurse's history of her marriage, and Tatyana's halting declaration of love and desire for solitude (3.17-21). At the same time, Tchaikovsky cuts the narrator's discussion of his love affairs, his admission of Tatyana's sincerity and his remarks about her bad Russian and his attitudes to language (3.22-27). Though Tatyana's letter in the opera follows Pushkin closely, small alterations reveal Tchaikovsky's experience with Antonina, especially at the beginning. In the opera, Tatyana declares, "Alas! I haven't the strength to control my own soul! Let it happen, whatever must happen to me!" which derives not really from Pushkin but from Antonina. Tchaikovsky moved the cherry chorus from Pushkin's Chapter III to his own Scene 3, which draws on Pushkin's Chapter IV. There is another startling omission. Onegin's remarks initially draw from Pushkin (4.12-14), but with "Mechtám i gódam nét vozvráta" Tchaikovsky moves to 4.16, cutting 4.15. No elimination has more personal significance for Tchaikovsky, since 4.15 is Onegin's indictment of loveless marriage, too cruel a mirror of Tchaikovsky's own situation with Antonina.

In Act II, Tchaikovsky's changes of Pushkin are equally detailed, drawing on the poem (5.31) for Onegin's angry frustration while achieving a directness not found in Pushkin. Pushkin's Triquet allusion (5.27) was expanded by Tchaikovsky's associate Konstantin Shilovsky with cliché French couplets. In the quartet Tchaikovsky uses Pushkin carefully in Tatyana's "I am lost!" (6.3) and in Onegin's "I am displeased with myself" (6.10), but in the brief Lenski/Onegin passages Tchaikovsky has Lenski realize, "I have found out that life isn't a novel," an awareness never granted him in Pushkin's poem. Unlike Pushkin, Tchaikovsky does not permit Lenski to visit Olga before the duel, increasing the pathos of the ensuing confrontation. Lenski's aria derives from 6.21-22, the poem Lenski addresses to Olga before his duel. Eliminated, however, are these caustic remarks by the narrator which frame the poem:

Vladimir shuts the book, and for writing

prepares himself; and then his verse,
compact of amorous trash, and worse, flows and reverberates.
So Lenski wrote, obscurely, limply
(in the romantic style, we say,
though what's romantic here I simply
fail to perceive—that's by the way).

For the fine Lenski/Onegin duet in Scene 2, Tchaikovsky used Pushkin's 6.28, the narrator's reactions, turning them into superb psychologizing as the former friends prepare to face each other. The changes in Act II brilliantly illustrate Tchaikovsky's handling of Pushkin's narrator, compelling him to suit the psychological intensity of the opera.

In its emendations Act III is the most radical in the opera. Onegin's long rumination at the beginning of the first scene joins sections 8.12-13 from Pushkin, even preserving the allusion to Chatsky, the hero of Griboedov's *Woe from Wit* (1824). As in the brief duet before the duel, Tchaikovsky transforms the narrator's reflections into direct psychologizing by his characters. Four years having passed, Onegin meets an earlier associate, Prince Gremin (in Pushkin only Prince N.). While their conversation follows Pushkin (8.17-18), Gremin's aria is entirely Tchaikovsky's creation, a subconscious idealization of the married life he did not know. Onegin's reaction derives from 8.20, but Tchaikovsky has transformed the narrator's reflections into Onegin's own psychologizing.

Tchaikovsky's alterations extend to the final scene, which in the poem takes place about five months later, in 1825. Here we find Tchaikovsky's most incisive inversions of his source. In Pushkin, Onegin's letter comes before Tatyana's justification, stanzas 8.42-44, but in the opera these *precede* Onegin's explanation, drawn from this letter. Especially since Tchaikovsky cut Tatyana's revelation in Onegin's library, he had to give her an immediate declaration of her beliefs in this final scene. He executes two dazzling maneuvers to increase the negative attitude toward Onegin, who at this point in Pushkin is given a moderate reprieve. First, in Tchaikovsky's adaptation of Onegin's letter, no reference is made to Lenski's death, as there is in Pushkin. In the letter, Onegin's declaration of Tatyana's virtues precedes his description of his agony, but in the opera these are reversed to increase Onegin's egoism. Furthermore, while Tatyana's admission that she still loves Onegin derives from Pushkin (8.47), Onegin's final words before the duet, "Forsake this hateful house," are in Pushkin Tatyana's rejected longing (8.46), a bitterly ironic shift by Tchaikovsky. Rarely has operatic transformation been done so precisely.

When Pushkin called his work a "free form novel" (8.50), he provided Tchaikovsky with a paradigmatic document of *mal du siècle*, for despite the alterations between the *Eugene Onegin* of Pushkin and that of Tchaikovsky there remains an undisguised similarity of outlook. Pushkin in 1824, when he had already finished the first two chapters of *Onegin*, when mentioning his work remarked, "I am taking lessons in pure atheism. [An English writer is] destroying in passing the flimsy evidence of the immortality of the soul. His philosophic system is not so consoling as it is usually thought to be, but unfortunately it is the most plausible." For writing this letter Pushkin paid dearly, being exiled to his mother's estate, Mikhailovskoye, when the police intercepted this document. It is scarcely an accident that atheism and *Onegin* are discussed in the same breath.

Similarly, while composing *Onegin*, Tchaikovsky wrote in 1877 to Nadezhda von Meck, "I am as full of such ideal longing as you are. Our sufferings are the same. Your doubts are as strong as mine. We are both drifting in the unbounded sea of skepticism, seeking a harbor and not finding it. Aren't these the reasons my music touches you so intimately?" For both Pushkin and Tchaikovsky, *Eugene Onegin* is a manifesto that while faith is dead, art lives. From neither work is there any other reassurance: unlike Pushkin, Tchaikovsky never mentions that Olga Larina married a cavalry officer five months after Lenski's death. "I feel that my soul is fully developed. I can create," Pushkin wrote in 1825. When he died in a duel over his wife in 1837, he fulfilled his own damning prophecy and became a Lenski. In reality, all duels are roulette. Pushkin's secret, that the soul exists to create, nevertheless survived. Tchaikovsky heeded that challenge in *Eugene Onegin*.

Legend of Lovers:
Zandonai and *Francesa da Rimini*

The premiere of Riccardo Zandonai's *Francesca da Rimini* in February 1914 represents the apex of a European cultural obsession with a couple of mythical stature since the thirteenth century. Dante Alighieri (1265-1321) immortalized Paolo and Francesca in his *Divine Comedy*, but this embodiment was far from the last manifestation of the ill-fated pair. Painters, writers and musicians recreated the story of the tragic lovers, the most legendary in history after Romeo and Juliet and Tristan and Isolde.

The fact that Paolo da Verrucchio and Francesca da Rimini were historical figures has increased their allure. The daughter of Guido Minore da Polenta, Francesca was married, for political reasons concerning Ravenna and Rimini, to Paolo's brother Gianciotto. After her marriage, however, she fell in love with her brother-in-law, himself married (to a woman named Orabile) and the father of two children. When Gianciotto learned of their passion, in or around 1285, he slew them both. In Dante they are found in the Second Circle of Hell, populated by the Lustful, and his placing of Paolo and Francesca with some of their legendary precedents locates the pair in a sequence of European traditions—*l'amour courtois*, the *dolce stil nuovo* of the Italian poets, artistic representations in the nineteenth century, the drama by Gabriele D'Annunzio of 1901 and Zandonai's opera.

The death of Paolo and Francesca took place at a time when Italian literature was undergoing the strong influence of the traditions of courtly love, *l'amour courtois*. This movement had received expression during the life of Marie de Champagne (1145-98), daughter of Eleanor of Aquitaine. In 1174 Marie's chaplain Andre codified the maxims of *l'amour courtois* into his treatise *The Art of Courtly Love*. Because marriages were rarely made for love, almost invariably for political strategy, courtly love was adulterous, providing an alternative to the loveless alliances of the nobility. As a *mariage de convenance*, the wedding of Francesca to Gianciotto historically fulfills this circumstance. "Marriage is no real excuse for not loving" was one of the central ideas of courtly love. This philosophy marks the first revolt against ecclesiastical authority which finally led to the Renaissance. To its adherents courtly love was ennobling, since fidelity originated in the individual rather than in social or religious coercion. To the Church, however, courtly love was unquestionably sinful.

The Italian poets of the thirteenth century soon became aware of this revolt in France. They seized on courtly love to found their own variation of the idea, the *dolce stil nuovo* or "sweet new style." The woman in the Italian tradition was more spiritualized and more democratic. This emphasis arose from the example of Francis of Assisi (1186-1226) and his creation of *madonna povertà*. This "Milady Poverty" purified the conception of women from *l'amour courtois*, serving as an intermediate stage between the French tradition and the emergence of the "sweet new style." The idea of *madonna povertà* meant that love was conceived as amor gentile-that is, any woman, not only the aristocratic woman, might bring gentility to the heart.

Two poets enormously important to Dante's conception of Paolo and Francesca were his immediate contemporaries Guido Guinizelli (c. 1235-76) and Guido Cavalcanti (c. 1255-1300), who originated the "sweet new style" and its welding of *madonna povertà* to courtly love. Influenced by his beloved Lucia ("light"), Guinizelli expressed the idea of the *donna angelicata*, a woman made angel-like. Though passionate, this woman is likened to a celestial being because she inspires gentility, a love elevated to the spiritual. In his canzone "The Gentle Heart," Guinizelli declares that "Love wore an angel's face," since "the truth in her eyes is glorified."

The emphasis on the eyes is highly significant for Zandonai's opera. In the first act it is a silent glance that overwhelms Francesca. Zandonai evokes a tradition that the souls of lovers traveled to each other along the invisible thread of their eye beams. (Ben Jonson's "Drink to me only with thine eyes" illustrates such pledging.) Cavalcanti, while supporting the idea of the *donna angelicata*, is yet more pagan in intellectually admitting his infidelities to his beloved Giovanna of Florence. To Cavalcanti, love is not only purifying but tormenting, a reinforcement of the two sides of Paolo and Francesca. The traditions of Guinizelli and Cavalcanti were advanced by Dante's friend Cino da Pistoia (c. 1270-1337), who emphasized the ennobling spirituality of love. He wrote to Dante on the death of Beatrice Portinari that "She was the face of our Redemption."

The greatest expression of the "sweet new style" in Italian literature apart from the *Comedy* is Dante's spiritual transformation of his love for Beatrice Portinari in *La Vita Nuova*, composed about 1292. Dante first met Beatrice in 1274, when she was nine years old, but it was his second meeting with her on May Day 1283 that revealed the nature of love, though he was recently married to Gemma Donati, to whom he had been betrothed by his father in 1277. Soon after this meeting, Dante began to compose the poems that would form *La Vita Nuova* (The New Life).

The poetry in the first half of *La Vita Nuova* is from an older, pagan tradition descending from Ovid and Propertius, where the woman scorns the man, and love is torment. Midway through this spiritual autobiography, however, Dante decides "to write of another matter, more noble than the foregoing," that is, to express the "sweet new style" and advance beyond courtly love. Love will no longer be earthly but transcendental. Dante was the first poet to use the verb *transumanar* (to go beyond the human), and *La Vita Nuova* records the elevation of Beatrice as Dante's *donna angelicata*, whom his spirit should "go hence to behold [in] glory" in Heaven. The "new life" recorded in *La Vita Nuova* is not only a great love but a rebirth to a new philosophy of life, the "sweet new style."

The story of Paolo and Francesca used by D'Annunzio and Zandonai derives from Dante's intense opposition of *l'amour courtois* to the *dolce stil nuovo* in the Second Circle of the *Inferno*, composed of "carnal sinners who subject reason to desire." Led by his companion poet Virgil, Dante asks these lovers "so light upon the wind" to speak with him. Describing the motivation of their passion, Francesca quotes two maxims of courtly love: "Love is quickly kindled in the gentle heart," and "Love absolves no one beloved from loving." In contrast to Dante, Francesca espouses courtly love rather than the "sweet new style." She describes how she and Paolo were reading from the tale of Lancelot and how, inspired by the book, they kissed: "That day we read no farther." *Lancelot* (c. 1220-25), with its story of King Arthur, Guinevere and Arthur's chief knight, is the very embodiment of courtly love.

This incident, the catalyst of D'Annunzio's treatment, is a famous confrontation of *l'amour courtois* and the *dolce stil nuovo*, as Dante uses the standards of the latter to criticize the former. A practitioner of the "sweet new style," he has Francesca utter the maxims of a code Dante could understand, pity and yet condemn. Dante does not lack compassion for the lovers—he is even moved to collapse after they depart. But he realizes from the tradition of Guinizelli that a love that is nothing but passion is in the end hell. By placing the lovers in the circle of carnality, Dante regards them as adulterous in the tradition of courtly love. Their wish to be inseparable has become their damnation.

If Dante found the lovers lacking in spirituality, it was left to painters of succeeding eras to note the physicality of the lovers and to add to it a spirituality that transfigured their carnality. This transformation of the lovers figures in the extension of the myth of Paolo and Francesca inherited by D'Annunzio and Zandonai, augmented by the revival of interest in ruined lovers like Romeo and Juliet (Gounod) and Tristan and Isolde (Wagner). Zandonai's *Giulietta e Romeo* (1921) shows that such stories continued to interest him after *Francesca da Rimini*.

Among the earliest of the pictorial predecessors of Zandonai and D'Annunzio were John Flaxman, the English sculptor, and his friend William Blake. For a translation of Dante in 1793, Flaxman delicately illustrated Paolo and Francesca reading *Lancelot*, spied by a page behind a pillar. The illustration for Canto Five shows a prostrate Dante and the lovers, like an infernal Adam and Eve, covering their eyes as they are whirled away. William Blake began a series of designs to the *Divine Comedy* in 1825, working on them until his death in 1827. Blake, who learned Italian to complete the assignment, left behind seventy-two water colors for the *Inferno*. That for Canto V shows the lovers in a fiery wind, with Dante collapsed on the ground, and a strange sunburst of the erotic encounter of the two, telescoping the reading and the damnation.

Prior to the time Blake began his watercolors, Jean Auguste Ingres, who knew Flaxman's illustrations, had begun painting the first of five canvases of the reading episode. With their graceful ardor and refinement, the influence of Ingres' idol Raphael is apparent. In the earliest, done around 1814, Paolo and Francesca are shown as he implants his first kiss on her cheek, as depicted in Zandonai's Act III. The figure of her husband is barely detectable, hand on sword, on the right. Like Blake, Ingres telescopes the reading and the murder. In the 1819 picture Ingres shows the lovers, Francesca now having dropped the book, with Gianciotto clearly visible. Two later pictures portray the reading, one with Paolo on the left, without the husband, the other showing the same placement as in 1814. A final picture, of 1857-58, recapitulates the earlier canvases.

In 1826, an artist of a different temperament, Eugene Delacroix, completed a watercolor of the lovers. The British artist Frederic Leighton, who knew Delacroix and Ingres, was obviously influenced by the latter in his canvas completed about 1861. Placed outside at sunset, with Rimini outlined in the distance, the figures reproduce the poses in three of Ingres' canvases. Here the drapery adds impulsiveness, and Francesca has already swooned.

For the remainder of the nineteenth century, artists would show either the reading, the damnation or, in a few cases, both episodes. English painting was particularly rich in depictions of Paolo and Francesca. One of the earliest was by Scottish painter William Dyce, who knew both the Flaxman and Ingres conceptions. Dyce's 1837 canvas details the lovers reading, with the leaning Paolo recalling Ingres. The fingers of the avenging husband are barely visible on the left. A later Scottish artist, Joseph Noel Paton, depicted the lovers twice, once in a canvas of 1852, *Dante's Dream*, which shows the poet brooding as the lovers appear in a vision against the sky. The other is intriguing for showing Paolo and Francesca reading outdoors by moonlight, with its unusual serenity suggesting the naturalness, possibly even the goodness, of the lovers, who look more like innocent adolescents than married adulterers, a good example of the Victorian sanitizing of the subject.

In contrast to Ingres and Dyce, who revered Raphael, Dante Gabriel Rossetti espoused a "Pre-Raphaelite" flatness of design and coloring. Prior to painting incidents from Dante, Rossetti translated other poets of the "sweet new style," as well as *La Vita Nuova* in 1848. Having been named for his illustrious Italian predecessor, Rossetti was saturated with his influence, even writing a sonnet about *La Vita Nuova* in 1870. Rossetti painted such subjects as Beatrice denying Dante a greeting, Dante's vision of Rachel from the *Purgatorio* and Beatrice transfigured in *Beata Beatrix*, in the tradition of the *donna angelicata*. Rossetti's watercolor of Paolo and Francesca is a triptych, the left panel showing the reading, the center Dante and Vergil staring at the lovers damned in hell on the right. Rossetti emphasizes the passionate kiss and the compassionate Dante. The pose of the lovers in the left panel inspired the sculpture of Paolo and Francesca by Alexander Munro.

Other English artists—George Frederic Watts, Aubrey Beardsley and Edward Burne-Jones—completed designs about Dante's lovers, of which Watts' are the most insightful. During his stay in Italy from 1843 to 1847, Watts experimented in fresco painting, doing a small study, inspired by Flaxman, of the reading scene. After completing this fresco, Watts did four canvases (1848-84) of Paolo and Francesca, all depicting the damnation. The four pictures are not alike. In the first, Francesca is naked; in the remainder, partially or completely clothed. Her eyes are open in the 1848 version but closed in the others, while Paolo's head, bent toward hers in the earlier versions, is raised and staring in the final canvas. The women whose features Watts portrayed in Francesca also changed. In 1865 they were those of Ellen Terry, Watts' first wife; in the last, those of Virginia Pattie, Countess Somers, with whom Watts may have been in love. The arrangement of the figures recalls the posture, in reverse, of the painting by Ary Scheffer of 1835, though Watts' Paolo is more subdued than the tormented man in Scheffer. Subsequently, Burne-Jones in an 1885 notebook sketch reversed the figures of Watts' paintings, making his lovers much younger than the progressively aging (and thus even more pathetic) figures of Watts' sequence. Around 1889 Beardsley did a head of Francesca that shows her anguished and malevolent, one of the *femme fatale* images of the *fin-de-siècle*, like Salome, a destructive female.

The German artist Joseph Anton Koch painted the lovers in the Cassino Massimo in Rome during 1825-29, leaving as well several erotic graphics of the youthful lovers floating in hell. Gustave Dore's famous *The Tortured Lovers* shows Paolo bending over Francesca in midair, bloodstains still evident on her naked bosom. The best known Italian representation is that of Gaetano Previati late in the century. Italian painting during the period concentrated on Greco-Roman subjects (Segoni, Dusi), Biblical stories (Ciseri) or contemporary history (Fattori, Bertini), so Previati's canvas is especially interesting. The lovers are shown neither reading nor damned, but instead just after their murder. The hilt of the phallic sword is prominent in the center of the canvas, piercing Paolo's back as he lies dead on the slaughtered Francesca. The turquoise dress against the gold-embroidered coverlet of the bed lends the picture a decadent intensity.

Through the influence of Walter Pater and from his own travels, D'Annunzio knew such pictorial representations, reproducing in Paolo and Francesca the violence of Previati's canvas. D'Annunzio's drama, performed in 1901 as a vehicle for his mistress Eleonora Duse, interprets the couple as descendants of Tristan and Isolde, metamorphosed by D'Annunzio into the obsessed lovers of novels like *Trionfo della Morte* (1894) and *Il Fuoco* (1900). In the former, permeated with Wagnerism and Bayreuth, Giorgio Aurispa and his mistress Ippolita are Italian versions of Wagner's lovers. At its climax, Giorgio hurls himself and Ippolita over a cliff, meriting Henry James' observation that D'Annunzio's characters are "erotically exasperated," "insanely demoralized" and "either homicidally or suicidally determined." The conclusion of *Il Fuoco* has the central character act as a pallbearer of Wagner's coffin in Venice, and D'Annunzio was to publish a pamphlet about Wagner's music in 1914. In these novels and in *Francesca da Rimini*, it is significant that death in Italian is feminine, *la morte*. As in many pictorial representations, women are bearers not only of love but of death, or of the love-death or *Liebestod*. Arthur Symons noted of Francesca,

"Violent deeds go on around her wherever she is."

D'Annunzio described *Francesca da Rimini* as a "poema di sangue et di lussuria," a poem of blood and lust. In both D'Annunzio and Zandonai the idea of *l'amour courtois* is persistent. The Jester sings of Tristan in the first act, the room of the reading is decorated with this legend, and it forms the song of the swallow dance. Though the play scarcely recognizes a spiritual element, emphasizing courtly love, for the opera D'Annunzio added verses to the Act III love duet that contain ideas of the *dolce stil nuovo*. For Paolo, love is both flame and lamp (familiar images from Guinizelli), while Francesca is conceived as an unearthly vision, slightly the *donna angelicata*.

On the eve of Italy's involvement in the First World War, Zandonai's *Francesca da Rimini*, a final linking of l'*amour courtois* and the *dolce stil nuovo*, marked the end of the 600-year European probing of the historical lovers, who had become legends. In this there is the solution of the famous riddle of the tenor's silence in Act I and in the final scene, where he dies without a cry. The concept of the *trobar cluz* from poetic tradition dictated that the lover must sing in secret and not name the beloved. Zandonai defies operatic convention to preserve the silence of the initial gaze as Paolo sees his *donna angelicata* in Act I, and as he last glimpses his *femme fatale* in Act IV, both lovers enigmas before the War that obliterated them forever.

The Scandal:
Verdi and *Hernani*

In 1843, with the double successes of *Nabucco* and *I Lombardi* behind him, Giuseppe Verdi received a request from Marquis Mocenigo, the Director, to create an opera for the Teatro la Fenice in Venice. Verdi debated many ideas for a text, including Shakespeare's *King Lear*, Bryon's *The Corsair* and *The Bride of Abydos*, and Bulwer-Lytton's *Rienzi* (already used by Wagner in 1842). During this period of indecision, Francesco Maria Piave, a young Venetian poet, wondered if Verdi would be interested in a text about Oliver Cromwell. Replying, Verdi was explicit about his demands for a libretto: "You know better than I that in this type of composition there is no effect unless there is action, so therefore let's have as few words as possible . . . I do insist on brevity because that's what the public wants."

Meanwhile, Mocenigo had brought to Verdi's attention another subject for an opera, Victor Hugo's notorious drama *Hernani*, which had had its premiere in 1830. This was far from unknown to Italian composers. In 1830 Bellini had undertaken an *Hernani*, for which sketches of five numbers exist. Some of his work eventually went into *Norma* and *La Sonnambula*, but only rigid censorship deterred Bellini from pursuing the project. Two minor composers, Vincenzo Gabussi in 1830 and Alberto Mazzucato in 1843, had already produced works based on the Hugo drama. However, Mocenigo's suggestion was to prove a turning point for Verdi.

On 5 September 1843, Verdi wrote the Director:

This *Cromvello* is certainly not of great interest, considering the requirements of the theatre . . . it lacks action. The fault perhaps lies more with the subject than with the poet.

Oh, if I could do *Hernani*, that would be a wonderful thing! It's true it would be hard work for the poet, but first of all I would try to compensate him, and then we would surely achieve a much greater effect on the public . . . In *Hernani* he would only have to condense and tighten: the action is ready-made, and the interest is immense.

Verdi offered to "write out all the scenes of *Hernani* that seem . . . suitable" to indicate the outline of the libretto. By November the censors had approved the text, demanding only that there be no drawing of swords, that the King's clemency be emphasized, and that the word "blood" be eliminated. *Ernani* was born.

However, if the birth of Verdi's *Ernani* involved some political and artistic skirmishing, it was nothing compared to the tumultuous origin of Victor Hugo's *Hernani*, which caused an artistic and political revolution at its premiere at the Comédie Francaise, for on 25 February 1830 "la batialle d' *Hernani*" was waged between the adherents of Classicism and the supporters of Romanticism. It is not extreme to call this night a "battle": it was in fact the final part of a war against the stifling traditions of the Classical tragedy as embodied in Corneille and Racine. In their tragedies, the specious three "unities" of Aristotle (time, place, action) were strictly observed, with noble characters debating, in elegant vocabulary, duty, honor, and passion in rigid twelve-syllable Alexandrine lines. The Classicists felt no change in these regulations was necessary—the Romanticists defied them.

Although the final battle was fought in the nineteenth century, small sorties during the previous century had begun to alter the nature of French drama. Marivaux (1688-1763) began to transfer tragic scenes into common life. Under the influence of Richardson, a new emotionalism appeared in literature that was to intersect with the plays of La Chaussée (1692-1754). In such works as *Mélanide* (1741), he evolved the *tragédie bourgeoise* or *comédie larmoyante* ("tearful comedy"), a form intermediate between tragedy and comedy, featuring ordinary people. With the bourgeoisie or "Third Estate" supporting these works, the hybrid form of the serious play or *drame* was established. In his writings about his play, *Le fils naturel* (1757), the philosopher Diderot (1713-1784), modifying the *comédie larmoyante*, advocated the *drame bourgeois*, a type of play written in prose but adhering to the "unities," featuring contemporary characters with realistic costumes and speech. Gone were the noble Greeks and Romans of Classical tragedy.

While more realistic staging and characters were evolving, during the 1760s there appeared another mixed form of play, the *mélodrame* or sensational thriller, compounded of music and drama. Violent emotions, gallows, dungeons, daggers, and last-minute rescues formed the basis of plays drawing on all classes of society for their virtuous heroine, valiant hero, and wicked villain. The major practitioner of this form, Pixerecourt (1773-1844), who wrote more than fifty melodramas like *Caelina* (1800), proclaimed, "I write for people who cannot read," and indeed thousands of the proletariat who had initiated the French Revolution were the supporters of *mélodrame*. One incensed official declared that with Pixerecourt's works "the vital principle of never portraying bloodshed on the stage has been absolutely thrust aside." Nevertheless, so popular was the *mélodrame* that the rue du Temple containing its theatres became the "Boulevard du Crime."

During the 1820s, however, the Romanticists, demanding new freedom for the individual and for the drama, found their real strategies. In 1823 two important events occurred: a group of English actors came to perform Shakespeare, and Stendhal published *Racine et Shakespeare*, a study protesting the rigidity of the unities of time and place and even the Alexandrine line. Shakespeare, everyone noted, was hardly concerned with the unities. In 1827, another group of English actors, including Kean and Kemble, brought more Shakespeare, importing *Hamlet*. In the same year, Victor Hugo, who had attended these performances, began work on *Cromwell* and more significantly on the famous "Preface to Cromwell," the Romantic "declaration of independence."

Hugo proclaimed that the *drame*, the fusion of tragedy and comedy, was the only genuine form of dramatic art for his era, a "natural combination of two types, the sublime and the grotesque, which meet in the *drame*, as they meet in life," the core of his concept of antithesis. As for the

Alexandrine line, Hugo argued its language should be more democratic and its form more varied. "Let us take the hammer to theories and poetic systems . . . there are neither rules nor models," he thundered. By 1829, Hugo's influence had been felt. Dumas *père's Henri III* was produced on 11 February, and although a prose drama it featured jealousy and murder in an historical setting. Present at this performance, Hugo realized that one more battle had to be fought to assure the vanquishing of the Classicists.

On 7 August 1829, King Charles X insultingly forbade the performance of Hugo's *Marion de Lorme* because he felt its portrait of Louis XIII disparaged the throne. Angry and bitter, Hugo began the composition of *Hernani* on 29 August, finishing the work on 24 September and reading it at the beginning of October to the actors of the Comédie Francaise. *Hernani* takes its origin therefore from both political and artistic discontent. In his "Preface" to the play, published after its premiere, Hugo observed that Romanticism was only "liberalism in literature" and that "liberalism in literature will not be less popular than in politics . . . Liberty in literature is the offspring of political liberty . . . For a new people, new art." Hugo's growing skepticism about royalty was confirmed when the July Revolution of 1830 forced the abdication of Charles X in favor of the "bourgeois king" Louis-Philippe d'Orleans.

In writing *Hernani*, Hugo was drawing on autobiographical experiences. In fact, this very element is a part of the Romantic revolt against the depersonalized effacement of the author in Classical drama. The title of the play derives from the small village of Ernani in northern Spain, where in 1811 when he was nine years old, Hugo and his mother stayed en route from Paris to Madrid to join his father. In adding the "H" to the village name, Hugo was endowing it with his own initial as well as with the word "hero." The third act setting in the portrait gallery of the Silva castle derives from the palace of the Prince of Masserano where the young Hugo played alone, subconsciously absorbing the atmosphere. In addition, many of the speeches of Hernani himself echo Hugo's letters to his fiancée Adèle Foucher, whom he married in 1822. Hugo took the name of his heroine Doña Sol (Elvira in the opera) and the nobleman revolting against his king from the *Romancero general* translated by his brother Abel in 1821.

On 25 February 1830 the "bataille d'*Hernani*" was waged. One may wonder that the censors passed the play, but they did "so that the public might see to what extremes of preposterous insanity the human mind may be driven, when it claims to be freed of all rules and conventions." Undaunted, the adherents of Romanticism, collectively called *Jeune France* (Young France) gathered at one o'clock in the rue de Richelieu to enter the Théâtre-Francais, dressed in contempt of the old guard: instead of wigs they wore their long hair, some down to the shoulders; instead of conservative evening dress, they wore satin and velvet. Théophile Gautier wore an immortally notorious outfit: scarlet vest (designed for the occasion), green trousers, black coat. In their hands Young France bore red passes on which Hugo had written their password *hierro*, in Spanish "iron," the final meaning of the "H" in *Hernani*. Gautier summarized the importance of this night: "Two systems, two parties, two armies, it is not too much to say two civilizations confronted each other, hating each other." Among the audience were Balzac, Mérimée (author of *Carmen*), and Berlioz. After the triumph, an exhausted member of Young France said, "If there had been a sixth act, we should all have collapsed." The verdict of success was best expressed by the famous ancestor of Romanticism, Chateaubriand, who wrote to Hugo the following morning: "I am going, sir, and you are coming."

What in *Hernani* caused the uproar and assured the Romantic triumph? First, the play realized the goals of the "Preface to *Cromwell*." As for the unities, those of time and place ceased to have meaning. While the year of the action is 1519, the span of events is indeterminate: Act II is twenty-four hours after Act I. The settings of the five acts are distinct: bedroom in the house of the Silvas, square at the Silva palace, Castle in the Aragon mountains, Tomb of Charlemagne at Aix-la Chapelle, and Hernani's palace. Hugo's innovation is significant since he emphasized the importance of spectacle and historical atmosphere by varying his locales, exotic ones in the true Romantic spirit of Young France. Although the common theme of love versus honor provides a unity of idea in *Hernani*, there is no single action (three men in love with Doña Sol, Hernani's vengeance for his father, Carlos' election as Emperor).

In addition to spurning the unities, *Hernani* extended the Romantic rebellion into language itself. The Classical outrage began at the opening line:

> Serait-ce déjà lui? C'est bien à l'escalier dérobé.
> (Has he arrived already? It *is* the secret stairway.)

At once, the audience noticed that the line did not stop at the end. Hugo had used *enjambement*, the run-on line, against all Classical practice! In further defiance, Hugo resorted to a shifting caesura (pause) in the previously rigid Alexandrine line, writing: "Je suis banni! je suis proscrit! je suis funeste," dividing the line at the fourth and eighth syllables instead of the Classical sixth. The greatest uproar occurred when the King, asking the time, inquired "Quelle heure est-il?" and was told "Minuit" ("Midnight"). To the Classicists, it was outrageous for a monarch to use ordinary instead of elevated language.

Hernani also created anger by its use of antithesis and contrast, preserved in Verdi and evident from the titles of Hugo's acts: The King, The Bandit, The Old Man, The Tomb, The Wedding. Contrasts also occurred within groups of characters (young versus old) and within individuals: Carlos alters from irresponsible rakish King to disciplined Emperor, Hernani is a bandit and a nobleman, the aristocratic Doña Sol receives an outlaw in her bedroom. To top it all, continual reversals in the fates of the characters, with constant coincidences and *coups de théâtre* and the presence of physical violence on stage, were the final flaunting of the Classical tradition. Hugo's influence on the nineteenth-century opera libretto is clearly incalculable.

It was the nature of the bandit nobelman, however, which most embodied the revolt of Hugo's and Verdi's era, the rebel sacred to Young France and the Risorgimento. In his great speech in Act III, Hernani declares: "Take the duke, take hell, take the king. Anything is better . . . I am an unchecked force, a blind and deaf agent of deadly mysteries . . . Where am I going? I do not know. I am hurled by a wild wind and a mad destiny." Descendant of Chateaubriand's *René* and Byron's *Childe Harold*, Hernani lives in an existentialist stage of siege, defying all authority, subverting every belief. From the beginning Doña Sol and Hernani are doomed, longing like Romeo and Juliet for death. Their end is a *liebestod*.

Ultimately, Hernani is one of the *hommes fatals* for whom the world is insufficient. So strong was the spirit of *Hernani* that one man died fighting a duel to defend it.

To understand the transformation of *Herani* to *Ernani*, it is essential to focus on the play's two alternative titles. Hugo had once called the work *Tres para una* and gave the drama the subtitle *l'Honneur Castillon*, denoting respectively the concepts of love and of honor. It is easy to see in the love of three men for one woman a reversal of the mythical Judgment of Paris, where the man chooses among Juno, Athena, and Venus. Doña Sol/Elvira confronts three men offering the same alternatives: power in Carlos, wisdom in Silva, passion in Hernani. It is appropriate that Hugo finally decided to retain *l'Honneur Castillon* rather than *Tres para una*, for in *Hernani* the emphasis in the end is on honor, which concerns Hernani more than love, even in the first act. For Piave and Verdi in *Ernani*, the reverse is true, with their emphasis of love more than on honor.

This shift had major consequences for the opera. The opening scene of *Ernani*, which is without basis in Hugo, presents Verdi's bandit as lover only. It is not until the trio of the second act that one learns of Ernani's father and the basis of honor, but it is submerged in the ensemble. Verdi's Act I, named The Bandit after Hugo's Act II, draws on the first two acts of *Hernani*, eliminating the humor of Hugo's Carlos and effecting only an awkward entrance for Silva. The excision of nearly all Hernani's speeches from Hugo's second act undermines Ernani's force in the opera, which is not helped by the fact that Verdi never wrote a great love duet for Elvira/Ernani. Verdi's Act II, named The Guest but deriving from Hugo's Act II, shows some of the same inadequacy, inexplicably: Hugo's fourth scene, containing the core of Hernani's Romanticism, would have made a superb duet. The setting in the portrait gallery has little meaning since Silva, unlike in Hugo, never addresses these ancestors.

Verdi's two final acts (The Pardon and The Mask) realize the source more successfully. Verdi's presentation of Carlo in "Gran Dio! . . . Oh, de' verdi'anni miei" is a perfect condensation of Hugo—and an improvement. In the final act of *Ernani*, Verdi makes significant alterations. In Hugo, both Hernani and Doña Sol take poison, dying together, with Silva stabbing himself in despair. In *Ernani*, Ernani stabs himself, Elvira falls "unconscious," and Silva gloats in triumph. Thus, the love and honor themes merge more suitably in Hugo, while the love-death remains muted in Verdi since Elvira does not commit suicide.

Nevertheless, *Ernani* was a turning point for Verdi, particularly since it was his first international success. In it, one sees the emergence of the great Verdi baritone roles in Carlo's "Lo vedremo, veglio audace" (Act II) and "O sommo Carlo" (Act III). The horn theme associated with Silva is Verdi's first genuine leitmotiv, sans Wagner. *Ernani* furthermore marks Verdi's first collaboration with Piave, which was destined to produce *Rigoletto*, *La Traviata*, *I due Foscari* (after Byron), *Macbeth*, and *La Forza del destino*. The outcast here was to reappear as Manrico in *Il Trovatore*, while the grandson of Carlo in *Ernani* became the protagonist of *Don Carlo*. Furthermore, Verdi like Hugo was to find his works the subject of politcal controversy, and two passages of *Ernani* especially demonstrate this politicization. In the Act III chorus "Si ridesti ii Leon di Castiglia," advocates of the Venetian republic substituted "Leon di Venezia," invoking the patron Lion of Saint Mark. In the "O sommo Carlo" of the same act, patriots replace "Carlo" with "Pio" to praise Pope Pius IX, elected in 1846, a liberal who encouraged Italian national aspirations. During the Italian unification movement, Verdi's name became an acronym for *V*ittorio *E*manuele *R*e *D'I*talia, with *Viva Verdi*! becoming a popular slogan.

After the premiere of *Ernani*, Victor Hugo bitterly condemned the "clumsy travesty" he believed Verdi had made of *Hernani*. When the work was performed in Paris in 1846, he forced its title to be changed to *Il Proscritto* and demanded that the setting and characters be Italian, with Ernani becoming Odraldo of Venice and Silva Elvira's father. Nevertheless, Verdi used Hugo's 1832 *Le Roi s'amuse* for *Rigoletto* in 1851, again at La Fenice, and as late as 1861 Verdi thought of Hugo's last great drama *Ruy Blas* (1838) for a text. Verdi recognized that opera in the nineteenth century would have to reckon with Hugo's revolt. He wrote in 1853: "I want plots that are great, beautiful, varied, daring . . . daring to an extreme, new in form." *Hernani* had set the standard.

The Cloak:
Puccini and *Il Tabarro*

The premiere of *Il Trittico* at the Metropolitan Opera in 1918 offered its audience a startling triptych of the world. *Il Tabarro* with its grim lovers' triangle, *Suor Angelica* with its anguished nun and *Gianni Shicchi* with its greedy vultures present stages of experience that disturb and aggravate, whether they are tragic or pathetic or comic. In particular *Il Tabarro*, with its presentation of proletarian boredom, frustration and desperation, seems a fitting commentary on the Bolshevik Revolution as well as on later modern despondency. Michele's original monologue, a longing for death and oblivion, is contemporary in its abject vision.

Il Tabarro, however, has endured for reasons beyond its contemporaneity. Its music, a heady impressionism of the Seine, ennui and danger, is more suggestive of character than creative of it. Its story, while fascinating, is one of the world's oldest—a young wife, an older husband, a young lover. Its conclusion, though powerful, is the signature of opera—revenge. The merit of *Il Tabarro* rests not so much on its matter as on its presentation.

By retaining the title *Il Tabarro* from Didier Gold's one-act play *La Houppelande*, Puccini at once located the work in an extensive tradition of the cloak as symbol. The opera is not only an apex of verismo but the culmination of a theme going back as far as Greek mythology, the Bible and the Middle Ages.

Both Greco-Roman and Hebraic tradition use the cloak in frankly sexual situations. Zeus, in the course of his amours, covers his wife Hera with a cloak as a symbol of his domination, protection and disguise. In the Book of Ruth, Boaz, to lay claim to Ruth and to symbolize his habitation with her, covers her with a cloak. Such a covering is completely symbolic in Ezekiel, where the ritual covering of a woman indicates God's concern for mankind. In these instances, Puccini found a ready archetype of the cloak in connection with sexual situations. In a realistic work like *Il Tabarro*, dealing with the passions of the working class, the cloak seems as inevitable as it is intriguing.

In the Middle Ages, while the cloak remained associated with love, it also became connected with suffering. The garment worn by Christ during the scourging emphasizes his lower-class origin; the robe of the crucified Christ, since it is seamless, must be distributed by lots. In *Il Tabarro* the cloak indicates Michele's class origin and suffering as well as his determination not to "rend" his family by condoning the affair of Giorgetta with Luigi.

In his reminiscence "Erano sere," Michele recalls evenings when he wrapped Giorgetta and their child "together in my cloak as though in an embrace." This protective cloaking derives from another favorite theme in the Middle Ages, that of St. Martin. Born in Hungary in the fourth century, Martin as a child ran away to a monastery. His father compelled him to join the imperial cavalry, and while in Amiens, France, he encountered a beggar suffering from the bitter winter. Martin took his cloak and divided it, giving half to the frozen beggar. Michele's brief recollection, with its longing to protect Giorgetta once again, has an archetypical connection with the protective covering of the beggar in St. Martin's life.

The other function of the cloak in *Il Tabarro*, as an instrument of revenge when Michele hides beneath it the slain Luigi, recalls the episode of Joseph and his brothers. Here the symbol of the cloak is connected with adultery as well. Because Joseph was "the son of his old age," Jacob made him "a coat of many colors," provoking violent jealousy among Joseph's brothers. After stripping Joseph of his cloak, his brothers sold him into slavery in Egypt: Joseph's coat, dipped in animals' blood, caused his father to think his child had been slain. While Joseph was in Egypt, he was tempted into adultery by the wife of Potiphar, a captain in Pharaoh's guard. One day, when Joseph was forced to escape her advances, he avoided her by slipping out of his coat. Later she used the coat as evidence against Joseph, who was imprisoned until he saved Egypt by predicting a famine. The situation of Joseph, Potiphar and his wife is a prototype of the triangle in *Il Tabarro*, with the beloved object being someone subservient to the husband—a fact of extreme irritation to Luigi when he rages against the backbreaking life of a stevedore forced to load sacks of cement. In both *Il Tabarro* and the story of Joseph, the cloak is associated with domination and adultery.

The relationship of the cloak to domination and suffering in the accounts of Joseph and Christ recurs in a story by Gogol, *The Overcoat*, published in 1842, sixteen years before Puccini's birth. Dostoevsky's remark, "We have all sprung from Gogol's *Overcoat*," signaled the arrival of new subject matter in the nineteenth-century literary world inhabited by Puccini. Gogol's central character, Akaki Akakievich, a minor government clerk, determines despite his meager salary to possess an overcoat, a symbol of dignity and stature in Petersburg. The first night he wears the cloak he is robbed, dies of mental anguish, and then haunts pedestrians of the city until he steals a coat from an official who refused to help him. The influence of the story was enormous, with its depiction of the oppressed, faceless masses. Luigi's anger in "Hai ben ragione"—"Our lives are worth no more, and every joy turns into punishment"—is equally expressed by Gogol. Lile is bleak, brutally monotonous, stifling in its meanness. Puccini reinforces the impression when Giorgetta, in her own "Hai ragione; e un tormento," responds to Luigi: "I'm a captive, I feel it more strongly than you, this chain!"

The cloak in *Il Tabarro* comes not only from Gogol but from an extensive tradition of Greco-Roman and Hebraic-Christian connotation. Puccini, however, did not accept this legacy blindly. In *Il Tabarro* he molded it in the light of the great movement in psychology that occurred during his maturity. His achievement—aligning the tradition of the cloak with latter-day psychological associations—makes *Il Tabarro* the peak of the coat symbol.

The sexual tension of the cloak symbolism is immediately apparent in

Giorgetta's remark to Michele, "No more smoke comes from your pipe." This suggestion of impotence is quickly countered by Michele when he notes, "Al vino ho rinunciato"—"I may have given up wine, but if my pipe is burnt out it doesn't mean my passion is too." The signal decided upon by Luigi and Giorgetta for their tryst, a lighted match, is a comment on Giorgetta's repugnance to sexual contact with Michele.

Gogol's association of the cloak with the poor is emphasized when Puccini depicts various solutions to their oppression. Tinca loses himself in wine ("In questo vino affogo"), while Frugola, the old ragpicker, advises Giorgetta ("E il più bel gatto") that "it's better to be master in a hovel/than to serve in a palace." It is with Giorgetta and Luigi, however, that Puccini explores the modern despair of existence. Luigi's statement "By morning the day is already dark" remains a powerful declaration of existential despair, while Giorgetta's "How difficult it is to be happy!" suggests Camus' statement from Caligula "Men die; and they are not happy." In *Il Tabarro* the longing for death is expressed by Frugola and by Michele, with the conclusion "La pace e nella morte." That "Peace is only in death" is the existential message of *II Tabarro*.

The association of the cloak with death is used by Puccini with considerable psychological insight. Early in the opera, Michele's cloak is connected with remembrance of Giorgetta, and in his final appeal to her, "Ah! ritorna, ritorna come allora," Michele desires her to be once again within his embrace in the cloak. Puccini, however, complicates his adulterous triangle with the well-known theory that in adultery the object really being sought is the beloved's spouse. When Michele conceals Luigi where Giorgetta had formerly been, Michele's "fascination with the abomination"—Luigi—becomes clear. This attraction is suggested by the Pietà posture in which Giorgetta discovers her dead lover rolling from her husband's lap. By such a device, Puccini associates his cloak symbol with Christ as well as probing modern theories of adulterous love. The novels of D. H. Lawrence being published at this time, especially *Sons and Lovers* in 1913, reveal the prevalence of these ideas. When Michele forces Giorgetta to kiss Luigi's corpse, this necrophilic, life-denying action is the image of despair.

The original monologue by Michele, "Scorri, flume eterno," while lacking the furious personal anguish of the 1922 "Nulla! Silenzio," shows that Puccini regarded *Il Tabarro* as much more than a depiction of a specific adulterous relationship. The pessimism of Michele staring at the Seine, with its dead bodies and eternal flow, is made universal by the cloak symbol: "How many people, ruined like me, have you calmed with your tide?" *Il Tabarro* has survived other verismo operas because its statement of anguish is comprehensive, total, unlimited. The cloak, in Frugola's words about her sack of rags, is "evidence of a thousand loves." The brief action of *Il Tabarro*, from sunset to night, draws the black cloak of death about the world.

The interpretation of *Il Trittico* as a modern Divine Comedy, with *Il Tabarro* the *Inferno, Suor Angelica* the *Purgatorio* and *Gianni Schicchi* the *Paradiso*, is intriguing but insufficient. Like most triptychs, *Il Trittico* is a variation on a single theme—despair at the human condition. *Il Tabarro*, first of the triptych panels, remains the determining element: the brutality exhibited in all three operas is continuing and eternal. The rage of Michele, the callousness of the Princess in *Suor Angelica*, the greed of Zita in *Gianni Schicchi* remain. Confronted with this vision, one can only imitate Shakespeare's Julius Caesar and draw the cloak over one's eyes.

Woe to the Vanquished:
Puccini and *La Bohème*

French novels of the 1840s were a gold mine for future operas: Mérimée's *Carmen* (1845) and Dumas' *Dame aux Camélias* (1848) led of course to *Carmen* and *La Traviata*. That so brief a literary period inspired two operas of distinction is remarkable. That it happened a third time is extraordinary. But it did, when Henry Mürger's *Scènes de la Vie de Bohème* of 1849 became the basis in 1896 of *La Bohème*. So attractive to composers was this novel that while Massenet was at work on *Werther* (1892) his publisher, Georges Hartmann, considered suggesting *Vie de Bohème* to him. Ruggiero Leoncavallo, who had a triumph in 1892 with *Pagliacci*, thought he could surpass himself using Mürger's novel. Puccini beat him, after a bitter episode. How did he do it?

Since *Cavalleria Rusticana* in 1890, advocates of verismo in opera had been on the lookout for "realistic" source material. Puccini had already gone to prose fiction, Prévost's *Manon Lescaut*, for such realism. When Puccini returned to his village of Torre del Lago, his friend Ferruccio Pagni told him he did not have to search for material: he just had to open his eyes. Pagni is reputed to have said, "Write about the Bohemians." Stinchi di Merlo's café in Torre del Lago had not been named Club Bohème by Puccini and his friends for nothing. When Carluccio Caselli lent him a copy of Mürger's book, the composer looked no farther.

In this book, Puccini found a spiritual predecessor. The son of a concierge and tailor, Henri Mürger (1822-1861) could not have failed to be a "realist." By the age of nineteen he had gone to the Latin Quarter of Paris, the world of students, artists, poets and journalists, to begin a literary career. Opening one's eyes was a sure method: the editor of a literary journal popular in the Quarter, *Le Corsaire de Satan*, solicited some stories, and in 1847 Mürger began to contribute the tales that became *Scènes de la Vie de Bohème*. (Baudelaire also began his career in the pages of *Le Corsaire*.) Most of these "scenes" were hardly fiction. Mürger was Rodolphe; his friend Alexandre Schanne (who later returned to the family business) was Schaunard; Champfleury was Marcel; another friend, Wallen, was Colline. Marie Christine Roux, who modeled for Ingres, inspired Musetta, while four grisettes (working girls), Lucille, Louisette, Juliette and Anaïs, led to Mimi.

Mürger himself said the book was not a novel at all but rather a series of "brief sketches," since his characters inhabited a world of disorder and were disordered among themselves: "Ce désordre même est une nécessité que leur fait la vie." For composer and librettist there was little plot to untangle but a wealth of incident to rearrange. Mürger declared there were four species of Bohemians: the unknown martyrs to "art for art's sake"; the proud but suicidal idolaters; the "amateurs," play-actors who eventually returned home to "marry their second cousins and become notaries"; and the true Bohemians, total nonconformists who publicly opposed traditions of both society and art.

Scènes de la Vie de Bohème has been described as "sentimental realism," the work of a "semi-realist." Upon its completion as a serial in 1849, with its transformation into a successful drama the same year and its appearance in book form in 1851, the work stands between the romances of the 1830s and the unrelieved documentary realism that the brothers Goncourt, Flaubert and Zola made famous in the latter half of the century. For Puccini's age, however, Mürger's depiction of free love (freely offered, freely ended), social defiance and the mercenary straying by Musetta and Mimi to silk shawls amid silk sheets seemed real enough. As late as the 1960s, an American critic could still call Mürger "the poet laureate of the gutter."

One crucial element of Mürger's tale, however, is strangely never mentioned in connection with Puccini—its overwhelming use of musical allusions and comparisons. *Lucia di Lammermoor*, *La Dame Blanche*, *Les Huguenots* and *Robert le Diable* all appear in its pages. The first Bohemian to figure in the novel is not Rodolphe the poet but Schaunard the musician; his first act is to compose at the piano one of those songs "that the composers of librettos rightly call monsters." As Schaunard sees it, the central problem in composition is "how the notes mate with the syllables." A young composer would naturally become engrossed with *Vie de Bohème* reading such an opening.

Further, Puccini would have recognized the comparisons of life with music throughout Mürger's novel. The affair between Rodolphe and Mimi is termed a "duet of affection." Seraphine, another mistress, is "a true Stradivarius of love." Rodolphe begins a rendezvous with Mimi thus:

> Then, as a musician, before beginning his performance, strikes a series of chords to test the condition of his instrument, Rodolphe took the youthful Mimi on his knees and bestowed upon her shoulder a long, resonant kiss, which imparted a sudden vibration to the budding creature's body. The instrument was in tune.

Musette tells her aristocratic lover Maurice, "I need to go back from time to time and breathe the air of that life. My foolish existence is like a song; each of my love affairs is a stanza, but Marcel is the refrain."

To a composer *La Vie de Bohème* would be far more than a good story. By its musical comparisons it was real not only in its content but in its treatment of that content. Albert Thibaudet said of Mürger, "He loved to talk, to write what he had said, as he had said it." More succinctly, Mürger himself said in his preface, "The vocabulary of Bohemia is the hell of rhetoric and the paradise of neologism." To put this new, even barbaric language on the opera stage became Puccini's goal.

The connection between Mürger and Puccini becomes fascinating when one examines how Puccini and his librettists confronted this "hell of rhetoric." Of the twenty-three chapters in the novel, ten were eliminated entirely, with a resulting sharper focus on essential experiences. The elaboration Puccini entrusted to the unusual combination of naturalism and lyricism that constitutes the score of *La Bohème.*

The fundamental alteration of novel into opera lies in the character of Mimi herself. In *La Vie de Bohème*, Musette is explained in detail before Mimi even appears. Presenting her in chapter eleven, Mürger spares no pains in describing Mimi's loud voice, her abandoned behavior at parties, her dislike of Platonic lovers and her fondness for consorting with prostitutes wherever she and Rodolphe happen to take up an abode. So vagrant is her life that she is called Lucille sometimes, Mimi others. By chapter fourteen, this portrait becomes more devastating: "Her features . . . assumed at certain moments of ennui or ill-humor an expression of almost savage brutality." In sum, she inflicts upon Rodolphe "all the unskillful tortures of the woman who does not love." Their existence becomes "a hell to both of them." At one point Rodolphe, suspicious, follows Mimi and sees her exiting from a tryst with an aristocratic lover, "her eyes surrounded by a halo of debauchery." In the course of the novel, she and Rodolphe separate—violently—several times.

From where then did the Mimi of *La Bohème* emerge? While Puccini and his librettists retained the name, the character in the opera originates in chapter eighteen, the episode of "Francine's Muff." Before recounting this tale, Mürger warns, "Bohemia is not cheerful every day." In the first part of this scene, Mürger describes how the seamstress Francine and the promising sculptor Jacques met. Here is the entire meeting Puccini was to use in Act I of *La Bohème*—the extinguished candle, the knock at the door, the lost key, the groping hands. In fact Francine is forward enough to kick the key under the bed: "She did not choose to find it." Puccini retained some of the minutest details of her death—the longing for a muff, the moving "Courage!" uttered by Jacques' friends. Puccini's attraction to this particular scene may have been prompted because Jacques has his own name, Giacomo. In the novel, after several reunions with Rodolphe, Mimi dies too, not in the garret but in a vile hospital ward, where she is nothing but a bed number.

This alteration in the character of Mimi causes the opera to have an effect much different from that of Mürger's book. It is obvious that much of the "gutter" is eliminated: one does not see Mimi with prostitutes or greedily staring at shop windows or emerging from an orgiastic encounter with a random lover. On the other hand, the omission of a detail like the wretched death in a hospital ward decidedly lessens the starkness of the realism Mürger exploited. Further, if the subsequent fate of Francine's lover Jacques is any indication, one can maintain little hope for Rodolfo in the opera after Mimi's death: when he falls weeping over Mimi's body, he is lamenting not only her passing but the bleakness of his future existence.

In *Vie de Bohème*, while workmen shovel dirt over Francine's corpse, the distraught Jacques cries out, "O my youth! They are burying you in that grave." (This statement in fact concluded the dramatic version of 1849.) And so it is: Jacques becomes an emotional and creative cripple who refuses to work and dies in another fetid hospital, buried unattended by friends while one observer declares, "Art before everything." The most brutal irony is the last: Jacques "was buried somewhere." The verismo of *La Bohème* is immeasurably enhanced by knowledge of these dark sides of the Left Bank.

Another consequence of this change in Mimi's character is the necessity for Musetta to assume completely the role of foil to Mimi's constancy and ill health in *La Bohème*. In *La Vie de Bohème*, Mimi and Musette are quite similar: several times they are associated with Manon Lescaut, so the original Mimi was not far removed from Puccini's first heroine. When Musette is introduced, in chapter six, Mürger recounts that she "often threw conventionality to the winds." For instance, the suggestion of marriage by one of her lovers prompts Musette to retort: "You would be much more likely to lose me if I was your wife." In Act III of *La Bohème* this becomes Musetta's declaration to Marcello: "I abhor that sort of lover who pretends he is your husband." Most of Musetta's character in Act II (her entrance and Marcello's jealousy) and in Act III (her quarrel with him) is detailed in chapter nineteen, significantly entitled "Musette's Whims." When in Act IV of the opera Mimi tells Marcello how good a woman Musetta is, one finds it difficult to believe after reading *La Vie de Bohème*. Musetta's pawning of her earrings is much more the hasty act of charity than Puccini liked to admit.

Puccini retained many details of Bohemian life in *La Bohème*; like Mürger, he believed such details completed the veristic canvas. In Act I, for example, the encounter with the landlord Benoit is compounded from chapters ten and nineteen. The account in Act III of Marcello's painting on house fronts derives from chapter sixteen, devoted to the fate of the painting "The Passage of the Red Sea," mentioned in the opening lines of the opera. This ambitious masterpiece ends up as a shop sign designating a sordid market. That this picture is referred to in the very beginning of *La Bohème* is surely Puccini's way of suggesting images of captivity and disaster, which the music itself comes to express. The entire second act of the opera originates in chapter eleven, "A Bohemian Café," recounting the Christmas Eve banquet at Café Momus. In the opera as in the novel, Schaunard is a heavy eater; in Act I, his account of playing music to rout an annoying parrot from an Englishman's residence was taken from chapter seventeen of Mürger. Throughout *La Vie de Bohème* the philosopher Colline is associated with his coat, which evolves into his coat aria ("Vecchia zimarra") in Act IV of *La Bohème*.

One section from the novel is particularly important, for it supplies not only detail but also a clue to the form of *La Bohème* itself. The burning of Rodolphe's manuscript for fuel (chapter nine) becomes a moment of both pathos and humor in Act I of the opera. Beyond that, the episode has a fundamental parallel to the structure of *La Bohème*, for the third act of Rodolphe's burning drama is described as "short," while the fourth is declared "all soliloquy." Quite broadly, this is the outline of the opera as well.

No less fascinating than what Puccini has retained from Mürger's novel is what he excluded, for such exclusions indicate what limit Puccini put to verismo representation. Some of these episodes, like the housewarming when Mimi and Rodolphe first live together or the initiation of a fool into the Bohemian *cénacle*, were cut because they supplemented rather than delineated the protagonists. The latter episode, however, showed the extent of the Bohemians' defiance of outsiders, which is barely suggested by the fleeting presence of Alcindoro in Act II of the opera. Giacosa and Illica wrote an entire act about a party given by Musette, recounted in chapter six of *La Vie de Bohème*, which Puccini never composed. Another element eliminated was Schaunard's mistress, Phémie; of all the women in the novel she is the most stupid and the most wanton. Schaunard even beats her, and Mürger suggests she enjoys it. Puccini refines the realism of *La Vie de Bohème* here, just as he has Mimi die in the garret rather than in a filthy hospital or as he avoids suggesting Rodolfo's probable demise after Mimi's death.

A particularly significant element not transferred to the opera is Marcel's denunciation of Bohemian life at the end of the novel. He deplores the way he and Rodolphe, for example, "make of the most futile things pretexts for recalling the past." He observes that Bohemian existence, dependent as it is on loutish clients and friends' handouts, is in reality anything but free. "True liberty is the power to do without the assistance of others and to exist by ourselves; have we reached that point?" He continues, "No! the first scamp that comes along . . . has his revenge for our mockery, and becomes our lord and master from the day we borrow a hundred sous of him, which he doesn't lend us until he has made us expend more than a hundred crowns' worth of ruses and of humility! To wear a summer coat in December is not enough to give a man talent; one may be a real poet or artist, even though he does keep his feet warm and eats three meals a day." The attractions of "Manons" like Mimi and Musette are sterile and futile. At the end of *La Vie de Bohème* Marcel utters devastatingly, "I am corrupted."

But if such a denunciation is absent dramatically from *La Bohème*, it is implied in Puccini's music and scene descriptions. The Barriere d'Enfer of Act III is the "gate of hell" its name describes. The disturbing fifths heard at the beginning of this act remain threatening; in fact, the consecutive fifths in *La Bohème* are the equivalent of Mürger's "hell of rhetoric and paradise of neologism." Like a neologism, they are new and barbaric when the subject demands. The movement from *andantino mosso* at the beginning of Act III to the *allegro vivo* of the opening of Act IV to the *grave* of the conclusion shows life as the Barrière d'Enfer.

Such music reflects what Mürger declared in his preface: "Bohemia is the stage of artistic life; it is the preface to the Academy, the hospital or the morgue." What Puccini did with this novel alters one's conception of *La Bohème*, which from this perspective is scarcely sentimental or reassuring.

The prostrate Rodolfo reminds one of the validity of Mürger's declaration that "la vie de Bohème is a fascinating yet terrible life . . . upon which no one should enter unless he has first resigned himself to submit to the pitiless law of *vae victis*."

That is the statement of *La Bohème*: Woe to the vanquished.

A World Apart:
Verdi and *La Traviata*

In February 1852, an enraged Frenchman thundered,

La Dame aux Camélias by Alexander Dumas *fils* is an insult to everything that judgment must respect. This play is a disgrace to the age that supports it, to the government that tolerates it, to the public that applauds it. Each evening at the Vaudeville Theater, women of the better class do not fear to sit in the loge. During its five acts. the Lady of the Camelias, otherwise known as a kept woman, displays before a civilized public the disgraceful details of a prostitute's life. Nothing is omitted from the presentation, not the go between, nor the gallant gamblers, nor the cynical words, nor the scenes taken from the most abject places. This play sweats vice and debauchery. All the characters are monstrous, those on whom the author has wished to spill his interest are ignoble. *La Dame aux Camélias* represents true love—and what love!

Count Horace de Viel-Castel hated the author as much as the heroine. His condemnation, however. was not the sole opinion. In 1895, Henry James was asked to write a commemorative essay about Dumas. As a little boy, James had been forbidden to see the play, but in maturity he made up for it by seeing nearly every famous actress who played Marguerite Gautier. James noted, "Her title had a strange beauty and her story a strange meaning" which "emphasized that bloom of youth (I don't say bloom of innocence—a very different matter) which was the signal-note of the work." The play, James wrote, "remains in its combination of freshness and form, of the feeling of springtime of life and the sense of the conditions of the theater, a singular, an astonishing production." Not surprisingly, Robert Johnson of the *Century* magazine rejected James' essay as unsuitable for a family publication. To lurid headlines, the piece instead appeared in the *New York Herald*. Dumas throughout his life, James observed, was "a man riding a dangerous horse without ever being thrown."

If indeed it was danger that repelled Viel-Castel and allured Henry James, Giuseppe Verdi was not immune to *La Dame aux Camélias* when he saw it. The play, written in 1849 after the sensational appearance of the novel in 1848, had not been produced—for censorship reasons—until February 1852. Its contemporaneity had been judged repellent, its realism too stark. However, the Duc de Morney, chief minister under Louis Napoleon, encouraged its performance to divert attention from the coup d'état of December 1851 by Louis Napoleon who made himself dictator and who became a year later Napoleon III and established the Second Empire (1852-70). Dumas' play had been running for a month when Verdi saw it in March 1852. The previous May he had signed a contract with the Teatro la Fenice in Venice for an opera, and *La Dame aux Camélias* proved to be its inspiration. Verdi's enthusiasm for the play was undoubtedly prompted because he saw it with his mistress, Giuseppina Strepponi, whose past bore resemblances to Dumas' Marguerite Gautier.

La Dame aux Camélias and *La Traviata* are two extremely important historical analyses of society during the Second Empire, the Golden Age of Courtesans. The names of Blanche d'Antigny, Anna Deslions, Apollonie Sabatier and Atala Beauchêne, although less illustrious than those of the legendary Diane de Poiters or Madame de Pompadour, deserve inscription in this hall of fame. In *Recollections*, Daniel Stern wrote of the Second Empire:

> During the reign of Louis-Philippe one saw the importation of Anglo-American customs: the club, sports, cigars, female dandies, hastening the collapse of the salons. Under the Empire. in the overthrow of traditions, in the rout of all ancient dignity, the woman whom one did not know how to designate, the woman whom one called "of the demi monde" entered the scene, with a disruption. It was she who gave it its tone: and what a tone! In place of discreet

intimacies and refined love affairs, she brought a crude and shrill familiarity. In place of careful language, slang; in place of elegance, gaudy money; in place of the refinements of the spirit, the grossness of the flesh.

The social critic Jules-Antoine Castagnary noted in 1866 that "prostitution was a constitutional state," with 40,000, perhaps 100,000, women parading their "insolent luxury" in the best circles. "Never in the history of any era has the courtesan occupied so great a place in the concerns of society. It is a world apart, a true world, with its own customs, language, norms." Inspiring this crude mobility, he felt, were two plays by Dumas, *Le Demimonde* and *La Dame aux Camélias*.

Louis Veuillot wrote that the theater was "the canal by which the *grand monde* and the demimonde flowed together," while Theodore Muret despaired that to distinguish between the two worlds became more and more difficult." A famous anecdote makes this clear. When a guest remarked to the courtesan Léonide Leblanc, "I have not seen Princess So-and-so here for a long time," she replied, "I no longer see her—she compromised me."

The world or Dumas' novel and play and or Verdi's *La Traviata* was indeed what Henry James called "a special order of things." In this order there were three levels—the *grand monde* or aristocracy, which provided protectors: the *petit monde* or the middle and working classes; and the demimonde, a "half-world," but half-acknowledged, or the kept woman (*femme entretenue*). Within the demimonde there was *la garde*, the inner circle, presided over by Adèle Courtois, which included the original Lady of the Camelias, Marie Duplessis. Various other subclasses might exist— the *grisette* or working girl (like Musette in Mürger's *Scènes de la Vie de Bohème*), the *lorette* beloved of clerks, the *cocotte* or free-living young married woman, and *les grandes horizontales* or glittering salon hostesses like Jan de Tourbey. Castagnary wrote, "This world is complex and has its own stockbrokers. It was never the subject of painting, now it is the vogue. It never had its own music, now it is invented on its doorstep. It never had a literature, now men race to fill the gap. Someone feared that its language might be altered—now we have its dictionary."

Castagnary was right: it did have its literature and its language.

Preeminent in this literature is *La Dame aux Camélias*, but the definition of this world was made in his later play *Le Demi-monde* in 1855. Napoleon III, Gustave Gelfroy wrote, was "an Emperor or the political ambush," and Dumas remains the chronicler or the courtesan and her no less lightning ambush of society. In *Le Demi-monde*, Dumas recounts the attempt or the demimondaine Suzanne d'Ange to marry Raymond de Nanjac to save herself from oblivion. She tells her protector, the Marquis de Thonnerins:

> I was nothing, and you made something of me. Thanks to you I have attained a position on the social ladder which might be considered a descent for women who started at the top, but which is for me, who started at the bottom, the apex. Now you can readily understand that since I have risen through you . . . I cannot help having certain ambitions. They are inevitable under the circumstances. Things being as they are, I must either fall lower than where I began or rise to the very top. Marriage is my only salvation.

Though Suzanne is only twenty-eight, she assesses her situation accurately. In her campaign to snare Raymond de Nanjac, however, she encounters a Machiavellian antagonist, her former lover Olivier de Jalin.

Olivier in Act II tells Raymond the true nature or the demimonde: it is a "modern creation," recognized "by the absence of husbands. It is full or married women whose husbands are never seen," he informs Raymond. In a famous simile, Olivier compares these women to baskets of peaches, which on the surface look of the highest quality. However, if one picks up the cheaper peach, Olivier remarks, turning it over one sees "on the bottom side a tiny black speck. That is the explanation of the lower price." He tells Raymond that he is in "the fifteen-sous peach basket":

> Every woman here has some blot in her past life, some stain; they are crowded close to one another in order that these blots may be noticed as little as possible. Though they have the same origin, the same appearance, and the same prejudices as women of society, they do not belong to it: they constitute the demimonde or "half-world," a veritable floating island on the ocean of Paris, which calls to itself, welcomes, accepts, everything that falls from the mainland—not to mention those who have been shipwrecked or who come from God knows where.

With this speech, Dumas defined for history the nature of the Golden

Age of Courtesans, Marie Duplessis, Marguerite Gautier and Violetta Valéry.

Dumas in *Le Demi-monde* explains a great mystery: how did these women form their "world"? Women who had erred began to band together, Olivier contends:

> The second followed the first, and the two gave the name of misfortune to what was really a fault: an error, to what was actually a crime. They began to console and excuse each other. With the arrival of a third, they invited one another to lunch; with the fourth, they had a dance. Then, about this nucleus came in turn young girls who have "made a slip," false widows, women who bear the name of the man they are living with. Today this irregular society functions regularly. This bastard society holds charms for the younger generation. "Love" is more easily obtained than higher up, and cheaper than at the bottom.

Like Valmont and Merteuil in Laclos' *Les Liaisons Dangereuses*, Suzanne and Olivier have a sexual war—she to secure Raymond, he to foil her. Though Olivier wins, Dumas treats Suzanne sympathetically in *Le Demimonde*: the ending remains ambiguous, since Olivier marries the virtuous Marcelle and remains unjudged, the double standard triumphing.

However, many citizens of the Second Empire saw *Le Demi-monde* as endorsing the rise of courtesans and their invasion of respectable society. Among this group was Emile Augier, after Dumas *fils* the greatest dramatist of the era. In his play *Le Mariage d'Olympe*, presented four months after *Le Demi-monde*, Augier used his favorite "intrusion" plot to condemn the rehabilitation of the courtesan Pauline, Countess de Puygiron, formerly Olympe Taverny. The Baron de Montrichard speaks for Augier, declaring, "These women have passed out of the lower strata of society and come into broad daylight. They constitute a little world of their own, which makes its orbit in the rest of the universe." Of the acceptance of these women. he says bitterly, "Like the city of Paris, society takes in new suburbs every fifty years. This latest is the Thirteenth Arondissement." Pauline's husband, young Count Henri, states defiantly that he will not be bound by "the prejudices and absurd conventions, the hypocrisy and tyranny of society." When the conniving Pauline threatens to expose a lapse by Genèvieve, the granddaughter of the Marquis de Puygiron, the Marquis shoots her, screaming, "God is my judge!" Augier's point is brutal. In 1866 he returned to this theme with a play, titled significantly, *Le Contagion*. Although Augier obviously misunderstood *Le Demi-monde*, veiled references to it and to *La Dame aux Camélias* condemn Dumas himself. So powerful was Augier's reputation that Napoleon III and his minister of the interior were present at the premiere of *Le Mariage d'Olympe*.

This pistol shot had many echoes. Dumas *fils* and Augier remain the great exponents of the *pièce à thèse*, the social-problem play intended not only to entertain but to instruct and reform society: the rise of the demimondaine was rich material for their lashes. In his preface to *Le Fils Naturel*, Dumas wrote, "By tragedy or comedy, let us inaugurate the theater of the useful, at the risk of the cries of the apostles of 'art for art,' three words absolutely devoid of sense." The age, he claimed, "does not need charm but salvation. All literature that does not have morality and utility as its end is, in a word, sick literature, stillborn." Dumas advocated the "clear and simple reproduction of actions and persons, a record and a photograph." Augier agreed, denouncing marriage for money, portraying aristocratic/bourgeoisie rivalry and proclaiming the need for divorce. Dumas pleaded for seduced women, censured the unjust treatment accorded illegitimate sons (which he knew first-hand), espoused divorce and condemned faithless wives.

In line with this policy of "art for truth," Dumas made no disguise of the fact that his novel *La Dame aux Camélias* was true, for on its first page he stated, "Not being old enough to invent, I content myself with narrating, and I beg the reader to assure himself of the truth of a story in which all the characters, with the exception of the heroine, are still alive." He contrasted his objectives with those of his famous father, the author of *Le Comte de Monte-Cristo* (1845): "My father was born in a poetic and picturesque epoch: he was an idealist. I entered the world in a materialistic time. I am a realist. My father took his subjects from dream; I take mine from reality. He labored with eyes closed; I work with mine open. He turned from the world; I identify myself with it. He sketched; I photograph." As the illegitimate son of a Belgian seamstress, Dumas had no choice: "Born of an error, I had errors to fight against," he wrote. Despite the fact that his father acknowledged him as his son, Dumas remained a crusader. In autumn 1844 he met Marie Duplessis, the original of Marguerite Gautier and Violetta Valéry, remaining with her until August 1845. After her death, Dumas wrote his novel in four weeks.

As he stated in its first sentence, the major events were true. Born Rose Alphonsine Plessis in 1824 to a vicious father, the future Marie Duplessis was sold by him to a man in 1837. By 1839 she was a grisette (similar to Dumas' mother) in a dress shop. With her name changed by 1842, she became the mistress of many famous men, including the Due de Gramont, Napoleon III's minister of foreign affairs; the Count de Stackelberg, who had been crucial at the Congress of Vienna; Alfred de Mussel; and Franz Liszt. After breaking with Dumas in 1846, Marie Duplessis married Edouard Perrégaux, like Augier's Olympe becoming a countess.

Already fatally ill, she died in February 1847. The disposal of her effects was a major event: Eugène Sue bought her prayerbook, Charles Dickens attended the sale. She was "one of the mysteries of our epoch," declared Jules Janin, while Dumas believed "she was one of the last and the few courtesans with a heart." When Verdi visited Paris in March 1852, he met men like Roqueplan, director of the Paris Opera, who had known Marie. The parallels of Marie's life with that of Verdi's mistress, Giuseppina Strepponi, could not be ignored, since she like Marie was a "strayed woman." Giuseppina not only had several illegitimate children; she also had a throat inflammation that portended consumption. Though she had been Verdi's Abigaille at the premiere of *Nabucco* (1842), to save her life she gave up her career.

The novel and the drama *La Dame aux Camélias* have two important literary predecessors. The first is the Abbé Prévost's novel *Manon Lescaut* (1731), which Dumas called "the prayerbook of courtesans":

Manon Lescaut is a touching story of which not a single detail is unknown to me. However, whenever I happen to find the book near at hand, my sympathy for it is such that I invariably open it and for the hundredth time live again with the heroine of the Abbé Prévost. And this heroine is so true to life that I always feel I once knew her.

In Dumas' novel, *Manon Lescaut* has a key function. The narrator goes to a sale of Marguerite Gautier's effects after her death. Among the items offered is "A volume beautifully bound, gilt-edged, entitled *Manon Lescaut*. There is something written on the first page." Unknowingly, the narrator outbids Armand Duval for the book, inscribed: "Manon to Marguerite, Humility," reflecting: "Now this heroine is so true to life that I feel as if I had known her; and thus the sort of comparison between her and Marguerite gave me an unusual inclination to read it, and my indulgence passed into pity, almost into a kind of love for the poor girl to whom I owed this volume." When Armand Duval asks the narrator to give him the book, the two meet, and Duval tells the story of Marguerite's life. In the drama the two lovers discuss Manon Lescaut in Act II, and Armand peruses it just before Maguerite sends the fatal letter at the end of Act III. All these references. unfortunately, are eliminated in *La Traviata* except for a pointless allusion at the end of Act II, Scene I, where "Alfredo opens a book."

The second key prototype for Dumas' novel was Victor Hugo's drama of a romantic hero, Didier, reformed by a fallen woman, *Marion Delorme* (1831). The plays of Hugo were well known to Verdi, since *Rigoletto* (1851) had been taken from Hugo's *Le Roi s'Amuse* (1832). *Marion Delorme* had been suggested to Verdi for an opera in 1844 during the first performances of *Ernani*, based on Hugo's drama of 1830. Verdi's reaction was dismissive: "I know the subject you suggest. The heroine is a character I don't like. I don't like prostitutes on the stage." By 1852, obviously, he had altered his thinking, perhaps since he and Giuseppina had become lovers in 1847.

Verdi's librettist Francesco Maria Piave (who had done the texts for *Rigoletto* and *Ernani*) worked from the drama Dumas had fashioned from his novel. In reworking his novel for the stage, however, Dumas had made a number of alterations, some not fortunate. First, he eliminated the chapters framing Armand Duval's narrative about Marguerite, happily focusing on her rather than on Armand but eliminating the parallel with the comparable structure of *Manon Lescaut*. The lovers in the play fall in love too rapidly, since the brooding introspection of the novel is gone. One loses also the narrative of Marguerite's final hours by Julie Duprat and Marguerite's journal account of her final days, both important psychological probings of her mind.

In particular, Dumas cut several notorious necrophilic scenes, closely modeled on reality. When Dumas returned after Marie's death in 1847, he witnessed her exhumation and reinterment, recording: "Of the eyes there remained but two empty sockets: the lips had disappeared. The long black hair, quite dry. Stuck to the temples and partly veiled the green cavities of the cheeks." This episode is transferred literally to Chapter Six of the novel, when the narrator accompanies Armand to the cemetery. Unlike the opera and the play, in the novel one experiences Marguerite dead before one encounters her alive, a strategy draining any residue of sentiment.

Dumas also eliminated the crucial Chapter Fifteen of the novel, which contains Marguerite's great discussion of herself in the most unsentimental terms. She tells Duval, "Well, my friend, you must either love me a little less or understand me a little better. We are sometimes obliged to buy the satisfaction of our souls at the expense of our bodies." She confronts him with part of her credo:

> Naturally we have no friends. We have selfish lovers who spend their fortunes not on us, as they say, but on their own vanity. We no longer belong to ourselves. We are no longer beings but things. We stand first in their self-esteem, last in their esteem. Our associates carry their friendship to the point of servility but never to that of disinterestedness.

It is the novel *Manon Lescaut* that Duval sends her after this confrontation, cementing their relationship. These excisions that Dumas made from novel to play never found their way into *La Traviata*.

Dumas' alterations were an attempt to impel *La Dame aux Camélias* to conform to the rules of the *pièce bien faite*, the "well-made play," whose master was Eugène Scribe and whose model was *Adrienne Lecouvreur* (1849; opera by Cilèa 1902). Scribe distributed the five acts rigidly: Act I, exposition: Act II, hero and rival conflict, alternately succeeding and failing; Act III, more reversals, with the hero reaching his peripeteia or point of lowest fortune; Act IV, the *scène à faire* (obligatory scene), a crisis, usually resulting from the hero's rising fortune over his rival; and Act V, resolution and denouement, with the hero or heroine generally gaining the upper hand. Today the "well-made play" survives in *All My Sons* or *Watch on the Rhine*. The key element is the machinery of complication, such as a letter or message, but the contrivance must always appear logical. Later in the century, Victorien Sardou (*La Tosca*, 1887) claimed that one established the crisis or *scène à faire* and then worked backwards. Dumas always believed the same: "A denouement is a mathematical total. If your total is false, all your operation is wrong. I would even add that one should commence writing at the denouement, refuse to begin until he has the scene, the action, and the words to be used at the end."

Indicating his awareness of these principles, Verdi wrote Cesare De Sanctis in 1855 about *La Traviata*, "The third act is the best, and so it should be." While Dumas was to admit that only Acts I and II of his play had actually taken place between him and Marie, he retained his initials in those of his protagonist, Armand Duval, realizing a "well-made play" that still had documentary truth.

Piave and Verdi worked rapidly on *La Traviata*. Act I was a distillation of Dumas' first act, but they eliminated entirely Dumas' second act, which contains the shreds of the psychology from Chapter Fifteen of the novel. Verdi's Act II is a welding of Acts III and IV of the play, while the final act of the opera follows closely Act V of the drama. To reinforce the idea of penitence and impending death, Verdi's final act occurs during Mardi Gras, unlike the New Year's Day of the play. The change of title from *La Dame aux Camélias* to *La Traviata* (The Strayed Woman) introduces a moralizing suggestion, deflecting the documentary nature of the Dumas text and removing the symbolism of the flowers. In Act I of the drama, Marguerite dances a polka, but Verdi wisely saw this would be false in a consumptive heroine. The two characters Olympe and Prudence were condensed into Flora Bervoix in the opera, but their hard Parisianism is lost. The decision to have Germont *père* appear at Flora's party is dramatically convincing but scarcely realistic, as the Duval *père* of the novel would never be present at such a gathering of the demimonde. The connection of Verdi to Dumas is especially critical, since the play had been performed in Venice the week previous to the premiere of the opera (March 6, 1853), forcing comparisons both acute and inevitable.

"A *whore* must remain a *whore*," wrote Verdi when purifiers tampered with the text of *La Traviata*. The opera was sufficiently documentary about the Second Empire demimonde that it was first presented with costumes of the 1700s and Louis XIV to avoid denunciations. While inadequate and unsuitable singers marred the premiere, Verdi wrote, "Time will judge." A definitive judgment belongs to Marcel Proust, who immortalized Odette de Crécy in *Remembrance of Things Past*; with *La Traviata,* Verdi turned *La Dame aux Camélias* into art. Violetta Valéry, like Manon Lescaut, Marion Delorme, and Marguerite Gautier, however strayed, cannot be lost.

The Eternal Swan:
Wagner and *Lohengrin*

"Suddenly the whole of my *Meistersinger* comedy took shape so vividly before me that I felt I must write it out. I therefore proceeded to do this, hoping it might free me from the thrall of the idea of *Lohengrin*. But I was mistaken. No sooner had I got into my bath than I felt an overwhelming desire to write out *Lohengrin*. This longing so overcame me that I ran home to write out what I had in my mind. I repeated this for several days until the complete sketch of *Lohengrin* was on paper." So Richard Wagner recalled the summer of 1845 in *My Life*. An obsessive interest in the Lohengrin legend had been recorded in his earlier *Communication to My Friends*: "Peace forsook me until I had sketched out the detailed plan for *Lohengrin*. The peculiarity of that subject itself makes plain to me why it was that *it*, of all others, so irresistibly attracted and enthralled me."

This enthrallment meant that *Lohengrin* was conceived and composed in a creative fury. Wagner completed a prose outline of the story by August 1845, reading it on November 17 in Dresden to a group that included Robert Schumann. Between the summer of 1846 and that of 1847, Wagner worked strenuously on the composition sketches of the opera, beginning with Act III, which he completed by March 1847. Act I followed by June, Act II by August. On August 28, Wagner finished the prelude. Working at fever pitch into the first four months of the following year, Wagner finished the autograph score by April 1848. By the time *Lohengrin* was completed, there had been political uprisings in Vienna, Berlin and Saxony. Because he became involved in the Dresden revolt of May 1849, Wagner could not attend the premiere of *Lohengrin* at Weimar in 1850: he and the swan knight had become identical in their alienated, exiled status. The intersection of *Lohengrin* with the complex significance of swan legends was an act of fate.

Wagner's immediate sources for *Lohengrin* suggest the thoroughness of his acquaintance with swan legends and their inferences. While living in Paris, 1840-41, Wagner studied the monograph *The Song Contest of the Wartburg* (1838) by C. T. L. Lucas, an important source for *Tannhäuser*; this monograph refers to Lohengrin. In July 1845 at Marienbad, Wagner read the anonymous *Lohengrin* epic written in Bavaria c.1260-90, which supplied him with key details for *Lohengrin*, including the name of its heroine, Elsa, and the *Gottesgericht* or trial by combat. In the same year Wagner studied the German epic *Parzival* by Wolfram von Eschenbach (c.1170-c.1220). Written between 1198 and 1209-15, its final lines summarize the life of Parzival's son, called Loherangrin (possibly "Garin the Lorrainer"). Eschenbach describes how Loherangrin was sent by God as spouse for the princess of Brabant. Included are such important elements as the *Frageverbot* (the forbidden question of the knight's origins), the sword, horn and ring Lohengrin gives Elsa as he leaves Antwerp.

Wagner also knew Eschenbach's *Titurel*, which recounted Loherangrin's deeds after leaving Brabant. An additional influence was *The Swan Knight* by Konrad von Würzburg (d. 1287); like the Bavarian *Lohengrin* saga, it includes the *Frageverbot* after the trial by combat. To emphasize the knight's mysterious origin, Wagner altered his sources and placed the prohibition before rather than after the clash between Telramund and Lohengrin. In their 1815 compilation of tales the brothers Grimm included *The Six Swans*, at the conclusion of which a sister is reunited with her brothers, who had been turned into swans by their stepmother, a parallel with Gottfried's reappearance at the end of *Lohengrin*. Wagner's "enthrallment" led to extensive research in German mythology.

To these German sources Wagner added the Old French *Chevalier au Cygne*, a manuscript of the late twelfth century recounting the deeds of a hero named Helyas. Like his counterpart in the Bavarian *Lohengrin*, Helyas arrives in a swan boat. Unlike the German hero, who is sleeping on his shield in the boat, Helyas stands in the boat on his arrival. In addition to this detail, Wagner derived a strong historical element for *Lohengrin*. In the *Chevalier au Cygne*, Helyas weds the daughter of the Duchess of Bouillon and becomes thereby the grandfather of Godfrey of Bouillon, hero of the First Crusade (1095-96). This grounding of the French swan knight in history led Wagner to place Lohengrin during the reign of King Henry I of Saxony (875-936).

A descendant of Charlemagne, Henry in 924 negotiated a truce with the Hungarians for nine years, during which he fortified the German states. When the Hungarians invaded at the end of the period, Henry defeated them at Merseburg in March 933. It is in defense against this invasion that Henry is recruiting the Brabantians at the opening of *Lohengrin*. Henry died in July 936, having consolidated surrounding territory into the German realm, including Upper and Lower Lorraine. The Loherangrin or "Garin the Lorrainer" of *Parzival* indicates this political alliance between the German states and Lorraine. This welding of history to swan legends was to have great significance in Wagner's century.

These German and French sources for *Lohengrin* suggest various interpretations of its legendary material—the impulse of German nationalism, the swan knight as emissary from a Christian to a pagan world, the necessity of absolute trust between men and women. Wagner himself indicated that these swan legends had to be incorporated into an extended mythical context. He wrote in *Communication to My Friends*, "Who does not know the story of Zeus and Semele? The god loves a mortal woman and, for the sake of this love, approaches her in human shape. But the mortal learns that she does not know her lover in his true form and demands that he show himself to her in the full substance of his being." In this legend, Zeus reveals his godhead to Semele in the form of lightning, destroying her for her fatal curiosity. The forbidden question of *Lohengrin* has important antecedents in Semele, Eve or Psyche.

The two most important sources of information about swans in the ancient world are the Greek philosopher Plato and the Roman poet Ovid.

In the *Phaedo*, Plato's dialogue recounting the death of Socrates in 399 B.C., Socrates rebukes those attending him by comparing himself to a swan—prophet of a lofty, more exalted world:

> Evidently you think I have less insight into the future than a swan; because when these birds feel that the time has come for them to die, they sing more loudly and sweetly than they have sung in all their lives before, for joy that they are going away into the presence of the god whose servants they are. It is quite wrong for human beings to make out that the swans sing their last song as an expression of grief at their approaching end. People who say this are misled by their own fear of death. I believe the swans, belonging as they do to Apollo, have prophetic powers and sing because they know the good things that await them in the unseen world. I consider that I am in the same service as the swans.

In ancient art, Apollo is depicted on the back of a swan or in a chariot drawn by swans. This linking of Apollo and swans indicates that swans are bearers of the soul to the other world. It also identifies them as partakers of the arts of the Muses, whose leader was Apollo. Since Apollo is conceived as the god of light (hence of prophecy and reason), the symbolic association of Lohengrin with the Light of Christianity in Wagner is appropriate: Lohengrin counters the pagan darkness embodied in Ortrud's Frisian, pre-Christian religion. (The name Helyas in the French epic may derive from the Greek helios or "sun.") The swan image appears in Plato's *Republic* in the Myth of Er, expressing the doctrine of the immortality of the soul. Er remarks that Orpheus chose to be reborn in the figure of a swan, avoiding another birth by woman because female followers of Dionysus had destroyed him. Here the swan is associated with art but not, as in its nexus with Apollo, in a saving sense. In this linkage of Orpheus and swan, the artist is seen as threatened by his own unusual status. Wagner's artist/savior Lohengrin is thus both exceptional and endangered.

Wagner's reference to Zeus and Semele indicates his recognition of a key source of classical mythology, Ovid's *Metamorphoses* (7 A.D.). Ovid recounts stories of two different characters, each bearing the name of Cycnus or "Swan," dealing with unrequited love. In one tale, Cycnus imposes tasks of love on Phylius, who finally refuses to perform any additional deeds. This

Cycnus, a son of Apollo, then throws himself from a cliff, whereupon he is transformed into a swan. In the second tale, Cycnus, a King of Liguria, is in love with Phaëthon, son of Apollo. When Phaëthon is destroyed by Zeus for his presumption in driving the sun chariot, Cycnus is transformed into a mournful swan, seeking shaded streams to avoid the wrath of Zeus. Both stories involve the swan in unfulfilled love, as does the opera. In the story of Phaethon, the swan signifies deference to authority, which marks the conclusion of Lohengrin's situation in Wagner.

The swan in classical mythology is associated with more explicit erotic contexts. In the tale of Leda and the swan, Zeus the immortal, in the form of a swan, couples with Leda, wife of Tyndareus, King of Sparta. The phallic neck of the swan emphasizes this aggressive sexuality. From this union came Helen (of Troy) and her brothers, Castor and Pollux, the Dioscuri. The swan legend in this variant becomes associated with combat through Helen, whose abduction by Paris caused the Trojan War. Through the legend of Leda, the swan is linked with transcendental power and with royalty in the form of Zeus. These elements of war, royalty and voyaging coalesce in *Lohengrin*. The erotic component of swan legends is emphasized in Greek art by the Pistoxenos Painter, whose cup from 460 B. C. depicts the goddess Aphrodite riding on a swan. Other Greek artists depicted the swan with griffins or Bacchic revelry. They suggest the opposition to violence and irrationality by the force of reason through affiliation with Apollo. *Lohengrin* embodies in a distilled form all the elements of classical swan legends: bravery before death, reason, light, the besieged artist, unrequited love, immortal authority, military invincibility.

Leda and the swan preoccupied Italian painters during the sixteenth century. The most famous early-Renaissance depiction was by Leonardo da Vinci, executed around 1503, telescoping two different time periods of the legend. Leda appears after coition with the swan, whom she gently moves aside. To her right, twin eggs hatch to reveal Castor, Pollux, Helen and her sister Clytemnestra (usually not considered the progeny of Zeus). More daring than Leonardo, Michelangelo in the lost painting *Leda* (c. 1530) depicted the actual moment of coition, removing all accessory detail of the offspring. Bartolommeo Ammanati finished a sculpture after the model of Michelangelo's canvas. Antonio Correggio follows Michelangelo in painting the moment of intercourse but places the episode against the natural scenery suggested by Leonardo's *Leda*. This same eroticism appears in the *Leda and the Swan* of Paolo Veronese, where Leda is shown as the wife of the King of Sparta, decked in jewels amid a sumptuous interior.

During the eighteenth and nineteenth centuries, artists continued to find inspiration in the Leda legend. Jean-Francois de Troy completed a *Leda* with two swans, now placed in marshy streams. During the rococo period, François Boucher could not fail to be attracted to the theme. Toward the end of the century, Jacques-Louis David painted a *Paris and Helen* that shows the daughter of Leda with her abductor, while on the bedstead behind them is a detail of Leda and the swan. With David the legend assumes a political cast, symbolically criticizing the morality of an aristocracy that was to be abolished by the French Revolution. A drawing by Théodore Géricault adapts one of the Parthenon sculpture figures to the pose of Leda as she reclines before an aggressive swan. Jean-Baptiste Gibert in his 1829 canvas *The Death of Adonis* includes the classical association of Aphrodite and the swan as the goddess alights from her chariot. The British artist William Etty, in an oil from a few years before, shows Leda in the posture originated by Michelangelo. Eroticism reappears in Frederic Leighton's canvas *The Odalisque* (1862), where a swan gazes longingly at the exotic woman above him, a welding of the classic legend to the Middle Eastern themes admired during the period. A late *Leda* was completed by Jean-Léon Gérôme in 1874, a swan nuzzling a somnolent Leda. The latent eroticism of *Lohengrin* would have been apparent to Wagner's contemporaries from both his Germanic literary sources and these pictorial representations of the amorous Leda legend.

The more brooding element of the swan legend, its association with death and isolation, appears in German painting during the early nineteenth century. In particular, three canvases by the romantic painter Caspar David Friedrich are significant. In *Swans in the Rushes*, two swans are shown in moonlight, with the evening star above them. Friedrich is recorded to have said, "The divine is everywhere, even in a grain of sand. Here I depicted it for once in the rushes." If one interprets the rushes as a cathedral and the moon and stars as symbols of death, then the picture links pagan and Christian concepts of swans which, as Socrates observed, confront death hopefully and fearlessly. This canvas was shown at Dresden in 1820 and 1842, so it may have been known to Wagner. A second canvas, *Swans at Sunset* of 1832, indicates two swans in early evening with a crescent moon, standing for death and the Christian hope of resurrection; red lotus flowers, indicating divine love, reinforce this joining of pagan and Christian ideas. In 1832 Gustav Carus painted his *Allegory on the Death of Goethe*, a picture having particular significance to *Lohengrin*, since the opera had its premiere on August 28, 1850, the anniversary of Goethe's birth. Carus depicts the lyre floating on a turbulent ocean to indicate the classic and romantic components of Goethe's poetry. The swans suggest an intricate system of significance reflected in *Lohengrin*—the divine mission of the artist, the fearlessness before death, the conflict with an alien environment, the lofty destination of the light-bearing soul, the isolation of the solitary genius.

During the nineteenth century, a final element of the swan legend appeared—its association with royalty and power. As early as 1800, Napoleon Bonaparte became interested in furnishing the chateau of Malmaison for his wife Josephine; a swan motif was prevalent, signifying imperial sovereignty through its relation to Zeus in the Greek legend. The decor set a precedent for Wagner's patron, King Ludwig II.

In the same year, 1832, that Friedrich and Carus were painting allegories of swans, King Maximilian II of Bavaria, father of the future Ludwig II, began the restoration of the castle of Hohenschwangau ("Lofty Swan Province"). Maximilian transformed the former dining room into the "Hall of the Swan Knight," with pictures of Lohengrin's arrival in the swan boat and his poignant departure. Ludwig spent most of his time at Hohenschwangau and received the composer there. Wagner never visited the other royal residences, Neuschwanstein and Herrenchiemsee.

The swan legend and its involvement with Ludwig II is the most famous identification of royalty with the swan icon during the century. Surrounded by swan murals at Hohenschwangau, Ludwig fed swans in the lake (painted doing so in 1850), drew swans, heard from Maximilian that Lohengrin had inhabited the castle, and signed his letters with a swan-and-cross seal. Soon after Ludwig became king in 1864, he began erecting castles that would bring the Lohengrin legend and its swan to life. The first of these was Neuschwanstein ("New Swan Castle"), begun in 1869. Just as the study was decorated with the legend of Tannhäuser, the living room had murals depicting aspects of the Lohengrin saga, such as his arrival in Antwerp. Throughout the castle, vases, ceramics and curtains replicated the swan motif. In 1870 Ludwig began the castle of Linderhof, inspired by a visit to Versailles in 1867. The ornate rococo interiors rivaled in splendor if not in scale the residence of the French kings. The most famous of the creations at Linderhof is the Grotto of Venus from 1876. In the paintings of 1881 by Heinrich Breling, Venus' swans accompany her boat, a linkage as ancient as the cup by the Pistoxenos Painter or as recent as the canvas by Gibert. After Ludwig stayed at Paris in 1874, he conceived the idea of erecting a German Versailles at Herrenchiemsee, begun in 1878. The identification with the heroism and royalty of the swan legends was pervasive during Ludwig II's reign until his death in 1886.

The remainder of the nineteenth century witnessed the expression of many aspects of swan legends, partially from the influence of *Lohengrin* and King Ludwig II. As an emblem of the isolated (sometimes self-exiled) artist or of the soul, the swan recurred in imagist and symbolist poetry, beginning with Charles Baudelaire (an enthusiast of *Lohengrin*) in 1861, continuing through Stéphane Mallarmé and Edmund Gosse, reaching into the next century with texts by William Butler Yeats, D.H. Lawrence and Marianne Moore. In his study of Leonardo da Vinci in 1869, Walter Pater conceived the *Mona Lisa* as "the symbol of the modern idea" in her amalgamation of virtue and treachery. Pater noted one of her destructive variants was Leda as mother of Helen of Troy. The image of the swan as exiled in an alien universe became central to the conception of the 1877 ballet *Swan Lake*, with music by Tchaikovsky. In contrast to the aesthetic isolation of the poets' image or the fearful icon of Pater, Odette embodies a dislocation of identity remarkable in the last great manifestation of the legend, the shattered Charles Swann in Marcel Proust's *Swann's Way* of 1913.

In her diary in October 1881, not long before the composer's death,

Cosima Wagner recorded, "As far as *Lohengrin* is concerned, R. says he is completely satisfied with it." Wagner's sources of satisfaction are found in the musical revolution that *Lohengrin* marked. It was characterized as *durchkomponiert* or "composed through," with relatively few traces of set pieces. *Lohengrin* realized Wagner's new style of writing for the voice, an amalgam of aria and recitative. But the greater source of Wagner's satisfaction undoubtedly rests on his belief that "the character and situation of this Lohengrin I now recognize as the type of the only absolute tragedy, in short, of the tragic element of modern life," the separation of the spiritual and the sensual. Wagner believed that this tragedy could be resolved only by "the full reunion of sense and soul, each in its utmost consummation."

Lohengrin of Monsalvat and Elsa of Brabant fail to reconcile these complementary aspects of the self. This tragedy Wagner recognized as inherent in the mythical system of the swan legends, depicting both the spiritual and the erotic dimensions of existence. Wagner recorded in *My Life* his first acquaintance with the *Lohengrin* story in 1840-41: "There suddenly sprang up before my eyes a *Lohengrin* complete in every detail of dramatic construction. The legend of the swan, which forms so significant a feature of the whole complex of myths with which my studies had familiarized me, exercised a singular fascination over my imagination." Proving the eternal power of the swan, this "complex of myths" converges in *Lohengrin*.

Beyond Reason:
Donizetti and *Lucia di Lammermoor*

"Our theaters go from bad to worse . . . Operas fail, the public hisses, attendance is poor. Now at the San Carlo we have Persiani's old opera *Danao*, then my *Lucia di Lammermoor*, which is now finished . . . Crisis is at hand, the public has indigestion, the Società Teatrale is about to be dissolved, Vesuvius is smoking, and the eruption is near." So wrote Gaetano Donizetti in July, a few months before the premiere of his signature work on September 26, 1835, in Naples. Donizetti had wanted his opera to wield "love, without which operas are cold—violent love." From this perspective, Walter Scott's novel *The Bride of Lammermoor*, published in 1819, proved a composer's dream.

The composition history of *Lucia di Lammermoor* is the material of legend. The earliest reference to the opera is contained in a letter by Donizetti dated May 18, 1835. The librettist, Salvatore Cammarano, had completed a synopsis by a week later. On May 29, Donizetti wrote the Società, "Time flies, and I assure you I can no longer remain in such perplexity, since I have other obligations." This threat was effective, and Cammarano proceeded with the libretto. The autograph score of *Lucia di Lammermoor* is dated July 6: within six weeks, Donizetti had composed a masterpiece. He recorded, "You know what my motto is? Quickly! It may be reprehensible, but the good things I have written were always written quickly, and often the accusation of carelessness is made against the music that cost me the most time."

Donizetti recorded on September 29, "*Lucia di Lammermoor* has been performed, and kindly permit me to shame myself and tell you the truth. It has pleased very much . . . I was called out many times . . . The king's brother Leopoldo, who was present and applauded, paid me the most flattering compliments. The second evening . . . every number was listened to in religious silence and spontaneously hailed with shouts of 'Evviva!'" Already famous as the composer of *Anna Bolena*, *L'Elisir d'Amore* and *Lucrezia Borgia*, Donizetti had survived the "eruption" to attain immortality by depicting "violent love."

The incredible aspect of this "violent love," however, was that it was drawn from life. Scott commented later, "Of all the murders I ever committed, there is none that went so much to my heart as the poor Bride of Lammermoor; but it could not be helped, it is all true." So powerful was this story that other composers had already set The Bride of Lammermoor—Michele Carafa with *Le Nozze di Lammermoor* in 1829, Ivar Bredal with *Bruden fra Lammermoor* in 1832, and in 1834, the year before Donizetti, Alberto Mazzucato with *La Fidanzata di Lammermoor*.

As Scott recorded in the introduction to *The Bride of Lammermoor*, the original of Lucy Ashton was Janet Dalrymple, daughter of James, Lord Stair, and Dame Margaret Ross. Without her parents' knowledge, Janet Dalrymple betrothed herself to Lord Rutherford. A short time later, her father and particularly her mother, forced her to break the engagement and marry David Dunbar, heir to David Dunbar of Baldoon. The wedding was solemnized on August 24, 1669. Scott records the result:

> The bridal feast was followed by dancing; the bride and bridegroom retired as usual, when of a sudden the most wild and piercing cries were heard from the nuptial chamber . . . On opening the door, they found the bridegroom lying across the threshold, dreadfully wounded, and streaming with blood. The bride was then sought for: she was found in the corner of the large chimney, having no covering save her shift, and that dabbled in gore. There she sat grinning at them . . . absolutely insane. The only words she spoke were "Tak up your bonny bridegroom."

On September 12, Janet died. Unlike Arturo Bucklaw in *Lucia*, David lived on until March 1682, when he was killed by a fall from his horse. Rutherford died in 1685, never having married. The "violent love" of this trio supplied Scott and Donizetti with a tale as harrowing as it was factual.

Lord and Lady Stair presumably tried to conceal the facts. Robert Law, once a pupil of Lord Stair, recorded in his *Memorialls* that Janet Dalrymple was "harled through the house by spirits." Another legend claims that Rutherford broke into the bridal chamber and assaulted Dunbar. In his *Notes to Law's Memorialls*, Charles Kirkpatrick Sharpe records that it was not Dunbar but in fact Janet Dalrymple who had been stabbed by her husband. *The Stair Annals* camouflage the whole affair: "Alas! the bride's health suddenly declined or gave way, and she died at Baldoon, probably of a broken heart, on September 12."

Since Scott conceived the 1707 Act of Union between England and Scotland as the central event of recent Scottish history, he advanced his story by more than forty years, to around 1710. By this Act, Queen Anne became the first sovereign of the new state of Great Britain. The hatred between the Ashtons and the Ravenswoods originates in the Civil War of 1689, by which Tory adherents of James II and the Stuarts were vanquished by the Whigs. In the novel, the ascendant bourgeois Ashtons are Whigs and Presbyterians, while the doomed feudal Edgar of Ravenswood is Tory and Episcopalian. Transferring the tale after the Act of Union, Scott demonstrates that the real Union is far from achieved, that factions are still manipulating the legal system for political ends.

Lucy and Edgar, representing opposing ideologies, are destroyed by intrigues that override their personal desires. The Whig Lady Ashton (modeled on Lady Stair) hates Edgar of Ravenswood because he represents the old Tory order. Though himself a person of some Tory allegiance, Scott shows both factions as dishonest, deceiving, scheming and ruthless. To emphasize the political chaos, Scott relocates events from Wigtownshire in southwest Scotland to the region of the Lammermuir Hills on the Lothian border, east of Edinburgh, the locus of independent Scotland. Scott retains echoes of several Shakespearean dramas to strengthen the universality of the story. The feuding Ashtons and Ravenswoods, with their doomed offspring, recall *Romeo and Juliet*; evil old Ailsie Gourlay, who aids Lady Ashton in undermining Lucy's mental stability, is associated with the Witches from Macbeth; and Edgar in his usurped situation suggests Hamlet, who must avenge his father.

Like Scott, Donizetti and Cammarano adapted history and legend to suit their own purposes. Instead of locating the tale in 1710, they reverted to the more historically authentic late seventeenth century. William III and Mary, who ruled until 1694, are made political enemies. The major events in the relationship of Lucy and Edgar are retained in *Lucia*. The vision at the fountain (Chapter XXIII) becomes the basis of Lucia's "Regnava nel silenzio" in the first act, though in Scott the vision is not of a phantom but of the old family retainer and prophetess Alice Gray, who appears to Ravenswood as an omen of the family's decline. Cammarano skillfully welds an earlier tale of doomed love in the Ravenswood family, an affair between a Lord and a "plebeian" maid/nymph (Scott's Chapter V), to the later ghostly visitation. Scott indicates that the joy in her love expressed in Lucia's ensuing cabaletta "Quando, rapito in estasi" will be fleeting indeed. Donizetti and Cammarano adapt Scott's political idea as Enrico Ashton decides to force his sister to marry Arturo Bucklaw, who would exert enough influence to sustain the imperiled fortunes of the Ashtons. In Scott, Arturo's prototype, Frank Hayston of Bucklaw, is a wild Tory and Jacobite rebel.

The development of Lucia and Enrico in *Lucia* derives from a superb reduction of the novel. In the opera, Normanno describes an episode from *The Bride of Lammermoor* (Chapter V) in which Edgar rescues Lucy and her father from the charge of a bull: the sexual symbolism of the episode is underscored as Lucy is awakened to love for her rescuer. The duet in Act I ("Sulla tomba che rinserra"), when the two pledge fidelity by the fountain, derives from Scott's Chapter XX, where the lovers break a piece of gold as a sign of commitment. Omitted from the opera, however, is the sinister episode in which a raven is shot by Lucy's brother immediately after the betrothal: "The bird fluttered a few yards and dropped at the feet of Lucy, whose dress was stained with some spots of its blood." Scott reinforces the doomed plight of the lovers at the very moment of their strongest emotional union.

The greatest alteration that Cammarano and Donizetti effected was the creation of Enrico Ashton as the lovers' sole opponent, a conflation of several characters in Scott. In *The Bride of Lammermoor*, Lucy and Edgar are constrained by many members of the Ashton family: Sir William, Lucy's father, concerned with the political fortunes of the Whigs and his heirs; Henry, Lucy's younger brother, who gives Enrico his name and who invades the lovers' privacy; Douglas Sholto Ashton, Lucy's older brother, who, like Enrico in the opera, swears enmity to the Ravenswoods; and Lady Ashton, more implacable against the Ravenswoods than anyone else in the novel. It is Lady Ashton who intercepts letters between Edgar and Lucy, assigns the vicious Ailsie Gourlay to unsettle Lucy's mind and sabotages the interview between Lucy and Edgar after she has signed the marriage contract. To emphasize Enrico's prominence, Donizetti gives him a double aria in the first scene—"Cruda, funesta smania" and its cabaletta, "La pietade in suo favore," wonderfully etching his nature. While one might regret the decision to excise Lucy's fierce mother, Cammarano prevents Enrico from being a pure villain when in the sextet he expresses remorse ("Chi raffrena il mio furore?") at the destruction of his sister.

From Scott's Chapters XXXII-XXXIII derives the climax of Act II, the signing of the contract, the return of Edgardo and the confrontation between the lovers that triggers the sextet. Scott, in fact, sketched the framework of an ensemble at this moment:

> Lockhard and another domestic . . . were seen standing on the threshold transfixed with surprise, which was instantly communicated to the whole party in the stateroom. That of Colonel Douglas Ashton was mingled with resentment; that of Bucklaw with haughty and affected indifference; the rest, even Lady Ashton herself, showed signs of fear, and Lucy seemed stiffened to stone by this unexpected apparition. Apparition it might well be termed, for Ravenswood had more the appearance of one returned from the dead than of a living visitor.

Since he supplied librettists and composers with such possibilities, there can be little surprise that Scott endured as a source of operas during the nineteenth century—Rossini's *La Donna del Lago* (1819) from *The Lady of the Lake*, Boieldieu's *La Dame Blanche* (1825) from *Guy Mannering* and *The Monastery*, Bellini's *I Puritani* (1835) from Old Mortality, Bizet's

La Jolie Fille de Perth (1867) from *The Fair Maid of Perth*, Sullivan's *Ivanhoe* (1891).

It is the mad scene that has made *Lucia di Lammermoor* a touchstone of the bel canto repertory. The dramatic legacy of mad scenes extends back to the dazed Agave in Euripides' *The Bacchae* and of course Shakespeare's Ophelia. The Romantic Movement emphasized individual states of consciousness and motivation, often as a component of Byronic egoism. Scott's Edgar is marked as Byronic by his "air of contempt" and "a mind naturally of a gloomy cast." In the wild wasteland of Wolf's Crag, symbolizing his outcast status, he stands on the margin of civilized life. Donizetti's final scene, in the tombs of the Ravenswoods, emphasizes Edgardo's brooding fate.

Just as Scott set forth a prototype for a romantic opera hero, he supplied composer and librettist with the perfect description to catalyze Lucia's mad scene. Portraying Lucy Ashton as "gentle, soft, timid and feminine," Scott emphasizes that "Her passiveness of disposition was by no means owing to an indifferent or unfeeling mind. Left to the impulse of her own taste and feelings, Lucy Ashton was peculiarly accessible to those of a romantic cast. Her secret delight was in the old legendary tales." Lucy is lost in destabilizing dreams,"involved in those mazes of the imagination which are most dangerous to the young and the sensitive." Donizetti and Cammarano follow Scott by emphasizing early in the narrative this susceptibility to imaginative fantasy; the vision by the fountain recurs in the mad scene when the delirious Lucia imagines the phantom preventing her marriage to Edgardo.

In *The Bride of Lammermoor*, Lucy's mind begins to deteriorate when she receives no letters from Edgar: "Lucy's temper gave way under the pressure of constant affliction and persecution. She became gloomy and abstracted . . . and sometimes turned with spirit, and even fierceness, on those by whom she was long and closely annoyed." After signing the contract, Lucy is "in a state of absolute stupor." To fashion the mad scene, Donizetti needed only Scott's account:

> Here they found the unfortunate girl, seated, or rather couched like a hare upon its form—her head-gear dishevelled; her night-clothes torn and dabbled with blood—her eyes glazed, and her features

convulsed into a wild paroxysm of insanity. When she saw herself discovered, she gibbered, made mouths, and pointed at them with her bloody fingers, with the frantic gestures of an exulting demoniac.

The popularity of *Lucia di Lammermoor* during the nineteenth century was reinforced through a strong involvement by painters and illustrators in the works of Scott. As early as 1809, engravings were made from *The Lay of the Last Minstrel* (1805) and *Marmion* (1808), while paintings from Scott's novels appeared as early as 1816. *The Bride of Lammermoor* was illustrated by William Allan in 1820 and C. R. Leslie in 1823, both portraying *Lucy and Ravenswood at the Mermaiden's Fountain*; Thomas Stothard's picture of the same title, dated 1820, like Leslie's shows the dead raven at Lucy's feet. In 1830 Thomas Duncan engraved *Ravenswood and the Gravedigger*, with its strong echo of Hamlet. An artist particularly attracted to the novel was Eugène Delacroix, who finished a *Self-portrait as Ravenswood* around 1821, the brooding romantic outcast in seventeenth-century costume. Delacroix also made an ink drawing of *Ravenswood and Lucy at the Mermaiden's Fountain*, with its suggestion of the ominous raven, while the 1824 pencil *Lucy Ashton's Bridal Night* depicts Lucy staring demoniacally as Bucklaw's body lies on the bed. The scene at the fountain was painted subsequently by Henry Liverseege in 1833 and Robert Herdman in 1875.

Between 1830 and 1870, over sixty representations of episodes from *The Bride of Lammermoor* were produced in England and Scotland. Having finished a *Lucy at the Fountain* in 1842, William Powell Frith completed *The Love Token* in 1854, which depicts Lady Ashton returning the broken gold piece to Ravenswood right after the signing of the contract; Lucy, on the brink of madness, stares listlessly before her. The Scottish painter Robert Scott Lauder in 1831 completed *"He is come—he is come!"*, a representation of the signing of the contract and Ravenswood's return: the light falls on the downcast Lucy and her mother while Edgar remains in romantic shadow. In 1878 John Everett Millais finished *The Bride of Lammermoor*, showing Edgar of Ravenswood and Lucy Ashton after he has rescued her from the bull. Even at this first meeting, Lucy clings to Edgar, whose frown indicates he has just sighted Lucy's father, despoiler of the Ravenswood estates. Millais drew details from Scott's description:

A shooting dress of dark cloth intimated the rank of the wearer, though concealed in part by a large and loose cloak of a dark brown color. A Montero cap and a black feather drooped over the wearer's brow and partly concealed his features, which, so far as seen, were dark, regular and full of majestic though somewhat sullen expression. Some secret sorrow, or the brooding spirit of some moody passion, had quenched the light and ingenuous vivacity of youth.

The potential dementia of Lucy was not lost on reviewers of the canvas, one of whom noted, "Her firmness can only act when she is driven to madness; but her stupor of clinging faintness is exquisitely rendered."

The plight of Lucy and Edgar became a cultural signpost during the nineteenth century. Queen Victoria recorded speaking to Lord Melbourne: "I said to him I was reading the first novel I have ever read—*The Bride of Lammermoor*; he said it was a very melancholy—a terrible story—but admires it." The queen and Lord Melbourne were not alone. Two weeks after the appearance of the novel, it was dramatized on the London stage. In Flaubert's *Madame Bovary* (1857), Emma Bovary, attending Donizetti's opera, "recognized all the intoxication and the anguish that had almost killed her. The voice of the prima donna seemed to her but the echo of her own consciousness." Edgar Allan Poe described Scott's novel as "that purest and most thrilling of fictions." The love depicted in *Lucia di Lammermoor*, however violent, has endured.

Dynamic Encounter:
Verdi and *Macbeth*

"For a long time, it has been an intention of mine to dedicate an opera to you, who have been to me at once father, benefactor and friend . . . Here now is this *Macbeth*, which I love in preference to my other operas and so deem more worthy of being presented to you." So wrote Giuseppe Verdi to his father-in-law, Antonio Barezzi, on March 25, 1847. The premiere of *Macbeth* had taken place at the Teatro della Pergola in Florence on March 14. Barezzi already knew of Verdi's triumph, since the composer's pupil Emanuele Muzio had written Barezzi on March 16, "Last night [sic] was the great performance of *Macbeth*, which, as usual with Verdi's operas, produced tremendous enthusiasm, Verdi having to appear onstage thirty-eight times in the course of the performance." Verdi had many reasons for preferring *Macbeth* to the nine operas he previously had composed. For Italian opera as well as for Verdi, this work signaled a revolution.

The difficult genesis of *Macbeth* symbolized the magnitude of the challenge Verdi confronted with this opera, though he was already the strikingly successful composer of *Nabucco* (1842), *Ernani* (1844) and *Attila* (1846). In May 1846, Verdi had indicated his willingness to compose an opera *sul genere fantastico* for Florence, perhaps following the supernatural examples of Meyerbeer's *Robert le Diable* and Weber's *Der Freischütz*. During the summer of 1846, he considered possible subjects, but the lack of a strong tenor at Florence decided the choice of *Macbeth*. On September 4, Verdi sent a synopsis to his librettist, Francesco Maria Piave, observing, "Here is the draft of *Macbeth*. This tragedy is one of the greatest creations of man! If we can't do something great with it, let us at least try to do something out of the ordinary."

Macbeth was to prove "out of the ordinary" in many respects. It is famous for being an *opera senza amore*, an opera without standard romantic love interest. It has no major tenor role. The leading lady is unsympathetic until the final act. Verdi himself recognized the radical nature of his experiment. To Felice Varesi, the first Macbeth, he wrote of the dagger scene in Act I, "This whole duet will have to be sung sotto voce, in a hollow voice such as to arouse terror." *Macbeth* was to emphasize drama over singing, reversing the priorities of the bel canto tradition of Rossini, Donizetti and Bellini. Verdi reiterated this distinction when he wrote to another of his librettists, Salvatore Cammarano, on November 23, 1848, when a production of *Macbeth* was planned at the San Carlo Theater in Naples:

> I know you are rehearsing *Macbeth*, and since it's an opera that interests me more than the others, permit me to say a few words to you about it. The role of Lady Macbeth has been assigned to [Eugenia] Tadolini, and I'm surprised she would deign to undertake it . . . Tadolini's qualities are far too good for that role! . . . Tadolini has a beautiful and attractive appearance: and I would like Lady Macbeth to be ugly and evil. Tadolini sings to perfection: and I would like the Lady not to sing. Tadolini has a stupendous voice, clear, limpid, powerful; and I would like the Lady to have a harsh, stifled and hollow voice. Tadolini's voice has an angelic quality; I would like the Lady's voice to have a diabolical quality!

Verdi wrote the first Lady Macbeth, Marianna Barbieri-Nini, "This is a drama that has nothing in common with the others, and we must all make every effort to render it in the most original way possible. Furthermore, I believe it is high time to abandon the usual formulas and procedures." Barbieri-Nini recalled that the duet "Fatal mia donna!" was rehearsed "more than 150 times, so that it might be closer to speech than to singing." Verdi forced the singers to rehearse it yet another time when the audience was already seated for the premiere. The soprano remembered, "Anyone who says that duet was received enthusiastically is saying nothing; it was something unbelievable, something new, unprecedented."

In the course of his career, Verdi was to consider several Shakespearean sources, including *The Tempest*, *Hamlet* and *King Lear*. Much later he produced a tragic and a comic masterpiece, respectively, with *Otello* (1887) and *Falstaff* (1893). *Macbeth* was the first major challenge. Verdi had not seen any Shakespeare onstage until he saw *Macbeth* in London in 1847, after the premiere of the opera. To develop his own conception, he had to rely on the 1838 prose translation by Carlo Rusconi; the play was not performed in Italy until 1849, in Milan. Verdi wrote Cammarano, "There are two principal numbers in the opera: the duet between the Lady and her husband and the sleepwalking scene." He became so frustrated with Piave's handling of some of the drama that he asked Andrea Maffei to rewrite the Witches' chorus in Act III and the sleepwalking scene before the premiere.

The origin of the story resides in Raphael Holinshed's *Chronicles of England, Scotland and Ireland*, first published in 1577. Shakespeare consolidated two narratives in Holinshed, the character of Macbeth and the murder of King Malcolme Duff by Donwald. Through "instigation of his wife," Donwald bribed four servants to cut the king's throat. The historical Macbeth came to the throne of Scotland in 1040. Holinshed records many incidents that later appear in Verdi and Shakespeare: the encounter of Banquo and Macbeth with the Witches, the murder of Duncan, the slaying of Banquo, the slaughter of Lady Macduff and her children, the folkloric traditions of the moving forest and the man not born of woman, the defeat of Macbeth by Macduff and Malcolm in 1057. In the *Chronicles*, Lady Macbeth is characterized as "very ambitious, burning in unquenchable desire to have the name of a queen." In Holinshed, Banquo is one of Macbeth's co-conspirators in the murder of Duncan, not the innocent father of future kings. Perhaps most significant, there is no sleepwalking episode by the Lady in Holinshed's version.

Shakespeare's *Macbeth* probably was written in 1606 and performed that July at Hampton Court before King James I and the visiting King of Denmark. Shakespeare undoubtedly altered the character of Banquo to suit the Stuart line's claim of descent from him. The supernatural element of the drama guaranteed the interest of James, who had written the treatise *Demonologie* in 1597. At his coronation in 1603, one tribute recorded James' escape from "traitor plots, black poison and the murdering knife contrived by hags of darkest hell." In November 1605, James was endangered by the Gunpowder Plot, and it is likely that the Porter's reference to an "equivocator" in Act II alludes to one of the participants, the Jesuit Henry Gamet, who was hanged on May 3, 1606, two months before the first performance of Shakespeare's play.

Verdi's *Macbeth*, while relying on Shakespeare, differs from its source. In the opera, for example, Duncan is murdered earlier than in the play. Verdi's Banco (Banquo) is a moral censor from the beginning he notes Macbeth's arrogance on first hearing the Witches' prophecy. Verdi conflates Shakespeare for Lady Macbeth's first-act cavatina "Vieni! t'affretta!" and its cabaletta, "Or tutti sorgete," but he alters Shakespeare by having Macbeth involve Lady Macbeth in the murder of Banco. Lady Macbeth's drinking song in Act II is Verdi's and Piave's invention. In the sleepwalking scene, however, the composer uses all he can of Shakespeare, and Macbeth's monologue "Pieta, rispetto, amore" in the last act condenses the similar speech from the play.

For the Paris production, in 1865, though key episodes of the 1847 version were retained (the sleepwalking scene, the dagger scene), Verdi believed the work was "at least a good third new," a claim not entirely justified. His changes, however, did radically alter the relative significance of Macbeth and Lady Macbeth. In the 1847 version, the two characters are in approximate balance, as in Shakespeare. In the 1865 version, Lady Macbeth dominates.

For the 1847 cabaletta "Trionfai! securi alfine" of Lady Macbeth, Verdi substituted a new aria, "La luce langue," based not on Lady Macbeth's words in Shakespeare but on Macbeth's when he contemplates the murder of Banquo, to which Lady Macbeth in Verdi is privy. Her diabolical nature is increased by her knowledge of Banco's imminent death and the application of Macbeth's words in Shakespeare to her in the opera. In Shakespeare, Lady Macbeth does not appear after the banquet until the sleepwalking scene. In fitting out the opera for Paris, however, Verdi again emphasized her dramatic function: in the 1847 version, Act III, Macbeth's return visit to the Witches, ended with his cabaletta "Vada in fiamme," based on Shakespeare, but in 1865 Verdi substituted a duet for Macbeth and Lady Macbeth, "Ora di morte." The consequence of this alteration is considerable and not necessarily praiseworthy. It is improbable that Lady Macbeth would follow Macbeth to the Witches' cave. Further, there is much less time for her mental disturbance to arise before the sleepwalking scene, for which Shakespeare accounts by her absence from his Act IV.

At the conclusion of the revised opera, Verdi eliminated Macbeth's 1847 solo "Mal per me," having him expire offstage without a death aria. Verdi may have cut this solo because its text is not in Shakespeare—and Macbeth in the play shows no repentance, though actor David Garrick interpolated a dying speech in his 1744 production. The result of Verdi's excision is that Macbeth and Macduff disappear from the stage, to be succeeded by the victory chorus, "S'affidi ognun al Re," Verdi substituted for Macbeth's death. Such alterations undermine Macbeth's presence in the 1865 version. Recognizing this situation, conductors frequently restore "Mal per me" before the victory chorus.

Many interpretations may be derived from Verdi's and Shakespeare's Scottish tale. The political theme of regicide had relevance for both dramatist and composer, since the tyranny of renegades like Macbeth applied equally to early seventeenth-century England and nineteenth-century Italy. The revolutions that convulsed Europe in 1848 were nationalistic endeavors to unify countries and rout oppressors, and the chorus of Scottish exiles speaks for the struggling masses of Verdi's own time. The drama also has considerable psychological resonance. Macbeth may be construed as the ego harassed by the demands of the anarchic id in the figure of Lady Macbeth and wearied with the idealism of the superego, Duncan. Psychoanalysis recognizes that the murder of Duncan to satisfy ambitious drives is clearly Oedipal, as Duncan represents the father whose place Macbeth usurps. Particularly in the 1865 version, Verdi's *Macbeth* etches the dominant Lady Macbeth as a nineteenth-century femme fatale.

Freud believed Lady Macbeth exhibits the neurotic behavior of those who fall ill after achieving success, since the ego, which can tolerate a reckless wish when it is fantasy, collapses when such a desire is actualized.

For Freud, Macbeth and Lady Macbeth constitute "a single psychical individuality . . . It is he who has the hallucination of the dagger before the crime; but it is she who afterward falls ill of a mental disorder . . . What he feared in his pangs of conscience is fulfilled in her; she becomes all remorse and he all defiance."

Freud recognized the theme of childlessness and its significance in the tale of Macbeth, as did both Shakespeare and Verdi. In the opera, Macduff rebukes Malcolm's idea that revenge will assuage his grief at the loss of his children by saying of Macbeth, "He has no children!," an echo of Shakespeare. It is plausible that Macbeth's ambition represents a sublimation of his repressed desire to found a line of kings: the Witches and their prophecies are only an externalization of this psychical situation. Frustrated in his desire, Macbeth destroys the fathers Duncan and Banquo, Macduff's fertile wife and her offspring. In Shakespeare it is suggested that Lady Macbeth once had a child, perhaps by a previous union, so in her case, ambition becomes a substitute for lost powers of motherhood. Her sleepwalking may be construed as the result of hysteria occurring because of this longing. Lady Macbeth's somnambulism is a state of awareness, not oblivion.

The psychological complexity of Verdi's and Shakespeare's representations of Macbeth is reflected in the increasing focus of Macbeth in the visual arts on the drama during the late eighteenth and nineteenth centuries. The Swiss painter John Henry Fuseli was especially drawn to this play. In his 1783 oil *The Three Witches*, Fuseli captures the three figures as demonic Fates. In 1793-94, Fuscli painted Macbeth confronting the fierce triad, and in 1812 one of his most daring images depicted *Lady Macbeth Seizing the Daggers*. Around 1780, George Romney painted *Macbeth Meeting the Witches*, where he appears apprehensive and stunned, in contrast to Francesco Zuccarelli's figure of 1767. Joshua Reynolds' *Macbeth and the Witches*, painted for the Boydell Shakespeare Gallery, emphasizes Macbeth's militarism and the fatal nature of the sisters. A sympathetic handling of Lady Macbeth appears in Richard Westall's *Lady Macbeth Prevented from Stabbing the King* of 1790. Here, because the sight of Duncan reminds her of her father, she refrains from the actual murder.

146

One of the few canvases depicting the banquet is almost contemporary with Verdi's opera—Daniel Maclise's 1840 representation, which shows Lady Macbeth restraining her husband. John Singer Sargent's 1889 portrait, *Ellen Terry as Lady Macbeth*, depicts an incident not in Shakespeare but based on Henry Irving's revival of 1888, when Lady Macbeth, foreboding the end, removes the crown from her head at the end of the banquet scene. Dante Gabriel Rossetti's pencil study of 1876 concentrated on the appearance of Lady Macbeth at her death, suggested by Shakespeare. In 1908, Talbot Hughes painted the sleepwalking scene in *Mrs. Siddons Playing Lady Macbeth*, with the famous actress crossing the stage.

Following the Paris production, Verdi wrote about various commentators, "It's said I didn't know Shakespeare when I wrote *Macbeth*. Oh, in this they are so wrong. Maybe I have not rendered *Macbeth* well, but that I don't know, don't understand and don't feel Shakespeare—no, by God, no! He is a favorite poet of mine, whom I have had in my hands from earliest youth, and whom I read and reread constantly." Verdi's reformation of opera in *Macbeth* marks a new integration of music and drama and attests to the influence of Shakespeare on his evolution as a composer. Verdi recognized as much when he noted in 1875, "I too have attempted the fusion of music and drama, and that in *Macbeth*; but I could not write my own librettos, as Wagner does." So dynamic was this encounter between Shakespeare and Verdi that, whether in the 1847 or the 1865 version, one still feels the force of Verdi's opera revolution in his *Macbeth*.

Bridge of Dreams:
Puccini and *Madama Butterfly*

The stage directions, by George Bernard Shaw, are precise: "when he opens it, he is confronted with a dainty and exquisitely clean young Japanese lady in a simple blue cotton kimono printed cunningly with small white jasmine blossoms."

The "he" is Alfred Doolittle; the "lady" is his daughter, Eliza, after her cleansing bath at the hands of Mrs. Pearce in Shaw's *Pygmalion* of 1913. It is the summation of a cultural revolution called *japonisme*, the kimono marking the heroine's transformation from Covent Garden seller of flowers to the flower itself.

Giacomo Puccini's *Madama Butterfly*, which received its premiere in 1904 at La Scala, was another manifestation of *japonisme*, a term coined by Philippe Burty in the periodical *The Renaissance* in 1872, meaning "the study of the art and genius of Japan." There can be little doubt that Eliza Doolittle's appearance in a kimono reflects the influence of Puccini's opera. Beyond that, however, both *Madama Butterfly* and *Pygmalion* signal the importance of an extraordinary East-West encounter, which found expression in art, literature, drama and music during the nineteenth century and into our own time. The fascination with all things Japanese came about for one reason—the mysterious exoticism of the country itself, what Herman Melville called "the impenetrable Japans."

This mystery arose from impenetrability. Under the Tokugawa shogunate (1603-1867), Japan pursued a policy of excluding Westerners and Western influences. In 1620, the shogunate banned all foreign travel. In 1622, Christians were persecuted in Japan; in 1624 all Spaniards were expelled. The Shimabara Rebellion of 1637-38 ended Christianity as an organized religion in the country. In 1638 it was decreed that no one could build ships large enough for ocean trade. After 1639, trading privileges were granted only to the Dutch, on the island of Deshima in Nagasaki Harbor. Though the ban on foreign books was lifted in 1716, this policy of national seclusion (*sakoku seisaku*) was rigidly enforced. Foreign sailors cast on Japanese shores were subject to execution.

All this was to change during the nineteenth century. On July 8, 1853, Commodore Matthew C. Perry anchored his black ships near Uraga in Edo (that is, Tokyo) Bay, determined to break this policy of isolation. His motives were strictly commercial. The U.S., with its ambition to expand economically in the Far East, was hampered because American ships could not refuel in Japanese ports. Perry carried with him a letter from President Millard Fillmore, stating that the Commodore's objective was "friendship, commerce, a supply of coal, and protection for our ship-wrecked people." Perry left the letter with the shogun, vowing to return.

When he did, Perry negotiated the Treaty of Kanagawa in March 1854. Under its provisions, American ships were granted permission to take on coal and wood at the ports of Shimoda and Hakodate, although there was to be no trade in Edo (Tokyo) proper. The stationing of an American consul at Shimoda was permitted. Consul Townsend Harris arrived to fill that post in August 1856. Harris was to conclude the Treaty of Amity and Commerce of July 1858, whereby Shimoda was closed but Edo was opened. Treaty ports at Nagasaki and Yokohama were granted, along with most-favored-nation trading status. European powers quickly followed the American example by establishing trade rights—England in 1854, Russia in 1855, France in 1858, Portugal in 1860, Germany in 1861.

Because of outbreaks against foreigners after these negotiations, all non-Japanese were placed under the protection of law in March 1868. The anti-foreign element, known by the name *Joi* or "Expel the Barbarian," gradually ceased. The most important alteration in Japanese politics was the abolition of the shogunate in November 1867 and the restoration in January 1868 of the power of the emperor in the figure of Emperor Meiji, whose name means "enlightened" or "illustrious." The government passed to direct rule of the emperor, who in 1869 moved his residence from Kyoto to Edo, now renamed Tokyo or "Eastern Capital."

With lightning intensity, Japan entered the modern era. Clans were abolished in 1871; a railroad was opened between Tokyo and Yokohama in 1872; the edict against Christianity was removed in 1873, the same year Japan adopted the Gregorian calendar. In 1877, telephones were first used, and perhaps most important, Japan established the bicameral Diet, the legislative branch of the government, in 1890. Thanks to its great military strength, Japaa was victorious in the Sino-Japanese War during 1894-95, and its triumph in the Russo-Japanese War of 1904-05 solidified its status as a world power. The annexation of Korea in 1910 marked the beginning of its imperialist ventures.

Japonisme was a product of this extraordinary transformation of Japan and the contacts with the West that catalyzed it. The Orient, as Europe described Asia, already had exerted an influence on Western culture during the eighteenth century, evident for example in the taste called *chinoiserie*, which marked the rococo style, with its attraction to figurines of costumed Chinese and to porcelain. During the nineteenth century, there was often no firm demarcation between China and Japan on the part of Western enthusiasts and critics. Japanese art itself was not entirely unknown, thanks to such works as *Voyage to Japan* (1831) by Philip Franz von Siebold, who had been a sur geon with the Dutch East India Company and lived in Japan from 1823 to 1829, amassing a great collection of Japanese art, which he donated to a public museum in Leiden in 1837.

There were many manifestations of interest in Asia prior to the 1850s and Perry's voyage. Charles Lamb's essay "Old China" of 1823, relates:

> I have an almost feminine partiality for old china . . . that world before perspective—a china tea-cup I love the men with women's faces, and the women, if possible, with still more womanish expressions.

Lamb deploys the contemplation of his china collection to evoke memories of a time when he was happier, though poor. In Stendhal's novel *Le Rouge et le Noir* (The Red and the Black) of 1830, one chapter entitled "The Japanese Vase" compares the ruined love of Julien Sorel for Mathilde de la Mole to a smashed blue porcelain vase. At the same time, Thomas De Quincey's *Confessions of an English Opium-Eater* of 1822 evokes in its revelations a sinister configuration of Asia by its account of drug addiction.

It was during the 1850s, nevertheless, that Asia in its manifestation of *japonisme* assumed major significance for the nineteenth century, as Japanese art began to be circulated and appreciated. The French printmaker Felix Bracquemond is reputed to have discovered one volume of *Manga*, the sketchbook of Katsushika Hokusai (1760-1849), in 1856. Soon thereafter, the famous shop La Porte Chinoise was opened in Paris.

Japanese art became known to Westerners in Europe and in the U.S. through exhibitions, among which the most important are: 1854, Old Society of Painters in Watercolour, London; 1862, International Exhibition, London, with its Japanese Court; 1867, Paris Exhibition; 1873, Vienna Exhibition; 1876, Philadelphia Centennial Exhibition (the first major American venue); 1878, Paris Exhibition; and 1893, Chicago World's Fair, which had a Japanese teahouse. Others followed again in Paris in 1900 and in St. Louis in 1904, the latter to commemorate the Louisiana Purchase.

This exposure led to a blossoming of interest in and adaptation of Japanese art on the part of Western artists. Qualities such as emphasis on line, the high horizon, the lofty viewpoint, asymmetry, flatness, balance of black and white areas, narrow verticality and omission of foreground/background distinctions stunned both artists and public. Motifs from Japanese art, such as bridges, fans, floral sprays, cranes, bamboo, butterflies, parasols and herons, began to appear in Western pictures. *Japonisme* became manifest in everything from paintings, pottery, ceramics, wallpapers, screens, furniture, panels and plates to sideboards, overmantels, textiles, bookbindings, and silverwork. Ebonized wood was labeled "japanned." The impact on British, American and French artists was overwhelming.

In particular, two Americans, James A. McNeill Whistler and John La Farge, were major enthusiasts of Japanese art. During the early 1860s, Whistler discovered ukiyo-e prints ("Pictures of the Floating World")—that is, woodblock prints of courtesans, artisans and landscapes—by Hokusai, Ando Hiroshige (1797-1858) and Kitagawa Utamaro (1753-1806). Soon thereafter, Whistler's own etchings and paintings began to reflect Japanese art, either in adoption of technical practices like asymmetry, or in the deployment of Japanese accessories, such as fans, kimonos and screens.

In *Symphony in White, No. 2: The Little White Girl* of 1864, Whistler posed his mistress Jo Hiffernan before a mirror: she holds a Japanese fan while gazing at a blue-and-white jar and red lacquer bowl. The poet Swinburne was so moved by the canvas that he wrote "Before the Mirror" to express his feelings. In his painting *The Artist's Studio* of 1865, Whistler is shown with two women, one with a fan whom he called "La Japonaise," while in the back ground shimmers his collection of blue-and-white porcelain. *Caprice in Purple and Gold: The Golden Screen* of 1864 represents Jo studying Hiroshige woodblock prints while seated before a screen. *Purple and Rose: The Lange Lijzen of the Six Marks* of the same year depicts a woman in Chinese garb holding a blue-and-white vase. The famous *La Princesse du Pays de la Porcelaine* of 1864, now hanging in the Peacock Room of the Freer Gallery, shows the Greek beauty Christine Spartali standing before a screen, holding a Japanese fan; objects such as the Chinese carpet and the blue and-white vase reveal Whistler's fascination with Asia. In *Variations in Flesh Colour and Green: The Balcony* (c. 1864), Whistler poses Western models in Asian robes before the Thames River, across which one can see the smokestacks and factories of Battersea. Accoutrements such as a tea service, a spray of blossoms and a samisen enhance its Asian impression. By 1870, with *Nocturne: Blue and Gold—Old Battersea Bridge*, the influence of Hiroshige has been assimilated in the close-up view of this landmark.

John La Farge is of particular interest because he married Margaret Mason Perry, a grandniece of the Commodore Perry who "opened" Japan. La Farge first acquired Japanese prints around 1856. Beginning in 1860, his art started to reflect Japanese influences, for example in *Calla Lily* of 1862, with its Asian asymmetry, or *Flowers in a Japanese Vase* of 1864.

Snow Storm of 1865 combines flatness of tone with asymmetry. In his landmark "Essay on Japanese Art" of 1870, La Farge praises "the use of marvellous decoration . . . a simplicity, a love of subdued harmonies . . .

their abstract power of design . . . a balancing of equal gravities, not of equal surfaces" in Japanese art, which he claims "takes a distinct place, never before filled in the logical history of art."

In Britain too, artists were imbued with *japonisme*. Dante Gabriel Rossetti's *The Beloved* of 1865-66 shows a woman in a green kimono. Frederick Sandys in his *Medea* of 1868 places his figure before a screen decorated with cranes. Whistler's friend Albert Moore in such pictures as *Azaleas* (1868) and A *Venus* (1869) uses vases, scattered petals and blossom sprays to mix Asian and classical motifs. Frederic Leighton includes a screen decorated with cranes in his *Mother and Child* of 1865, while Edward Poynter in his *Lady Elcho* (1886) surrounds his subject with a Japanese screen and a goldfish bowl. Reviewing the Royal Academy exhibition of 1868, where *japonisme* was in evidence, Swinburne recorded of Moore's *Azaleas*, "The melody of colour, the symphony of form is complete: one more beautiful thing is achieved." Aubrey Beardsley with his illustrations to Oscar Wilde's *Salome*, 1894, juxtaposed black masses and white spaces in a dazzling experiment.

The influence of *japonisme* on writers was no less decisive. When a Japanese delegation came to the U.S. in 1860, Walt Whitman welcomed it to New York City with his poem "A Broadway Pageant": "Over the Western sea hither from Niphon come,/Courteous, the swart-cheek'd two-sworded envoys," he wrote. "Superb-faced Manhattan!/Comrade Americanos! to us, then at last the Orient comes . . . Today our Antipodes comes." Whitman praises Asia as the "Originatress," as "the nest of languages, the bequeather of poems with ample and flowing garments," not failing to note "the singing-girl and the dancing-girl." The economic element of Perry's expedition is not forgotten: "Commerce opening, the sleep of ages having done its work, races reborn . . . the Asiatic renew'd as it must be." Whitman commemorates Asia but simultaneously celebrates American economic expansion.

Many poets saw the aesthetic as well as the economic elements of East-West contact. William Ernest Henley in 1888 praised the prints of Utagawa Toyokuni (1769-1825) in his "Ballade of a Toyokuni Color-Print," wondering if he was a samurai, an actor, a priest in ancient Japan:

I have forgotten clean, I know

That in the shade of Fujisan,
What time the cherry-orchards blow,
I loved you once in old Japan . . .
I see you turn, with flirted fan,
Against the plum-tree's bloomy snow . . .

Henry Wadsworth Longfellow in his "Kéramos" (1878) muses on pottery, especially that of China and Japan:

The leaves that rustle, the reeds that make
A whisper by each stream and lake,
The saffron dawn, the sunset red,
Are painted on these lovely jars . . .
The stork, the heron, and the crane
Float through the azure overhead,
The counterfeit and counterpart
Of Nature reproduced in Art.

In his "Lapis Lazuli" of 1938, William Butler Yeats contemplates a Chinese sculpture: "Two Chinamen, behind them a third,/A symbol of longevity . . . There, on the mountain and the sky,/On all the tragic scene they stare." Oscar Wilde's poems "Symphony in Yellow" and "Impression du Matin" deploy tones of yellow and blue, inspired by Whistler's Japanesque paintings.

At the same time, the sterotype of sinister Asia appears in the inclusion of opium as a subject in works like Wilkie Collins' mystery *The Moonstone* (1868), Dickens' unfinished *The Mystery of Edwin Drood* (1870), Wilde's *The Picture of Dorian Gray* (1891) and Arthur J Conan Doyle's Sherlock Holmes tale *The Man with the Twisted Lip* of 1891, where the detective disguises himself to enter a London opium den. (Doyle was to write the non-Holmes tale *The Japanned Box* in 1899.)

It is literature in fact that prepares for Puccini's *Madama Butterfly*, particularly via three works: the French novel *Madame Chrysanthème* of 1887 by Pierre Loli; the tale *Madame Butterfly* by the American writer John Luther Long, which appeared in the *Century Magazine* of January 1898; and the drama *Madame Butterfly* by David Belasco, introduced in New York in 1900, adapted from Long's story and itself the inspiration for Puccini's opera, with its libretto by Luigi Illica and Giuseppe Giacosa. Each of these works, however, is equally a manifestation of Western *japonisme* and must be grasped in that context.

Madame Chrysanthème was the first novel to record a foreigner's affair with a Japanese woman, based on the experience of Loti (born Julien Marie Viaud). The narrator acquires an eighteen-year-old temporary bride for two and a half months during his residence in Nagasaki. The arrangement is purely a business transaction. The narrator views Japan and his mistress as the Other: different by virtue of race, sex and culture. To the Frenchman, the Japanese appear as "monkeys," "idiots" and "toys," marked by being "little," "grotesque" and "childlike." Long's story *Madame Butterfly* recounts how the American B. F. Pinkerton takes Cho-Cho-San as a temporary wife.

The basic elements of the tale as evolved in Puccini's opera are in Long: the birth of a child, the consul Sharpless, the faithful servant Suzuki and the long, futile vigil. Pinkerton's wife, here named Adelaide, calls Butterfly a "plaything," in line with the racism of *Madame Chrysanthème*. In Long's story, however, Suzuki seals Butterfly's wound from her attempted suicide, and Cho-Cho-San and the child escape the Americans. In Belasco's drama, which Puccini saw in London in 1900, the suicide takes place.

One of the most disturbing elements about *japonisme* is that as the nineteenth century progressed, enthusiasm for things Japanese was paralleled by Western racist beliefs, especially after the abolition of slavery led to increased immigration from Asia. Americans viewed Asians as a source of cheap labor, "the yellow peril"; such attitudes were reflected in the anti-Asian policy of the Hearst newspaper corporation. The opera *Madama Butterfly* underwent two revisions, in 1904 and 1906, one result of which was that Puccini altered the character of Pinkerton, who in the original is racist, brutal and coarse, like the narrator of *Madame Chrysanthème*. The arietta "Addio, fiorito asil," added for the production at Brescia's Teatro Grande, recasts the American lieutenant as a remorseful lover. While this underplaying of Pinkerton's racism may protect audiences' sensibilities, it also falsifies history.

Following *Madama Butterfly*, the twentieth century has continued to probe East-West relations, often with erotic subtext. Franco Leoni's opera *L'Oracolo* (1905) is set in an opium den in San Francisco, ending in violence and murder. The East-West encounter is frequently eroticized following the pattern set by *Madama Butterfly* of the Western man and the Asian woman, especially in films of the post-World War II era, such as Henry King's *Love Is a Many-Splendored Thing* (1955), Joshua Logan's *Sayonara* (1957) and Richard Quine's *The World of Suzie Wong* (1960).

The prevailing ethos at the end is Western, however impartial such pictures pretend to be. Occasionally the genders are reversed, with an Asian male and a Western female, as in Samuel Fuller's *The Crimson Kimono* (1959) or the masterful Alain Resnais' *Hiroshima Mon Amour* (1959). Each of these negotiates the minefield of miscegenation. David Henry Hwang's drama *M. Butterfly* (1988) demonstrates that the West has constructed so powerful a fantasy of Asia as female, dependent and passive that a French male diplomat can be deluded by a Chinese male spy into believing he is a woman.

In 'The Decay of Lying" of 1889, Wilde declared, 'The whole of Japan is a pure invention." The same year Rudyard Kipling recorded that "East is East, and West is West, and never the twain shall meet." Whistler stated in 1885 at the end of his Ten O'Clock Lecture: "The story of the beautiful is already complete—hewn in the marbles of the Parthenon—and broidered . . . upon the fan of Hokusai—at the foot of Fujiyama." Whistler's equation of Greek architecture with Japanese art is revolutionary.

Amid these three statements abide the fervor of *japonisme*—and the truth of *Madama Butterfly*.

The Verismo Movement:
Leoncavallo and *Pagliacci*

On May 19, 1890, a young man in Rome wrote to his father, "I feel as though I'm losing my mind. It was really overwhelming." The young man was Pietro Mascagni. Two nights before, at the Teatro Costanzi, he had started a revolution. Though Italy had endured a major political upheaval, the Risorgimento, during the nineteenth century under Garibaldi and Mazzini, it took the first performance of *Cavalleria Rusticana* to revolutionize opera. Mascagni's sixty curtain calls would echo, damningly for him, the remainder of his life. Verismo had arrived.

While *Cavalleria Rusticana* was enjoying unprecedented success, another struggling Italian composer was in great frustration. Ruggiero Leoncavallo, commissioned to compose a trilogy on the Italian Renaissance by the publisher Ricordi, produced *I Medici*, only to have it rejected by Ricardi as too costly for performance. Irritated at Ricordi and inspired by the fact that Ricordi's rival Sonzogno had sponsored *Cavalleria Rusticana*, Leoncavallo in four months composed *Pagliacci*, which Sonzogno accepted. It was mounted in triumph on May 21, 1892, at the Teatro dal Verme, Milan, conducted by Toscanini.

Corresponding to the statements by the Goncourts, Zola and Verga, Leoncavallo gave verismo opera its manifesto in the prologue to *Pagliacci*, following the suggestion of the first Tonio, Victor Maurel. Much influenced by Wagner, in the prelude Leoncavallo establishes four themes—those of the players, of Canio's despair, of love and of suspicion—before Tonio emerges from behind the curtain to address the audience. One recognizes immediately how similar and yet how different are Mascagni and Leoncavallo: the siciliana in *Cavalleria Rusticana* is sung with the curtain down: in *Pagliacci* the prologue breaches the space between audience and stage, a daring strategy, to enforce the idea that life and art are identical. Leoncavallo titles his opera *Pagliacci* to provide a documentary universal reference, that all mankind are "players." Mascagni, on the other hand, with the title *Cavalleria Rusticana*, describes and interprets rather than documents the action of his opera. Both the prologue and the siciliana, nevertheless, have the veristic spontaneity of Verga, intruding into their preludes. This spontaneity is reinforced by confining the action to two holidays, Easter in *Cavalleria* and the Assumption of the Virgin, August 15, in *Pagliacci*.

Costumed as Taddeo for the forthcoming commedia dell'arte, Tonio in the prologue declares, "The author has taken a slice of life . . . The artist is a man and writes for men—and he tells the truth." Several words recurring in the prologue, particularly "spasimi" (griefs), "vedrete" (you'll see) and "uomini" (mankind), stress Tonio's—and Leoncavallo's—idea that the stage and life are not separate. The music, he declares, originated "un giorno" (one day), an expression connoting the spontaneous nature of life, the occurrence of the opera on a single day, and especially, the fact that such events happen every day. That life and the stage are one is emphasized by Leoncavallo's brilliant idea of having Nedda's lover, Silvio, be not a part of the troupe but one of the village spectators.

Leoncavallo had not only the illusion of reality but actuality itself on his side when he composed *Pagliacci*. After the performance of *Pagliacci*, Catulle Mendes charged that Leoncavallo had plagiarized from his drama *La Femme de Tabarin* (1887), involving a murder by a man playing a role on the stage. In 1874, however, Paul Ferrier had produced his own *Tabarin*. Leoncavallo noted, in a response to these charges in 1894, that the idea of a man in stage character committing murder was quite old, dating as far back as *Drama Nuevo* by the Spanish writer Estabenez earlier in the century. In this same letter to Sonzogno, furthermore, Leoncavallo revealed, "In my childhood, while my father was a judge at Montalto in

Calabria (the scene of the opera), a jealous player killed his wife after the performance." At the trial, presided over by his father, young Leoncavallo had heard the enraged husband declare, "I repent nothing! If I had to do it over again, I'd do it again!" Those words he never forgot. The murderer in fact offered to defend Leoncavallo if Mendes pressed his accusation. Verga's story "The Mystery Play," moreover, recounts how Nanni killed Venera's lover Cola, with whom she fell in love while he was performing in a play during Easter. The fact that Leoncavallo knew of one actual murder gave him the impetus to compose the prologue to *Pagliacci*.

It is from the prologue that the tension of *Pagliacci* emerges. In his address to the villagers ("un tal gioco"), Canio declares, "The stage and life are not the same thing." This assertion, clearly made in ignorance, shows how far Canio is from the brutal truth revealed in the prologue. His "Vesti la giubba," therefore, has unbearable power, because a masker, and actor, has been unmasked—about life. Leoncavallo makes this particularly evident in Canio's repetition of words from the prologue, "uom," "singhiozzo" (sob) and "spasimo." His confused identity from "Tu se' Pagliaccio" to "No, Pagliaccio non son" exposes the terrifying similarity between the stage and life. The original score and Leoncavallo's widow attest that the final line of *Pagliacci*, "La commedia e finita!," was to be sung, not spoken, by Tonio, ending the opera as he began it. When uttered by Canio, however, its bitter truth is revealed. In fact *Pagliacci* used the ancient comedic characters of the *alazon* (braggart, Canio) and the *eiron* (ironist, Tonio) to subvert comedy itself: life is not what it seems.

The contrasts between *Cavalleria Rusticana* and *Pagliacci* indicate that the term verismo is relative and arbitrary. Veristic operas ultimately are a created, not a representational truth. Puccini, even in *Il Tabarro*, never used street or regional language and was never attracted to genuine *paesani*. Mascagni rarely dealt with Italian subjects, and few verismo operas ever had their setting in Italy or among the lower classes. It is true that verismo cornerstones like *La Bohème*, *Tosca*, *Adriana Lecouvreur* and *Andrea Chenier* depict artist figures ruined by sordid life, but their contexts scarcely correspond to the paesanismo al *Cavalleria* or *Pagliacci*.

"I found your successor in your predecessor, Verdi," Hans von Buelow once remarked to Mascagni. From the perspective of the twentieth century, one realizes that the revolution inspired by *Cavalleria Rusticana* and *Pagliacci* had marked antecedents. From *Rigoletto* came the idea of the "jester jested" in *Pagliacci,* atmospheric music and a romanticized "low life" appear in *Carmen*; *Cavalleria Rusticana* with its impassioned passage recalls *Il Trovatore* and in its local color even *Aida*. Opera in modern dress had already taken place with *La Traviata*, while the exchanges between Canio and Tonio in *Pagliacci* parallel in *Otello*.

"It is a pity I wrote *Cavalleria* first. I was crowned before I became king." So confessed Mascagni later in life. But the revolution he initiated remains one landmark of the transition from the nineteenth to the twentieth century, with *La Boheme, Il Tabarro, Andrea Chenier, Tiefland, Louise*, even *Wozzeck* and *Katya Kabanova*, revealing its significance. In his story "Ieli" Verga wrote, "Anybody who knows how to write is one who keeps words in a tinder box." Like Mt. Etna brooding over Sicily, such explosions occur—as did *Pagliacci* and *Cavalleria Rusticana*.

The Dark Side of Chivalry:
Wagner and *Parsifal*

Having completed the autograph score of *Tannhäuser* in April 1845, Richard Wagner took a vacation to Marienbad in July, recorded in *My Life*:

> I had intended to follow the easygoing mode of life . . . and had selected my books with care, taking with me the poems of Wolfram von Eschenbach as well as the anonymous epic *Lohengrin*. With my book under my arm, I hid myself in the neighboring woods and, pitching my tent by the brook in company with *Titurel* and *Parzival*, lost myself in Wolfram's strange yet irresistibly charming poem. Soon, however, a longing seized me to give expression to the inspiration generated by this poem, so that I had the greatest difficulty in overcoming my desire to give up the rest I had been prescribed . . . The result was an ever increasing state of excitement. *Lohengrin* . . . stood suddenly revealed before me.

Lohengrin had its premiere in 1850, but that opera was not the sole consequence of this reading of the great medieval German epic poem *Parzival*, composed c. 1197-1210 by Wolfram von Eschenbach (c. 1170- 1220), itself based on *Perceval li Gallois* (c. 1175) by Chrétien de Troyes. Wolfram had appeared in the *Sängerkrieg auf der Wartburg* of c. 1208, during the reign of Landgraf Hermann of Thuringia (1190-1217), memorably registered in *Tannhäuser*. Wolfram's influence endured for another thirty-seven years.

The story of Lohengrin ("Loherangrin" in the epic), however, occupies only a fraction of the material in *Parzival*, whose sixteen books chronicle the story of the *reine Tor* (pure innocent) and his quest for the Grail. Already Parzival (not spelled "Parsifal" until February 1877 by Wagner) had figured in Lohengrin's narration "In fernem Land" at the conclusion of *Lohengrin*, and he almost appeared in the final act of *Tristan und Isolde* when Wagner was planning the opera in 1854: "I introduced an episode which I did not work out later: namely a visit to Tristan's sickbed by Parzival, on his quest for the Grail. Tristan, ill from his wound and unable to die, had become identified in my mind with Amfortas in the Grail legend." Amfortas and Tristan were to be the knights of the flesh, Parzival the knight of the soul.

Then, in April 1857, Wagner had an epiphanic revelation:

On Good Friday I awoke to find the sun shining brightly . . . The little garden was radiant with green, the birds sang . . . I suddenly remembered that the day was Good Friday, and I called to mind the significance this omen already once had assumed for me when I was reading Wolfram's *Parzival*. Since the journey in Marienbad, I never had occupied myself again with that poem; now its noble possibilities struck me with overwhelming force, and out of my thoughts about Good Friday I rapidly conceived a whole drama, of which I made a rough sketch, dividing the whole into three acts.

Although the 1857 sketch is lost, the sketch Wagner completed in August 1865 for King Ludwig II has survived, as well as a crucial letter the composer wrote to Mathilde Wesendonk on May 30, 1859. In March and April 1877, Wagner completed the libretto, composing the music between 1877 and 1879. The scoring was finished during an intense year—Act I in April 1881, Act II the following October, Act III on January 13, 1882—with the premiere on July 26, 1882, at the Festspielhaus at Bayreuth.

Parsifal received a unique designation by Wagner as a *Bühnenweihfestspiel*, a "festival work to consecrate a stage." Since the premiere, the persistent question has been: what ideology is being consecrated on that stage? Myriad alternatives have presented themselves. It may be a ritual enactment of the death and rebirth of a fertility deity (harking back to Attis/Adonis/Christ); it possibly embodies art as the new religion; it suggests an Aryan racist program with anti-Semitic connotations; it enshrines a philosophical amalgam of Schopenhauer's negation of the *Wille*, Buddhistic doctrines of metempsychosis and Christian self-sacrificial compassion. Each of these interpretations may find partial validation in the opera, but the central component of *Parsifal* remains the chivalric code and its purpose.

Particularly persuasive is the fact that nearly all Wagner's works partake of some dimension of this coding. Wagner himself had indicated the affiliation of *Parsifal* with its predecessors *Tannhäuser*, *Lohengrin* and *Tristan*. He was to write Mathilde Wesendonk in 1859 about Amfortas, "To myself of a sudden it has grown too appallingly clear: it is my Tristan of the third act, with an inconceivable increase."

In that same letter, Wagner writes deprecatingly about Wolfram von Eschenbach:

> Never mind his understanding simply nothing of the inner content; he strings incident to incident, adventure to adventure . . . and leaves the earnest seeker with the question what he really meant . . . Wolfram is an utterly raw phenomenon, the blame for which must largely be laid on his barbaric, altogether confused era, hovering between primitive Christendom and the newer secular State. Nothing in that age could be carried right through . . . Our poet . . . merely took his subject from the sorry French chivalric romances of his age . . . With [Parzival] himself, Wolfram knows not what to do . . . Parzival must be accorded that main interest, unless he is merely to come on at the end as a cold *deus ex machina*.

Wagner solved this dilemma brilliantly by the excisions and compressions he made from Wolfram's 25,000 lines of verse.

Of the sixteen books in the poem, six are devoted to Gawan [Gawain], and while Wagner only hints at his presence, he does transfer characters from Gawan's adventures to *Parsifal*, especially the evil sorcerer Clinschor and the seductive Orgeluse de Logrois. Kundry is an amalgamation of several characters in Wolfram—Parzival's cousin Sigune, who tells him his name; Cundrie the sorcerer, the Grail messenger (*Kunde* = news); and Orgeluse, the temptress who inhabits the magic garden, whom Gawan loves and Parzival rejects. Gurnemanz derives from Wolfram's Trevrizent of Book 9, who recounts the mysteries of the Grail to Parzival. "I have no broad scheme," wrote Wagner, "such as Wolfram could command; I must so compress it all into the three main situations of drastic substance that the profound, ramifying meaning is presented clearly and distinctly; for *thus* to work and put across material is, after all, *my* art."

Wagner made crucial modifications in the *Parsifal* narrative. To begin with, the Grail, a stone in Wolfram, takes on the twofold function of the chalice used at the Last Supper by Christ and the cup that caught Christ's blood at the crucifixion, preserved by Joseph of Arimathaea, the latter element recorded in Robert de Boron's *Joseph d'Arimathie* (c.1202). Furthermore, Wagner annexes the spear that the soldier Longinus used to pierce the side of Christ. In Wolfram, Anfortas [sic] is cured when Parzival asks in Book 16 "Uncle, what is it that troubles you?" In Wagner, the application of the sacred lance restores Anfortas. In Wolfram, Anfortas suffers for a liaison; in Wagner, for violating the vow of chivalric celibacy.

Of particular significance is the fact that in Wolfram both men and women are servants of the Grail at Munsalvaesche; in Wagner, only males may serve. Finally, in Wolfram, Parzival actually has a wife, Condwiramurs, and two sons, Kardeiz and Loherangrin. Two conclusions may be drawn: in Wagner there is an importation of Christian mythology (chalice, lance) accompanied by a virtual erasure of the feminine. The knights are bound by celibacy; Parsifal has no wife or offspring; and no women exist at the conclusion of the opera with the death of Kundry at Montsalvat, despite the fact that Lohengrin in Wagner's own opera had declared himself the son of Parzival.

In fact, Wagner has appropriated and Christianized chivalric coding to serve a new ideology—that of an all-male, hyper-masculine, male-parthenogenic *Verbindung*, symbolized by the male chastity that does not appear in the medieval *Parzival* epic. It is to serve the ideology of this league that Wagner has coopted the myths of Christianity, Buddhism, Schopenhauerian philosophy, primitive ritualism and aestheticism. The chivalry of *Parsifal* sustains an Aryan idea, yes, but in Léon Poliakov's *The Aryan Myth*, "The true Aryan appeared to be a Westerner of the male sex . . . who could be defined equally by reference to colored men, proletarians or women."

This entrenched ambivalence about women, which yields the fantasy of their total elimination in *Parsifal*, delineates a cultural moment of nineteenth-century Europe. The medieval *Parzival*, however, already incorporates elements that exhibit cultural misogyny or gynephobia:

I know a thing or two about poetry, and I am a tongs at holding my anger against a woman. This one has offered me such an offense that I cannot do other than hate her. On account of this the others hate *me*. Though their hatred troubles me, it is their womanhood that is to blame. (Book 2)

It grieves me that so many share the name of woman. (Book 3)

O, the grief one woman is causing me! (Book 6)

I have had but scanty rewards from women. (Book 6)

Women are always women. Even the strongest man they have conquered in a trice. (Book 9)

This anti-female subtext obviously influenced Wagner's thinking when creating *Parsifal*, but even earlier it had its effect on *Lohengrin*. In Wolfram, Loherangrin marries and has children by the princess of Brabant before she asks the fatal question that leads to his departure. In the opera, she asks the question before the marriage is consummated, so connection with women is repudiated as early as *Lohengrin* in 1850.

The prescription of male chastity—this symbolic repudiation of women—results from a misogynistic indictment of potential female venality. In the 1865 prose sketch for *Parsifal*, this emphasis is apparent: "But only he who preserves himself from the allurements of sensual pleasure retains the power of the Grail's blessing: only to the chaste is the blessed might of the relic revealed." The severe demand of this vow of chastity is reflected in Klingsor's self castration in order to join the Grail order:

[Klingsor] is said to have mutilated himself in order to destroy the sensual longing that he never completely succeeded in overcoming through prayer and penance. Titurel refused to allow him to join the Knights of the Grail, for the reason that renunciation and chastity, flowing from the innermost soul, do not require to be forced by mutilation.

Wagner describes the women surrounding Klingsor as "she-devils," to one of whom, Kundry as siren, Amfortas succumbs. Kundry, for laughing at the crucified Christ in one of her previous incarnations, is cursed "in a manner reminiscent of the Wandering Jew [Ahasuerus]. . . to bring to men the suffering of seduction . . . to fall victim anew to the power that drives her to be reborn as a seductive woman." In the opera she is addressed first by Klingsor as "Namenlose"—nameless woman, already en route to effacement. In both the 1865 prose sketch and in the libretto, the swan killed by Parsifal is described as seeking its mate, so from his first entrance Parsifal is destroying things that are coupled.

There can be little doubt that *Parsifal* reflects components of the Oedipus complex . The motif of castration appears twice in the opera. In Wolfram (Book 13), Clinschor does not castrate himself but is castrated for seducing the wife of a king; in Wagner this becomes an extreme act of self-emasculation. In Wolfram (Book 9), Anfortas' wound is cited as "through the testicles." In *Parsifal*, Amfortas' wound, euphemistically described as in his side, is castration for violating knightly chastity.

Castration is the penalty for sexual connection with the mother (e.g., Sophocles' *Oedipus*). Although Wagner's Amfortas is Parsifal's uncle, he is his symbolic father (his natural father being unknown to him), since Parsifal ultimately succeeds him to the kingship of the Grail order. This means that Kundry, with whom Amfortas has had sexual connection, is symbolically Parsifal's mother. Wagner makes this explicit in the 1865 scenario and in the opera.

Kundry is described in the prose sketch as evoking Parsifal's memories of the "fond embraces of his mother," telling him that "the last breath of motherly longing is the benediction of the first kiss of love." In Act II, when Kundry tells Parsifal that his mother, Herzeleide ("Heart's Sorrow"), is dead, Parsifal recalls "Truest, dearest mother!," after which Kundry delivers her kiss, declaring that "Love sends you now a mother's blessing, greets a son with love's first kiss." Parsifal's reaction is to recall Amfortas' wound and to shout "Torment!"

From this perspective, the motivation for the all-male world of the Knights of the Grail is clear. The sole absolute guarantee of avoiding the consummation of the Oedipal desire is to repudiate not only the mother's body but the female body in general. Male chastity exists to circumvent Oedipal fear. From the Schopenhauerian angle, male chastity symbolizes the negation of the Will to Life.

Wagner's 1865 sketch and the opera itself, however, indicate that Schopenhauer is a screen for the genuine motivation of this super-masculinist ideology. In Amfortas, Parsifal perceives the actualization of the Oedipal fantasy: Amfortas has slept with the symbolic mother, Kundry, and his refusal to uncover the Grail has led to the death of his father, Titurel. (To reify the Oedipal scenario, Wagner has altered Wolfram's *Parzival*, where Titurel is Amfortas' grandfather, not father.)

To deny the mother it is necessary to deny the birth trauma, to deny birth itself. At the end of *Parsifal*, no woman participates, and the order is sustained by the Grail alone, a fantasy projection of male self-generation, parthenogenesis. Parsifal's *rite de passage/Bildungsreise* is from repudiated mother to all-male league. It is the ultimate expression of male negation not of Will but of woman, in Poliakov's terms the quintessential Aryanist program.

In a diary entry for 1882, Wagner laments "racial declines through wrong marriage"; in *Parsifal* he repudiates not only Blacks and Jews but women, marriage and birth itself. The ultimate guarantor of racial purity is male self-generation. Men then will not intermingle with alien elements, which their fallible sensual nature might drive them to do, especially since women are both venal and powerful. Parsifal's baptizing of Kundry at the conclusion of the opera empowers him as woman's rescuer, redeemer, ruler, and effacer—the epitome of male dominance.

Parsifal then is the summation of nineteenth-century misogyny, an attitude enforced through chivalric and medieval contexts. Anticipating Wagner's Kundry, Keats' "La Belle Dame Sans Merci" of 1819 is one distillation of this attitude, where the knight, seduced by a femme fatale, has a vision of her previous victims and is left ruined. The medieval locus appears in Tennyson's "The Lady of Shalott" of 1842, where the woman at first conforms to male conceptions: she is performing a domestic task (weaving). She symbolizes the male idea that the woman should be within the *hortus conclusus* or "enclosed garden" in a double sense: not only is she enclosed within the walls of her castle; she is also on an island.

Furthermore, the Lady perceives the world only through a reflection in a mirror. When she turns to view the actual Lancelot, the Lady violates the male mandate, yields to sensuality and must die. She passes from being the Angel in the House to being the fallen woman. Tennyson's *Idylls of the King* (1859-86) constructs the same ideology about woman. Either she is self-sacrificing, like Elaine or Enid, or she is venal, like Ettarre, Guinevere or Vivien. Arthur is the patriarchal law-giver.

The chivalric code in *Parsifal* was reinforced during the nineteenth century by medievalizing representations of male and female roles. Keats' "La Belle Dame" was frequently painted by such artists as Arthur Hughes (1863), Walter Crane (1865), John William Waterhouse (1893) and Frank Dicksee (1902), in the last with unbound red hair, code for a prostitute. "The Lady of Shalott" was portrayed by such painters as Crane (1861), William Holman Hunt (1905) and Waterhouse, the last no fewer than three times (1888, 1894, 1915).

Valiant knights rescuing imperiled women defined the male mission in such can vases as John Everett Millais' *The Knight Errant* (1870) and Dicksee's *Chivalry* (1885). The pure *Sir Galahad* (1862) of G. F. Watts embodied male chastity, as did the solitary knight of John Pettie's *The Vigil* (1884).

The self-sacrificing woman, such as Elaine, was depicted by Sophie Anderson (1870) and Atkinson Grimshaw (1877). Of intense interest were the threatening females of Frederick Sandys' *Morgan-le-Fey* (1863), *Vivien* (1863) and *Iseult* (1862), and Edward Burne-Jones' *The Beguiling of Merlin* (1874). The pictorial record also chronicled male heroic warfare in Dicksee's *The Two Crowns* (1900), showing the return of a victorious knightly regent. The globalizing epitome of the code was the oath taken by the Boy Scouts, founded by Sir Robert Baden-Powell in 1908.

Parsifal inscribes chivalric codes to reinforce male dominance and exclusivity in an extreme form of the nineteenth-century ideologies of masculine supremacy. John Stuart Mill in *The Subjection of Women* in 1869 indicated this chivalric encoding as inimical to women:

> We have had the morality of submission, and the morality of chivalry and generosity; the time is now come for the morality of justice . . . The chivalrous ideal is the acme of the influence of women's sentiments on the moral cultivation of mankind; and if women are to remain in their subordinate situation, it were greatly to be lamented that the chivalrous standard should have passed away. But the changes in the general state of the species rendered inevitable the substitution of a totally different ideal of morality for the chivalrous

one . . . Chivalry left without legal check all forms of wrong which reigned unpunished throughout society.

Mill perceives that the chivalric code as revived in the nineteenth century was actually a mode of enforcing male empowerment. In *Parsifal*, Kundry exemplifies this encoding by being an amalgam of servant in Act I, seductress in Act II and penitent in Act III. Conceiving men as heroic rescuers, like Lohengrin or Parsifal, implicitly defines women as resourceless victims or dangerous opponents.

The *Blutbruderschaft* of the Grail knights at the conclusion of *Parsifal* is the undiluted paradigm of the male supremacist chivalric code in nineteenth-century Europe. The central symbols of chalice and spear, of blood and phallus, conjoin in a solipsistic vision of eternal self-renewing maleness. For this reason, Parsifal declares in his final utterance "Nur *eine* Waffe taugt" (*One* weapon only serves). The vaunted *Mitleid* (compassion) of *Parsifal* constitutes its self-legitimating narcissism. How fitting is this entry from Cosima Wagner's diary of April 5, 1882, three months before the premiere of *Parsifal*: "R. ended the evening's conversation about religion with the remark that *Parsifal* certainly would have to be his last work, the fellowship of the Grail knights expressed the idea of communion."

In *Parsifal*, Wagner consecrated masculinity as divinity.

The Aesthetic Movement:
Gilbert & Sullivan and *Patience*

The opera *Patience; or, Bunthorne's Bride*, with music by Arthur S. Sullivan and book by William S. Gilbert, had its premiere at the Opera Comique, London, on April 23, 1881, where it ran for 578 performances before being transferred to the new theater, the Savoy, the first theater in Britain to use electric light. There it continued its great popularity. The opera was produced by Richard D'Oyly Carte (1844-1901). His new theater, the Savoy, led to the name Savoyards, designating the performers of Gilbert and Sullivan operas.

What was the source of the wild enthusiasm which greeted *Patience* in 1881?

Richard D'Oyly Carte himself stated the following: "In satirizing the excesses of these (so-called) Aesthetes, the authors of Patience have not desired to cast ridicule on the true aesthetic spirit, but only to attack the unmanly oddities which masquerade in its likeness. In doing so, they have succeeded in producing one of the prettiest and most diverting musical pleasantries of the day." Patience is, indeed, a brilliant satire of Aestheticism. In fact, the work was subtitled "An Aesthetic Opera." The question is: What exactly *is* Aestheticism?

Aestheticism may be seen as a nineteenth-century cultural phenomenon. It was actually experienced in three different ways. First, Aestheticism was an attitude toward life. This meant that life was treated in the spirit of art, that life itself was an object of art. The result was that beautiful form and being surrounded by beautiful objects were genuine goals in a person's life. Second, Aestheticism was an attitude about art itself. It meant that an artist produced art not to express moral ideas but to depict beautiful forms and colors. Art did not exist to teach a lesson or inculcate a moral. Third, Aestheticism denoted certain qualities of actual works of art and literature. Art which was "Aesthetic" could be identified by various elements. These might include such pictorial motifs as the lily, blue and white Oriental china, peacocks, carnations, dresses inspired by Greek drapery, sunflowers, Japanese screens and prints, and bands of color, frequently pastel, placed next to one another for formal effect.

To summarize, Aestheticism was a philosophy that elevated artistic values over all others in the culture, claiming that individuals must cultivate their perceptions of the beautiful rather than devote their attention to ordinary, mundane activity. Aestheticism is an implicit critique of the materialism of the culture generated by the Industrial Revolution. To an Aesthete, the pursuit of beauty was more important than the pursuit of money or power. The Greek word, *aisthesis*, means perception, and Aestheticism emphasized the refinement of individual perception by contemplation of beauty.

The origins of the Aesthetic movement in England can be located in France, in a movement now identified as Art for Art's Sake, or *l'art pour l'art*. The idea of Art for Art's Sake is that the only concern of art is art, that morality, philosophy, and religion have nothing to do with art. The term was first used as early as 1804. The writer Victor Cousin stated in 1818 that art is not a means to an end but is an end in itself. Theophile Gautier declared in 1832 that art was divorced from anything useful, that as soon as something became useful it ceased to be beautiful. As he wrote in 1847, "*L'art pour l'art* signifies a work disengaged from all preoccupation other than with the beautiful in itself." For Gautier, art advanced no doctrines.

French ideas came into England through the early essays of Algernon Swinburne. In 1862 Swinburne wrote an essay about the writings of the French poet Charles Baudelaire, who had published *Les Fleurs du mal*, or *The Flowers of Evil*, in 1857. Swinburne believed that art was independent of any obligation other than to be beautiful, an idea he emphasized in his 1868 essay on the English artist and poet William Blake. This essay was a turning point in British culture, as it was the first statement of *l'art pour l'art* in English. In 1868, also, Swinburne reviewed some paintings, praising the art of Albert Moore and James McNeill Whistler, who were crucial artists for expressing the idea that art was concerned with beauty, not with morality.

Aestheticism derived from *l'art pour l'art* but was not identical to it. Whereas *l'art pour l'art* emphasized the beauty of a work of art independent of any observer, Aestheticism felt that the observer was crucial to the complete realization of the work of art. The observer of a beautiful object was to cultivate the refinement of his or her perceptions, growing in self-awareness as a result.

In England the key statement of the value of beautiful perception was Walter Pater's collection of essays entitled *The Renaissance*, published in 1873. Pater emphasized that individuals should live for intensity of experience, a philosophy that he called the New Cyrenaicism. It is important to note that this was not Hedonism, which includes all experience. Pater's philosophy emphasized the refined and the highest experiences, not every experience. The purpose of criticism, Pater noted, was to convey impressions and appreciations, not judgments.

By the time of the premiere of *Patience* in 1881, Aestheticism had been very influential in British culture. A number of events produced this situation, several involving figures, ideas, and institutions directly satirized in Gilbert and Sullivan's opera.

Many prominent persons in the artistic world of London contributed to the formation of Aesthetic attitudes. One of these was an American, James McNeill Whistler (1834-1903), who had left the United States for Paris in 1855. Whistler imbibed his interest in things Japanese around 1856 while living in France when a Parisian dealer found some Hokusai prints. The emphasis on form, beautiful color, and delicate line became decisive. Asian vases and prints, which were considered beautiful without reference to dogma or morality, were highly valued. In 1862 Whistler met the Pre-Raphaelite artist Dante Gabriel Rossetti, whose art exhibited traits of medievalism, mystery, and symbolic suggestiveness that strongly appealed to the Aesthetes. Both Whistler and Rossetti began to collect blue china. The cult of blue china had been given impetus in 1862 when Japanese porcelain, lacquer, and bronze from the personal collection of Rutherford Alcock, the first British Minister in Japan, was exhibited at the International Exhibition in London. Whistler and Rossetti, needing little encouragement, inaugurated the cult known as Chinamania, alluded to several times in *Patience*. The opening of a shop by Arthur Liberty in 1875 provided a prime location for the sale of Asian art.

In 1863 Whistler met Swinburne and the artists William Morris and Edward Burne-Jones. Morris was at the heart of the Arts and Crafts Movement during the nineteenth-century, emphasizing the importance of beautiful and tasteful furnishings to the mass of mankind. Burne-Jones, a disciple of Rossetti in his early paintings, became a focus of Aesthetic interest after nine of his paintings were exhibited at the Grosvenor Gallery on its opening in 1877. In *Patience*, Bunthorne refers to the Grosvenor Gallery in Act Two during his duet with Grosvenor, who is specifically named after this Gallery, which exhibited the work of Whistler, Burne-Jones, and other artists deemed Aesthetic. Whistler called his paintings by such titles as *Symphony in White No. III* and *Nocturne in Black and Gold* to emphasize that they had no other motive than the expression of beautiful color. This in itself caused a furor. In 1878 Whistler took John Ruskin, the famous "moralistic" critic, to court for libel. Although Whistler won only a farthing in damages, he had successfully challenged the idea that art existed to instruct. It was Aestheticism's greatest moment.

In the opera *Patience*, the character of Reginald Bunthorne is a satiric portrait of Whistler and of Oscar Wilde. Wilde came to London in 1879 after a dazzling career at Oxford University, where he had already indulged in the Aesthetic appreciation of blue and white china and Japanese art. Wilde and Whistler had met in 1881, and for a brief period they had lived as neighbors in Tite Street, Chelsea. Wilde derived much of his attitude about art from Whistler, who proclaimed the separation of art and morality in no uncertain terms. It was Wilde who emphasized the attraction of the lily and the sunflower, which were valued for their exquisite formal beauties.

Wilde is closely associated with *Patience* not only because he is satirized in the figure of Bunthorne but also because he was sponsored by Richard D'Oyle Carte's American representative on a lecture tour of the United States from December 1881 until December 1882. These lectures coincided with the American premiere of *Patience* in New York. Thus, Wilde popularized the opera as well as explained the movement behind it. Wilde's popularity was extraordinary. Crowds flocked to his lectures; polkas, mazurkas, and gallops were named after him. Wilde clarified Aestheticism for the American audience, telling them: "Love art for its own sake and then all things will be added to you. The secret of life is art." The popularity of *Patience* in America was greatly enhanced by having one of the objects of the satire present in the flesh.

Gilbert and Sullivan's *Patience* is a work full of satiric appraisal of Aestheticism. The inspiration for the satire partially came from the work of a famous illustrator, cartoonist, and author of the period, George du Maurier (1834-1896). Born in Paris, du Maurier studied art in that city and at Antwerp. He came to England in 1860 and briefly shared a flat with Whistler. He was elected to the staff of *Punch*, the famous British satiric weekly, where he was required to do two cartoons a week on topics of the day. Du Maurier discovered that Aestheticism was a glorious object for satire.

In 1879 du Maurier introduced an artistic family, the Cimabue Browns, to the British public. The family name itself is a joke—linking the famous painter (c. 1240-1302) from Florence with the most ordinary of British names. The Cimabue Browns aspire to an aesthetic life. In many cartoons they are accompanied by the poet, Jellaby Postlethwaite and the painter Maudle, based on Whistler, Wilde, and a bit of Swinburne. Postlethwaite appeared for the first time in 1880. The cartoons are filled with Japanese "'effects'" such as fans, screens, vases, pots, and black furniture, in fact everything associated with Chinamania. Characters are shown admiring Japanese art, contemplating lilies, and pontificating on aesthetic matters. Representing the skeptical attitude of the British public is a figure called The Colonel, who wonders at the peculiar obsessions of the Aesthetes. Another skeptic is a man known as The Squire, who doubts the sanity of the Aesthetic adherents.

Du Maurier's cartoons indicate the influence of Aesthetic taste on room decoration and dress. Women appear in dresses modelled on those worn by women in the paintings of Burne-Jones. These are unusual amalgams of classical, medieval, and Renaissance costume. The women have the elongated necks, large lips, and bushy hair of the women represented in the paintings of Dante Gabriel Rossetti. All the Aesthetes appear swooning, languid, melancholy, contemplative, or brooding. Above all, Aesthetic characters were to be "intense." Another famous *Punch* cartoonist, Linley Sambourne, caricatured Oscar Wilde as a sunflower in 1881, the same year as the premiere of *Patience*.

In *Patience*, the chief representatives of the Aesthetic Movement are the two poets, Reginald Bunthorne and Archibald Grosvenor. Bunthorne is described as a "Fleshly poet," meaning that he writes about his emotions; Grosvenor, named after the famous "Aesthetic" gallery, is a pastoral poet. The epithet "Fleshly" had been used by Robert Buchanan, a minor critic and poet, to denounce Rossetti's poetry in 1871 as being too concerned with sexuality. In their duet in Act II, Bunthorne and Grosvenor summarize most of the key traits of the Aesthetes in several key stanzas:

A most intense young man,
A most soulful-eyed young man,
An ultra-poetical, super-aesthetical, Out-of-the-way young man!

A Japanese young man,
A blue-and-white young man, Francesca di Rimini, miminy, piminy,
Je-ne-sais quoi young man!

A pallid and thin young man, A haggard and lank young man,
A greenery-yallery, Grosvenor Gallery,
Foot-in-the-grave young man!

Such lyrics as these brilliantly focus the object of the satire in *Patience*. The plot itself, involving the attraction of the women for the two Aesthetes, catches the enthusiasm with which Aestheticism was embraced in some circles during the 1870s and 1880s in England. Those more skeptical of the movement include Colonel Calverley, Major Murgatroyd, and the Duke of Dunstable, officers in the Dragoon Guards. Hoping to win the affection of the ladies, these military men adopt Aesthetic attitudes and dress in the second act. In trying to appear "angular and flat," as the officers sing in their trio, the men are imitating the much admired "Primitive" style of the early Florentine painters such as Cimabue and Fra Angelico. This style was much admired by the English painters known as the Pre-Raphaelites, who flourished during the mid-nineteenth century.

At the end of the opera, Grosvenor abandons his Aesthetic ideas and thereby gains the affection of the sensible dairymaid Patience. Patience herself is in a long line of lower-class characters who demonstrate common sense when the upper-class characters are lost in delusions and fantasies, a pattern used frequently in Roman comedy. On hearing Bunthorne's first poem, Patience states, "Well, it seems to me to be nonsense."

Much of the language in *Patience* is a satire on Aesthetic speech. In the first act, Lady Jane declares: "There is a transcendentality of delirium— an acute accentuation of supremest ecstasy." Angela declares, "Our tastes have been etherealized, our perceptions exalted." Later she refers to the transformed officers as "perceptively intense and consummately utter." Jane later states the ultimate Aesthetic attitude: "I droop despairingly; I am soulfully intense; I am limp and I cling!" All this language captures the self-consciousness of the Aesthetic Movement. Much of this mocking language comes from du Maurier's cartoon Aesthetes in *Punch*. Bunthorne advises the women to "think of faint lilies." Medieval art, blue and white china, lilies, the Grosvenor Gallery—all are satirized. Bunthorne is left alone at the end, but for consolation he still has his lily.

Patience always enjoyed considerable popularity among the Gilbert and Sullivan operas. Its satire is so focused, its object is so clear, that it has remained, along with du Maurier's cartoons, the most vivid critique of Aestheticism. Aestheticism itself passed out of existence in the early 1880s, being succeeded by the Decadent Movement of the late 1880s and the 1890s. Decadence espoused the indulgence of any experience, not only the beautiful experience emphasized by the Aesthetic Movement.

Aestheticism, considered seriously, did much for Britain and America. It encouraged people to think beyond the money, power, and greed that marked the capitalism of the Industrial Revolution. It sought to provide standards of taste for people, emphasizing the importance of the domestic environment on human character. In this respect, *Patience* is a satire of a movement that did influence other generations to maintain a sense of beauty in existence.

Nineteenth Century Gamble:
Tchaikovsky and *Pique Dame*

"Blessed are they who do not gamble and regard the roulette-wheel with loathing." This new beatitude was coined by Fyodor Dostoyevsky in 1863 after his initial gambling experiences at Wiesbaden. He wrote his brother Mikhail, "Here tens of thousands are won in jest. With four napoleons I won thirty-five in half an hour. This extraordinary luck tempted me. I risked the thirty-five and lost them all." When Dostoyevsky wrote his novel *The Gambler* in 1866, he was addicted to roulette and faro, remaining this way for five more years. Dostoyevsky was writing not only of himself but of his era, "the contemporary moment of our inner life. All the hero's vital juices, forces, impetuosity, daring have gone into roulette. He is a Gambler and not a mere gambler, its own kind of hell." His obsession ruined his honeymoon in 1871. His wife recorded that in Baden-Baden Dostoyevsky "used to return from roulette pale, exhausted, ask me for money, leave, and after a half-hour return, still more disconcerted, for money, until he had lost everything we had." Dostoyevsky even pawned his wedding ring, surviving only through friends' generosity. For considering the relationship between Alexander Pushkin's *Pique Dame* (1834) and Peter Tchaikovsky's opera (1890), Dostoyevsky's *The Gambler* is the key. Pushkin at the beginning of the century, Dostoyevsky at its middle, and Tchaikovsky at its end are the focal points in this horrific nineteenth century addiction to gambling.

Tchaikovsky's opera is the culmination of an entire tradition particularly conspicuous in Russian culture. Not only Pushkin's *Pique Dame* but also his story "The Shot" (1831), Lermontov's *A Hero of Our Time* (1840), Gogol's play *The Gamblers* (1843), and Tolstoy's *War and Peace* (1863-1869) form the background of the opera. In 1870 Tchaikovsky experienced this culture firsthand when in Wiesbaden he visited Nikolay Rubinstein, a compulsive gambler who conducted the premieres of *Romeo and Juliet* and the Second Symphony. "He was in the act of losing his last rouble at roulette . . . He is quite convinced that he'll break the bank before he leaves," recorded Tchaikovsky. In the person of Rubinstein, Pushkin's Hermann had come to life. Although the composer dedicated his Piano Trio in A-minor to Rubinstein in 1882, the opera *Pique Dame* is a more astute memorial. It is not surprising, therefore, that Tchaikovsky was greatly moved by his Hermann, about whom he noted in 1890: "He was not a pretext for music but a living man who deserved sympathy. I cried terribly when Hermann died." Tchaikovsky's intense reaction reveals the power of this cultural obsession.

The Russian writer Gavril Derzhavin (1743-1816), whose poem "If Darling Girls" is included in the final scene of the opera, wrote about the era: "In these days politics, justice, intelligence, conscience, law, and logic hold banquets, staking the golden age on cards. Gambling with the destinies of mortals, they bend the universe." The first circumstance contributing to this age of gambling was historical. Two elements generally thought conflicting produced a new philosophical attitude toward existence. First, the Enlightenment or "Age of Reason" chipped away at the idea of a universe guided by Providence. Instead, Chance or Luck became the only definite factor. Following the Enlightenment, Romanticism added to this neurosis by its cult of egoism. It is well known that compulsive gamblers are megalomaniacs whose aggressive instincts produce fantasies of omnipotence and grandeur. A key element of this egoism is noted in Pushkin's *Pique Dame* when Tomsky tells Lizaveta Ivanovna: "This Hermann is a truly romantic figure: he has the profile of a Napoleon and the soul of a Mephistopheles. I think there must be at least three crimes on his conscience." Significantly, the epigraph to the fourth chapter alludes to a man "sans religion," so in fact Pushkin's Hermann combines elements of the Enlightenment and of Romanticism. Inheriting both these traditions, Pushkin noted: "The passion for gaming is the strongest of all passions."

Several consequences crucial to Pushkin and Tchaikovsky arise from these historical elements. Gambling with cards actually entails two aspects. Cards are used not only for games as the title *Pique Dame* indicates, but also for fortune telling as the epigraph to the story ("The Queen of Spades betokens the Evil Eye—*Modern Guide to Fortune Telling*") signifies. Pushkin, it is known, had several books about chance and probability in his library from which to gather information. Card games could involve two forms: "games of bidding" like whist, which were considered respectable and relied on calculation; and "games of chance" which were dangerous and disreputable, which trusted to Luck. The essential difference between the two forms is that in games of bidding the player has sufficient information, whereas in games of chance the player has little or none. The punter or player in games of chance plays not with another person but with Chance/Fate/Destiny, and these games become models of man's struggle against the Unknown and causelessness.

In the game of faro central to Pushkin and Tchaikovsky, there are thus two opponents. The first is the punter who must make decisions without having the necessary information. The banker becomes the representative of the Unknown, that is, the state of existence, which does not supply enough information for one to decide with certainty. Frequently in Russian literature, as with Silvio in Pushkin's "The Shot," the banker/Unknown is a central figure. In Pushkin and Tchaikovsky, this structure is evident, since the Countess is the banker/Unknown, Hermann the punter/man, with the subliminal analogy of the punter/Napoleon confronting the banker/Destiny. In Pushkin, in fact, the narrator describes how after the Countess's death, Her mann "bore a remarkable likeness to Napoleon." Thus the historical circumstances of the Enlightenment, Romanticism, and Napoleon converge in Pushkin's tale.

The pervasive belief in Chance during the period influenced many social attitudes. For example, the widely-dispensed favoritism of the aristocratic circles became a factor of Chance, superseding effort: one could "rise" with luck. Pushkin's age through favoritism made Chance an element of the social fabric, ignoring law and merit. Moreover, like advancement in a career, obtaining money became associated with Chance. Thus, deceivers became representative of the consciousness of the era in figures like Chichikov in Gogol's *Dead Souls* (1842) or Ikharev in *Gamblers*, while those who tested Destiny, like Pechorin in Lermontov's *A Hero of Our Time*, embodied fatalism. This risking was so pervasive that in one famous instance in 1802 Prince Alexander Golitsyn staked his wife in a game and lost: her divorce and subsequent remarriage became a scandal. Pushkin was quite justified in noting: "It is impossible for the mind to foresee Chance—the powerful, instantaneous instrument of Destiny."

In addition to these historical and philosophical components, the obsession with gambling during the nineteenth century had deep psychological causes. In his essay analysing Dostoyevsky and his "pathological passion" for gambling, Freud isolated four traits he associated with sinners or criminals like gamblers: Tomsky's remark about Hermann being a criminal from this perspective is not a jest. There are two basic urges, Freud observed; first, a boundless egoism that is characteristic of megalomania; and second, a strong destructive impulse. These persons are often also marked by an absence of love and an inability to feel love. In Gogol's *Gamblers*, for instance, a deck of cards is named after a woman, while in *Pique Dame* the Countess is not a person but a card, a live/dead thing. A fourth quality is a strong masochistic tendency and sense of guilt, which leads to sadism in social relationships. Tchaikovsky's brilliant decision in Act III when Liza is driven to suicide by Hermann perfectly elaborates this sadism.

The case of Dostoyevsky exposes further psychological consequences. Dostoyevsky's father had been murdered by peasants in 1839. When Dostoyevsky had an epileptic seizure, he experienced death, identifying with his father whom he in fact wanted dead. The epilepsy, Freud observes, has two sides in that Dostoyevsky subconsciously kills his father while simultaneously punishing himself by suffering a seizure. In this construct, Fate is the projection of the father. Dostoyevsky's compulsive gambling is a guilt manifestation in the shape of debt, a method of self-punishment. The gambler is characterized by his conscious wish to win and his unconscious wish to lose, rebelling and then punishing himself for the rebellion.

When the punter/player dares the banker/Fate/father, however, one has a visible manifestation of the Oedipus complex. In challenging Destiny, the ultimate father-surrogate, the gambler is denying the "reality principle" of maturity and those who taught it, most likely the parents. Thus in Pushkin Hermann, a man of the 1830s, challenges the Countess, representing the 1770s, in both an historical and an Oedipal way, as Napoleon challenged the ancient regime. In Tchaikovsky and Pushkin, Hermann's confrontation with the Countess, deliberately mirroring Hamlet's with his mother Gertrude, includes a strong Oedipal incest wish: he watches her toilette, comes to her bedroom, thinks of her past lovers, pleads with her as lover and mother, and is the fatal third lover to whom she discloses the secret. In Pushkin's story, in fact, an observer at the Countess's funeral marks Hermann as a "natural son" of the Countess.

This plea to the mother, however, has even stronger implications. Freud noticed that an obsession with hands links gambling to onanism. Both actions are compulsive, repetitive, pleasurable, and guilt-associated, often accompanied by resolutions not to repeat the action. These are associated with the idea of being rescued by the mother, since the boy surmises that if the mother sexually initiated him, he would be relieved of onanism. In *Pique Dame*, Hermann goes to the Countess, the surrogate mother, to be saved. The identification of Luck or Chance with a woman, as in the expression "Lady Luck" or in naming a woman after a card, has psychological validity, while the aphorism "Lucky in love, unlucky in cards" is profound, since gambling becomes a substitute for sexual activity. Thus, when Hermann in Tchaikovsky's Act III meets Liza, he flees to the gambling tables in a daze, asking her "Who are you? I don't know you!" His compulsive gambling masks the severest psychological neurosis.

Several texts in Russian literature, coming after Pushkin's story but preceding Tchaikovsky's opera, present variations of these historical and psychological factors that concern *Pique Dame*. Gogol's drama *Gamblers* develops the idea of the cheater cheated when the card-sharp Ikharev, coming to a provincial town to swindle the inhabitants, ends up deceived by even more clever rogues. Gogol's world is a universe populated by gamblers and ruled by Chance: people play for six nights straight, winning thousands in minutes. The gamblers represent the myriad defenses of such people: Shvokhnev declares that not gambling is like not fighting, valuing nothing but risk; Glov warns young men against the addiction; Uteshitelny asserts he has quit for good. In these men Gogol parodies the moralists, since all of them are compulsive gamblers. Gambling is an Oedipal challenging of the Fate/father: "Play is impartial; it is no respecter of persons. Let my own father sit down at a game with me—I'd skin him the same as any stranger. Who tells him to play? At the card table all are equal." The idea of gambling as a metaphor for existence is explicit in Gogol: "Of course you either win or lose. What of it? That is the beauty of it—the risk, man, the excitement, the uncertainty." So destitute is the world of *Gamblers* that Ikharev states: "Well, suppose it is faking? What of it? Can you live without it? It's necessary—in a sense a precaution." When he is ruined by the gang, he raves, "Such bastards! To think that the world is full of them! First thing you know, some scoundrel is there, cleverer than you, gets the best of you! Rotten world, that's all! Just rotten! All swindlers. Only fools have luck." He throws the deck of cards, named after a woman, on the floor, a bizarre form of symbolic matricide that is the key to Hermann's killing of the Countess in Pushkin and Tchaikovsky.

Lermontov's *A Hero of Our Time* is important to Tchaikovsky since at one time he and Chekhov discussed an opera based on "Bela," one of the tales in the novel. In Lermontov the central character Pechorin recounts in the final episode "The Fatalist" a harrowing testing of predestination. In a gambling room Pechorin encounters Lieutenant Vulich, a legendary player. When Vulich challenges someone to bet, Pechorin wagers a stack of gold coins that there is no predestination. At random Vulich selects a pistol and has Pechorin throw a card into the air. On its descent, he fires the gun at his own head. The pistol snaps, making everyone think it was not loaded. Testing it again, Vulich finds it was loaded and only misfired. After Pechorin tells Vulich he will die anyway, Vulich is killed by a mad Cossack later that night. Deciding to test fate himself, Pechorin risks his life to disarm the Cossack. When he survives, Pechorin muses: "How can one escape becoming a fatalist? How can a man know for certain whether or not he is really convinced of anything? And how often we mistake for conviction the deceit of our senses or an error of reasoning. I like to have doubts, about everything." The connection to gambling is clear, since Vulich compares such challenging to faro. By pursuing this idea of faro as existence to its limit, Lermontov underlies Tchaikovsky's treatment of Pushkin's tale.

Following Gogol's *Gamblers* and Lermontov's "The Fatalist," Dostoyevsky and Tolstoy used gambling for intricate symbolic purposes. In *War and Peace* Tolstoy writes a gambling episode which is metaphoric of his debate concerning causality and free will in a deterministic universe. Young Nicholas Rostov plays with the rakish Dolokhov, who has a propensity when bored "to escape by some strange and usually cruel action," symptomatic of this neurosis. Despite the fact that Dolokhov tells Rostov "only a fool trusts to luck, one should make certain," Rostov to save face wagers. During the game Rostov notices repeatedly Dolokhov's "short reddish fingers and hairy wrists, which held him in their power." This Freudian recognition of onanism and Oedipal father-domination is reinforced when Dolokhov repeats the proverb "Lucky in Love, unlucky in cards." When he loses heavily, Rostov is forced to abase himself masochistically in front of his actual father. This episode in the novel, however, is only a microcosm of Tolstoy's intense skepticism about the existence of causality. Dolokhov is the infernal Unknown/banker cruelly destroying man.

Dostoyevsky's masterful *Gambler* is a treatise on the subject. Its hero Alexis Ivanovich thinks, "It appeared to me that pure calculation means fairly little" when he notices that those who calculate lose as much as those who risk. His obsession begins consciously: "I ought to have left at that point, but a strange sort of feeling came over me, a kind of desire to challenge fate." The woman he loves, the enigmatic Paulina, tells him, "You let yourself be driven to absolute frenzy and fatalism," and his masochism is so great that he is "ready to gnaw my hands off" when he thinks of her. Desperate to win money, he plays "as if it was a dream . . . almost mechanically, without thinking." He knows he "has simply destroyed himself," exhibiting the compulsive gambler's unconscious desire to lose.

In textbook precision, he loses the Paulina whom he loves, wasting his fortune on a prostitute. Still, he thinks: "The point here is this—one turn of the wheel and everything can be different." Caught in a neurosis that Dostoyevsky himself had experienced, Alexis Ivanovich cannot change. By focusing on roulette rather than on faro as in Pushkin, Dostoyevsky removes every shred of the possibility for calculation, hurling it all to Chance. While operas like Verdi's *La Traviata* and Massenet's *Manon* reveal this nineteenth century obsession, it is Prokofiev's The *Gambler* (1929) from Dostoyevsky and Tchaikovsky's *Pique Dame* from Pushkin that remain the major operatic studies of this pathology.

In creating *Pique Dame*, Tchaikovsky inherited a tradition that included such luminaries as Dostoyevsky, Lermontov, Gogol, Tolstoy, and of course Pushkin. Pushkin's novella had already been given dramatic treatment. Alexander Shakhovsky in 1836 wrote his play *Chrysomania, or The Passion for Money*, while Halevy in 1850 did an opera with a text by Scribe. In 1888 Modest Tchaikovsky, himself a minor dramatist, began work on the libretto for Nikolay Klenovsky, a pupil of Tchaikovsky's. When that plan failed in 1889, Tchaikovsky decided to undertake the opera himself. In Florence the work proceeded rapidly: by March 15 the sketch was completed, with the piano score finished by April 5 and the orchestration by June 5, 1890. The score of *Pique Dame* reflects a paradox apparent in Tchaikovsky's correspondence about the opera. On February 19 he wrote A. P. Merkling that "Today I wrote the scene in which Hermann goes to the old Queen of Spades. It was so gruesome that I am still under its horrible spell." Five days later he said, "If, God willing, I finish the opera, it will be something *chic*." The completed work is at once tragic in its final act, rococo in its second act recreation of the eighteenth century. Regarding the work as "a masterpiece," Tchaikovsky confessed on March 31 that the composition had been a delight, despite his having been "in a dreadful state of mind." He remarked, "I was never before so deeply moved by the sorrows of my hero." For this reason Tchaikovsky contributed a number of pieces to the text, including Prince Eletsky's aria in Act II and Liza's famous aria in Act III.

He and Modest, however, did not follow Pushkin precisely. First of all, perhaps to gain the chic as well as the tragic, they removed the action to the late eighteenth century instead of using Pushkin's 1830s. As a result Tchaikovsky introduces the Pastorale "The Faithful Shepherdess" in Act II (which counterpoints the Hermann/Liza relationship), has the Countess recall an aria from Grétry's *Richard Coeur-de-Lion* (1784), and uses a polonaise by Koslovsky. Texts by Gavril Derzhavin, a favorite poet during the era of Catherine the Great, inspired the final chorus of Act II and Tomsky's aria in the final act. "At times it seemed to me as though I were living in the eighteenth century, and that after Mozart there was nothing," Tchaikovsky wrote in his diary.

Perhaps the most important change Tchaikovsky made from Pushkin is in the fates of his protagonists. In Pushkin Lizaveta disappears from the story after the Countess's death; one learns in the conclusion that she married a civil servant. Tchaikovsky, however, felt that "Liza's part cannot be finished in the fourth scene," so in Act III he supplied the embankment episode which concludes with Liza's suicide. If there is a false element in Tchaikovsky's adaptation, it is his emphasis on a love compulsive gamblers cannot experience; still, when Hermann parts from Liza he is so obsessed that in clinically accurate fashion he does not even know her. At the conclusion of Pushkin's *Pique Dame*, "Hermann went out of his mind. He is now in room number 17 of the Obuhov Hospital where he insanely repeats, 'Three, seven ace! Three, seven Queen!'" In the opera, however, Hermann stabs himself when the fatal Queen of Spades turns up instead of the crucial ace. The result of these alterations is a heightening of sharply contrasted moods, the elegantly rococo and the violently tragic, which underscores the psychological conflict between the "pleasure principle" and the "reality principle" that is basic to the gambling neurosis.

The greatness of *Pique Dame* is in fact this paradoxical juxtaposition, which perfectly accords with the nature of Hermann himself. Being both German and Russian, Hermann combines the two alternative strategies of gambling, calculation and chance. As a German and a member of the corps of engineers, he is presumably rational: thus, in Pushkin, after Hermann hears the story of the Countess from Tomsky, he scoffs, "A fairy tale!" Yet by the end of the second chapter he is at the Countess's house "as though some supernatural force drew him there." In one poem Pushkin wrote, "Imagination deals its varied faro," and it is this Russian superstitious, fiery imagination that is the other part of Hermann's character. In the psychological combat between calculation and chance, it is Lady Luck who leads Hermann to symbolic matricide and finally death. Before playing his last card, Hermann wonders "What is our life?" He concludes, "A game! Good and evil are dreams! Work, honesty, old wives' tales! Give up the battle, seize the moment of good fortune. Let the unlucky man weep, cursing his fate!" This despairing moral relativism suggests the nihilism of Turgenev's Bazarov in *Father and Sons* (1861) or Flaubert's Moreau in *The Sentimental Education* (1869).

This nihilism was very much Tchaikovsky's own. During the composition of *Pique Dame* he wrote Glazounov: "I am passing through a very enigmatic stage on my road to the grave. Sometimes I feel an insane anguish, but not that kind of anguish which is the herald of a new tide of love for life; rather, something hopeless, final." In basing his last great opera on the gambling neurosis, Tchaikovsky is the culmination of a crucial factor of nineteenth century culture: Existence = Faro.

Perspectives:
Alfano and *Risurrezione*

Franco Alfano's *Risurrezione*, with a libretto by Cesare Hanau, had its premiere on November 30, 1904, at the Teatro Vittorio Emanuele in Turin. *Risurrezione* was the third opera by Alfano (1876-1954), having been preceded by *Miranda* (1896) and *La fonte di Enschir* (1898), with a ilbretto by Illico. Although he created two ballets, *Napoli* (1900) and *Lorenza* (1901) between his second and third operas, *Risurrezione* was Alfano's first great success. Later operas included *L'ombra di Don Giovanni* (1914), *Le leggenda di Sacùntala* (1921), *Madonna lmperia* (1927), *Cyrano de Bergerac* (1937), and *Il Dottor Antonio* (1949). In addition, Alfano is remembered for completing Puccini's *Turandot* in 1924. His stature in the world of Italian opera of the early twentieth century was considerable, including managerial positions at the Bologna Liceo Musicale (1919-1926), the Turin Liceo Musicale (1926-1937), and the Rossini Conservatory in Pesaro in 1937, after the completion of *Cyrano de Bergerac*.

Risurrezione, however, established Alfano's reputation and secures it today. While Alfano is thought of as a verismo composer, in fact his work was directly concerned with escaping the influence of veristic composers like Mascagni and the early Puccini. Along with Respighi, Zandonai, and Pizzetti, Alfano derived his musical idiom not only from Italian sources but also from Wagner and Strauss. In this respect, be reverts to an earlier generation of Italian composer, that of Arrigo Boito (1842-1918) and

Alfredo Catalani (1854-1893) and the *scapigliatura* era, in welding Italian to Germanic elements, apparent in *Mefistofele* (1868), *Lorelei* (1890), and *La Wally* (1892). Alfano studied for a long time in Germany, especially under Jadassohn at Leipzig, a decisive formative experience. Alfano, then, is not so much a part of the Italian veristic Pentarch (Mascagni, Leoncavallo, Puccini, Cilea, and Giordano) as he is of a stage of development which considered verismo in light of Weber, Wagner, and Strauss, a group including, in addition to Alfano, Zandonai, Pizzetti, and Respighi, particularly Ferrucio Busoni (*Doktor Faust*, 1925) and Ermanno Wolf-Ferrari (*I Quattro Rusteghi*, 1906), both of whom were Italian/Germanic in origin. *Risurrezione* is far different from its popular misconception.

Risurrezione is also unique in the manner of its origin. Its source, Leo Tolstoy's *Resurrection*, had appeared in 1899, only five years before the opera itself, an exceptionally swift transition from the literary to the operatic world! Alfano's interest in the work was generated by the extraordinary reaction *Resurrection* caused, not the least of which was Tolstoy's sensational excommunication from the Russian Orthodox Church in 1901 (by a national proclamation affixed to the door of every church in Russia). This excommunication, a direct result of anti-clerical elements in *Resurrection*, influenced hundreds of people to read the novel. Alfano's attraction to the work, and indeed the success of *Risurrezione* itself, was enhanced by the notoriety of its source.

The novel Alfano used for creating *Risurrezione* had its origin in a story Tolstoy heard from a lawyer who visited him in June, 1887. The lawyer had been asked to deliver a letter from a young aristocrat to a convict, Rosalie Oni. As it turned out, while serving as a juror at the trial of Rosalie Oni for theft, the young man had recognized her as a young house servant he had seduced when she was sixteen. When she became pregnant, Rosalie was driven out of the estate and became a prostitute. The young aristocrat offered to marry her, but Rosalie Oni died of typhus in prison. This woman became the model for Alfano's and Tolstoy's Katerina Mikhailovna, called Katiusha, and the young man the model for Dimitri Nekludoff.

Tolstoy was overwhelmed by the account of this unhappy woman. In fact, in his own youth he had seduced a young servant, Gasba, and he even had a bastard child by a peasant woman. In December, 1889, he began the novel, but set it aside until 1895, when he completed a rough draft. During the summer and autumn of 1898, Tolstoy finished the work. It appeared, to sensational notice, on March 13, 1899, serialized in a journal. An incident in 1895 in Russia, involving the Tsarist persecution of a dissenting religious sect, the Dukhobors, caused Tolstoy to resume *Resurrection*. These Dukhobors or "Spirit-fighters" believed in chastity, abstinence from alcohol, vegetarianism, and communal ownership of property. A violent raid against them occured in 1895, arousing Tolstoy to write *The Persecution of Christians in Russia*. Tolstoy gave the 80,000 rubles he earned from *Resurrection* to a fund permitting the Dukhobors to emigrate to Canada, where their descendants still live. This intolerance, and the excommunication, made *Resurrection* a *cause célèbre*.

In his opera *Risurrezione*, Alfano preserves the core of Tolstoy's novel, presenting the plight of victimized servants and tyrannous masters; the dehumanization of prisons and bureaucracy; and the futility of political and religious institutions to help ordinary people. Having passed through a religious crisis in the 1880s, Tolstoy came to believe in the power of the solitary human spirit to be reborn despite its past, to "rise" above its degradation to a new life, hence the title "Resurrection" in both Tolstoy and Alfano. Both Katiusha and Dimitri undergo this spiritual regeneration, a "resurrection" not dependent on the Christian Resurrection so much as on their capacity to be reborn, to "resurrect" themselves in the Tolstoyan sense.

Tolstoy's novel was a great shift from his previous work, especially from *Anna Karenina*, which had dealt with sexual behavior among the aristocracy. *Resurrection*, in contrast, emphasizes the brutality of the aristocracy to the lower classes, a prophecy surely of the Bolshevik Revolution of 1917. The law which sentences Katiusha to prison in Act III of *Risurrezione* was scathingly criticized by Tolstoy, who believed that "All law courts are not only useless but criminal." Who, argued Tolstoy, can judge another person? From the novel, one learns that the prosecutor in Katiusha's case sought convictions regardless of innocence or guilt to advance his own career. The presiding judge, a known adulterer, doesn't even listen to the arguments; he even neglects to give complete instructions to the jury, which results in Katiusha's conviction.

Risurrezione follows Tolstoy's novel carefully. Instead of beginning with the trial, as does Tolstoy, Alfano, to great dramatic effect, uses the seduction on Easter Eve for Act I. From the novel, one learns that Katiusha is about 18, Dimitri about 27. The name Katiusha is particularly significant, since as a nickname for Katerina it is not so harsh as Katka nor so endearing as Katenka—a stark indication of Katiusha's exact status in the Nekludoff household. From the novel, one learns that Katiusha read ("Ole leggere amavi") Turgenev and Dostoyevsky. She is, then, capable of understanding the desperation and the brutality which affect her. Act II of *Risurrezione*, like Act I, follows carefully Part I of Tolstoy's novel.

Between Acts II and III about seven or eight years pass, during which Katiusha has become a prostitute, a fairly successful one ("Io vivea nel lusso!"). Act III shows particularly the cynicism Tolstoy felt about the aristocratic arrogance of the nobility, and Alfano preserves much of this: the lustful judge ("E il Presidente"), the futility of religion ("Ed ora parla di Dio!"), the despair at existence ("Ah, perchè non sono morta?"). Alfano uses the episode of the photograph from Part II, chapter 13 of Tolstoy's novel for the strong climax of Act III. Act IV, preceded by a remarkable Prelude, occurring on Easter as had Act I, introduces the important character of Simonson from Part III of *Resurrection*. Simonson expresses the Tolstoyan doctrine of universal brotherhood ("Li sentite, Katiusha? /Viver per consolare ogni dolore umano"). His moving petition to Dimitri about his love for Katiusha ("Non credite almeno che sia un volgare capriccio") derives from the powerful confrontation in the novel between the aristocrat Dimitri and the noble peasant. Tolstoy's novel clarifies the strange situation in the final duet ("Ah, Dimitri!") when Katiusha, though admitting she still loves Dimitri, leaves for Siberia with Simonson—her once passionate love for Dimitri has been altered by her spiritual love for Simonson, the agent of her "resurrection." Thus, even though he loses her, Dimitri can say she is "redeemed" ("Si, tu sei salva, tu sei redenta!") and Katiusha can respond: ("Si, risorta son io!" "I am risen.")

The appeal of the role of Katiusha is unquestionable. Mary Garden first heard *Risurrezione* in Nice and determined to do it in Chicago, which she did. Later, she cajoled the Opéra-Comique to stage it in Paris. She agreed to do twelve performances of *Pélleas et Mélisande* if they would give her *Risurrezione*. Alfano himself came from Turin to hear it in Paris. Of *Risurrezione*, Mary Garden wrote: "Each act was different, each about a different woman, really, yet about the different woman that is potentially in all women, and to each act I gave a different voice. What a role, Katiusha!" No one has disputed that opinion.

Nearly three-quarters of a century after its premiere, *Risurrezione* stands as one of the finest results of Italian opera "crossing the Alps." Its chromaticism, its welding of Germanic to Italian elements, remains striking. Its subject matter, with its remarkable focus on the lower classes, anticipates the Russian Revolution and the dramas of Gorki and Chekhov. To paraphrase Mary Garden, "What an opera, *Risurrezione!*"

La Maledizione:
Verdi and *Rigoletto*

Rigoletto or *La Maledizione*? Verdi's first choice for a title was the latter. After the premiere of his opera at the Teatro La Fenice, Venice, on March 11, 1851, the Gazzetta di Venezia recorded a triumph: "An opera like this cannot be judged after one evening. Yesterday, we were, so to say, overwhelmed by the novelty of it all . . . We could not take it all in at one hearing . . . Never was sound so eloquent." A year earlier, Verdi had been contracted to compose an opera for this theater. He had noted as early as September 1849 his interest in the source, a powerful romantic drama: "Suggest Victor Hugo's *Le Roi s'Amuse*. A wonderful play, with tremendous dramatic situations and two magnificent roles in it." Verdi composed and orchestrated in forty days the opera that became *Rigoletto*, finishing it on February 5.

The transition from *Le Roi* was a veritable hell. Verdi wrote librettist Francesco Maria Piave (who had supplied the texts of *Ernani* and *Macbeth*), on April 28, 1850:

> I have another subject which, if the police would allow it, would be one of the greatest works of art in the modern theater. Who knows! . . . Try it! The subject is great, immense, and it contains a character who is one of the greatest creations to be found in the theater of all countries and all times. The subject is *Le Roi s'Amuse*, and the character I speak of is Triboulet [Rigoletto].

By May 8 his enthusiasm became a command:

> Oh, *Le Roi s'Amuse* is the greatest subject and perhaps the greatest drama of modern times. Triboulet is a character worthy of Shakespeare! . . . Now, as I was reflecting on various subjects, *Le Roi* came back to my mind like a thunderbolt, an inspiration, and I said, "Yes, by God . . . that one can't go wrong." So then, get the president of the theater interested, turn Venice upside down and force the censorship to allow this subject.

Would that it had been so simple. When the libretto, first entitled *La Maledizione* (The Curse), was submitted to the censor in Venice (then under Austrian domination), its title proved too subversive. The governor banned the work, denouncing composer and librettist for "not having chosen a more worthy field for their talents than a plot so revoltingly immoral and so obscenely trivial." Verdi's reaction: "The letter that arrived with the decree completely banning *La Maledizione* was so unexpected that I almost went out of my mind!," he wrote the president of La Fenice.

Piave rewrote the libretto, changing the title to *Il Duca di Vendome* to appease the Austrians, who disliked the anti-royalist presentation of King Francis I of France (1515-47) as a debauched libertine, particularly after the democratizing revolutionary period of 1848. Making the libertine a duke, however, did not satisfy Verdi, who again addressed the president of La Fenice on December 14:

> I have had very little time to examine the new libretto. I have seen enough, however, to know that in its present form it lacks both character and significance, and finally, its most dramatic moments now leave one completely cold . . . All the rage of the courtiers against Triboulet doesn't make sense. The old man's curse, so terrible and sublime in the original, is made ridiculous here, because the motive which drives him to utter the curse no longer has the same importance, and because it is no longer a subject who speaks so daringly to his king. Without this curse what point, what meaning is left to the drama? The Duke has no character: the Duke absolutely must be a libertine. Otherwise there is no reason for Triboulet's fear that his daughter might leave her hiding place, and the whole drama is impossible.

This letter is renowned for its general relevance to Verdi's theory that dramatic motivation is the foundation of his music. The censors objected to a hunchback as protagonist, but Verdi responded, "A singing hunchback? Why not? . . . Will it be effective? I don't know." Then he added:

But if I don't know, then neither, I repeat, does the person who proposed the change. That is just what seemed so wonderful to me: to portray this ridiculous, terribly deformed creature, who is inwardly filled with passion and love. It was precisely because of all the original traits that I chose the subject, and if they are cut out I shall no longer be able to compose the music . . . I declare quite plainly that my music, whether beautiful or ugly, is never written at random, and that I always try to give it character . . . My artistic conscience will not permit me to put this libretto to music.

In the end, a compromise was effected. Hugo's Francis I became the Duke of Mantua, Blanche became Gilda, Triboulet became Rigoletto, Saltabadil (the assassin) became Sparafucile, and his sister Maguelonne became the lure Maddalena. These changes, however, did not transform the opera to nearly so great an extent as did the shift in title from *La Maledizione* to *Rigoletto* (from the French rigoler, "to have fun"; a parody of Hugo's drama had appeared in 1838, entitled *Rigoletti, ou Le Dernier des Fous*). Verdi's letter indicates that the curse, not Rigoletto or Gilda, is ultimately the opera's desideratum. In Hugo the jester falls over his daughter's body exclaiming, "I have killed my child!" In Verdi he cries out, "La maledizione!"

With his explosive drama *Hernani* of 1830, Hugo already had supplied Verdi with one of his earliest successes, *Ernani* in 1844, premiered at La Fenice. As architect of French romanticism, Hugo had issued its manifesto in the famous preface to his *Cromwell* of 1827, in which he repudiated the classical unities of time and place and the strict demarcation of tragedy and comedy, noting that Shakespeare cared for none of this. (A performance of *Romeo and Juliet* in Paris in 1824 led Hugo to this realization.) While *Hernani* often is cited as the quintessential illustration of his theories, *Le Roi s'Amuse* (The King's Diversion) is the true gloss of the romantic manifesto, especially of these lines:

The modern muse . . . will realize that everything in creation is not humanly beautiful, that the ugly exists beside the beautiful, the unshapely beside the graceful, the grotesque on the reverse of the sublime, evil with good, darkness with light . . . Poetic art . . . will set about doing as nature does, mingling in its creations—but without confounding them—darkness and light, grotesque and sublime; in other words the body and the soul, the beast and the intellect. It is of the fruitful union of the grotesque and the sublime types that modern genius is born . . . Antiquity could not have produced *Beauty and the Beast*.

The deformed Triboulet is the Beast, Blanche the Beauty—the grotesque with the sublime. *Le Roi s'Amuse* cuts to the heart of Hugo's romanticism in its linkage of contraries. While they are contraries, they share a horrifying similarity: both are the king's "diversion," the Beast being the bitter jester, Beauty the susceptible daughter. But if Triboulet and Blanche are diversions, what do they divert the King/Duke *from*?

Starkly and simply, from the curse—the only one that matters, existence itself. The key to this idea is a letter Verdi wrote in April 1853: "I prefer Shakespeare to all other dramatists, including the Greeks. As far as dramatic effectiveness is concerned, it seems to me that the best material I have yet put to music . . . is *Rigoletto*. It has the most powerful dramatic situations, it has variety, vitality, pathos; all the dramatic developments result from the frivolous, licentious character of the Duke." The title *Rigoletto* has obscured Verdi's intentions: it is not Rigoletto or Gilda but the Duke who is the focal character of the opera.

Verdi makes this indisputable by its construction. At the beginning of each act, the Duke has an aria signifying his catalytic function in all that follows. It becomes clear that the renaming of the opera is only an accident of Austria's domination of Venice in 1850. What then is the connection between the curse and the Duke? What is it that the Duke *knows*?

In his first-act ballata "Questa o quella" (not derived from Hugo), Piave and Verdi have distilled this libertine's nature. One woman is the same for him as another; fidelity is detestable.

In one stroke, the Duke repudiates centuries of *l'amour courtois*. By any conventional moral code, the Duke is *im*moral, but he despises all codes, for there is no love without absolute freedom. He is not immoral from his perspective, since in the world as he grasps it there is no morality. Instead, he is that truly shocking figure, the *a*moral anarchist, recognizing no code, acknowledging no responsibility. His second aria, at the beginning of Act II, often is construed as humanizing the Duke by showing his regret at Gilda's abduction. This is untenable. "Parmi veder le lagrime" is not a reversion from "Questa o quella" but an insidious exemplum of it. The Duke's regret is not for Gilda's plight but only for the momentary non-gratification of his wishes, instantly signaled when he goes to his bedchamber and seduces the imprisoned Gilda.

At the commencement of Act III, the Duke warbles the canzone "La donna e mobile," based on Hugo's Act IV, Scene 2. But note the words: he declares that a woman is always "lying," and that any man who believes her perforce is wretched. He denies responsibility, blaming women for his debaucheries. From the Duke's perspective, there is no victim, since in an amoral universe there can be no such thing. Verdi illustrates the Duke's position that the world is amoral by several *coups de théâtre* in the final moments of the opera: first, "La donna è mobile" recurs just as Rigoletto is gloating about his "victory" over the Duke; second, Gilda confesses, as if to drive home the point, "I deceived you . . . I was guilty"; third, the curse motif resurges as Rigoletto, the jester jested, howls "Ah! la maledizione!" The world is an amoral (not immoral) realm: there are no moral codes.

Without meaning, there can be no evil. As if any proof were necessary, the Duke survives scot-free, passing on to other prey. He alone has the awareness Verdi and Hugo saw in this tale: the curse is existential meaninglessness, and the only possible response is diversion, the only "freedom" one can have. Under sentence of death (for some a priori, unknown failing), mankind is condemned to life. The Duke is determined, in such a situation, to get it all.

A striking confirmation of this condition is presented in the opera and the play, for this world is pervaded by so much untruth and disguise as to make any "meaning" absurd. When Gilda first meets Rigoletto in Scene 2, the audience gets a shock: they are father and daughter, but she does not know his name! In an echoing of this episode, Gilda then asks the Duke, disguised as a poor student, *his* name—again a lie, "Gualtier Maldè." Since she does not know the true identity of either father or lover, Gilda's aria "Caro nome" is sabotaged. Commentators regard "La donna è mobile" and

"Questa o quella" as fatuous, but it is "Caro nome" that merits the term. The Duke's arias, on the contrary, are chillingly incisive. Just as he is a student in Act I, in Act III the Duke is a cavalry officer. What's in a name? Profoundly—nothing.

What are the true natures of Rigoletto and Gilda? Rigoletto is, in brief, despicable. In the first scene, he has no compunction about telling the Duke, who lusts after Countess Ceprano, to get rid of her husband by any means—exile, imprisonment, beheading. Even the callous Duke observes, "You always force the jest to extremes." Rigoletto then jeers at Count Monterone, whose curse is the first shard to penetrate his consciousness. Note: *not* his conscience. Verdi makes this clear at the beginning of the second scene when Rigoletto encounters Sparafucile, whose instinct for slaying matches Rigoletto's own, as he realizes: "We are equals! I with my tongue, he with a dagger." The recitative "Pari siamo!" shows Rigoletto at his most corrupt—he blames all his trials on the courtiers, believing, "If I'm wicked, it's only because of you." Although Rigoletto imagines himself a moral person, this kind of evasion is the height of hypocritical immorality.

If Rigoletto did not encourage vice and mock its victims, such as Monterone, he would not have to keep his daughter locked away. At the end of Act I, when Rigoletto, disguised and blindfolded, has assisted in the purported abduction of Ceprano's wife, his corruption is confirmed. Mistaken identities and disguises become the agents and symbols of the curse of meaninglessness. The Duke locks Gilda in his bedroom and violates her, but this incarceration replicates the captivity that Rigoletto already has initiated.

Toward the disturbing conclusion of Act II, Monterone, reappearing briefly, addresses the Duke's portrait: "Since you were cursed by me in vain and no thunderbolt or sword struck your breast, you will live happily still, Duke." Rigoletto swears to avenge himself and Monterone, but in the end, Monterone's doomed words are the true ones, confirming not the moral world the human race wishes it were but the amoral world the Duke knows *is*.

In the final act, the question of identity recurs when Sparafucile asks his victim's name. Rigoletto would like to believe "He is Crime, I am

Punishment"—but the Duke does not acknowledge crime, and Rigoletto never exacts punishment. The disguises are not finished: Gilda, dressed as a man, commits suicide by offering her body to Sparafucile's knife. Finally, an identity is queried when Rigoletto, hearing the Duke's song, wonders, "Who can be here in his stead?" When he discovers it is Gilda, the opera's point is made: identity, that is meaning, is death. Only diversion, that is meaninglessness, is life. Thus the last word and the last music in *Rigoletto* is the curse. We never know the fate of the Duke, for to know it would identify him. Verdi was fiercely correct in recognizing him as the core of his idea.

This idea, however, conceals a last tormented nexus in *Rigoletto* and *Le Roi s'Amuse*. While Piave remained fairly faithful to Hugo's text in condensing it, he eliminated the most explosive scenes, those in Hugo's Act III. The king, asking who is locked in his room, hears from a courtier that it is "the mistress of Triboulet." The king replies, "Indeed! God! To rob his mistress from my fool!" The courtier responds "His mistress, or his wife!," and the king rejoins, "A wife, a daughter!" There follows another scene in which the king attempts to conciliate Blanche before violating her. He tells her, "Someday we must age, and life, this condition,during which a few moments of love shine, is only a rag without such spangles." Beneath this lurks the final subtext of *Rigoletto*.

So meaningless is life, declares the king, that seduction, his greatest diversion, pays no regard to its object—wife, daughter, mistress. But it is this very melange of wife/daughter/mistress that links king and jester in a powerful erotic scenario. The mating of woman with hunchback is specifically referred to in Hugo's drama when, in Act I, Triboulet mocks Saint Vallier (Monterone) for having married his daughter Diane de Poitiers to "an ill-favored hunchbacked seneschal . . . As hideous as the vilest dwarf e'er known . . . A shape like that! An ugly hump like mine!" Triboulet seems to realize the parallel of this incident with the situation of him and his daughter.

In Verdi, both ruler and jester imprison the girl, focusing on her as an erotic object—the Duke to possess her, Rigoletto to protect her virginity. But by imprisoning his daughter, Rigoletto symbolically possesses her as much as does the Duke. Note the absence of the mother, who might otherwise prevent the daughter's seduction by the father. Ruler and jester are each other's alter egos. In the end, Rigoletto does not avenge his daughter's seduction—a psychodynamic evasion that validates the incest paradigm.

Such is the universe of *Rigoletto*, one of disguise, deception, indeterminacy, nonidentity but not nonexistence. Verdi's recognition of this amoral condition is the brief motif of the curse, the D-flat-minor chords of which strafe the opera at its conclusion. As it was at its origin, *Rigoletto* is really *La Maledizione*.

Deathless Love:
Gounod and *Roméo et Juliette*

I read over this duet, I read it again, I listen to it with all my attention; I try to find it bad; I'm afraid of finding it good and being mistaken! And yet it fired me! It still does! It was born of sincerity. In short, *I believe in it*. Voice, orchestra, everything plays its part; the violins turn passionate; it's all there: Juliet clasping her lover, Romeo's anxiety, his delirious embraces.

So declared Charles Gounod on May 2, 1865, about the duet "Nuit d'hyménée" from Act IV of his new opera, *Roméo et Juliette*. Already well known for *Faust* (1859) and *Mireille* (1864), Gounod sensed his greatest moment was coming: the premiere of *Roméo et Juliette* in April 1867 at the Théâtre Lyrique proved a sensation, the only unqualified success he enjoyed during his lifetime. Since *Roméo et Juliette* was performed the same year as the Exposition Universelle, Paris was thronged with foreigners, who carried word back home. It was given ninety consecutive performances to packed houses. Gounod's delirium was shared by the world.

Famous lovers are part of the legacy of human culture—Tristan and Isolde, Paolo and Francesca, Hero and Leander, Pyramus and Thisbe, Orpheus and Eurydice, Dido and Aeneas. No pair, however, is more legendary than Romeo Montague and Juliet Capulet, doomed lovers of fourteenth century Italy. The power of this story has made it extremely attractive to writers, composers, and artists. The challenge for Gounod was to create a work good enough to dare the competition. To begin with, there was William Shakespeare.

Probably written around 1595, Shakespeare's *Romeo and Juliet* proved extremely popular. Three quartos of varying quality were printed in 1597, 1599 and 1609. The corrupt first quarto of 1597 must have engendered even greater enthusiasm, as the many references after that date attest. Shakespeare's principal and possibly only source was Arthur Brooke's *The Tragicall Historye of Romeus and Juliet* of 1562. Like Gounod, however, Shakespeare worked in an extensive tradition.

The first version of the story was in a collection by Masuccio Salernitano, *Il Novellino*, published in 1476. This version recounts the story of Mariotto of Siena, who through the aid of a Friar secretly marries Gianozza. Having killed a man in a street fight, Mariotto is exiled to Alexandria. As in *Romeo and Juliet*, the hero manages to have a final meeting with his wife before departing. Being forced into a marriage, Gianozza takes a sleeping potion concocted by the Friar. The Friar's message explaining the plot miscarries. Mariotto is arrested at the tomb and subsequently beheaded. His young widow enters a convent. Masuccio's version contains no suicides. The outline of the story itself is even older, appearing in a romance, the *Ephesiaca* of Xenophon of Ephesus (fifth century A.D.), which contains the story of a woman separated from her husband who takes a potion to avoid another marriage.

For Shakespeare and Gounod a crucial distant source was Luigi da Porto's version of the tale in *Istoria Novellamente Ritrovata di Due Nobili Amanti*, c. 1530. Da Porto gave the legend the elements most familiar to it: the setting in Verona, the names of the warring families (the Montecchi and the Cappelletti), the meeting at the ball in the hostile house, the Friar Lorenzo skilled in potions, the wooing at the balcony, the secret marriage, the slaying of a man named Thebaldo, the forced marriage, the sleeping potion, the undelivered letter and the suicide of the man, identified as Romeo, by poison. The two lovers have a brief conversation before his death. His beloved Giulietta deserves renown for the manner of her death: "She drew in her breath and held it long, and then, uttering a great cry, fell dead on the corpse of Romeo." Da Porto's version of the story was widely imitated.

Matteo Bandello included the legend in his *Novelle* (1554), adding the role of the Nurse and including the rope ladder and the sinister sorcerer who became Shakespeare's Apothecary. Though his prototype had appeared in Da Porto's Marcuccio, in Bandello the true Mercutio exists. Two subsequent versions deriving from Bandello were adapted, one in Pierre Boaistuau's treatment in 1559 in the *Histoires Tragiques*, which introduced the disturbance of the Capulet ball. More significantly, Romeo is dead before Juliet awakens. William Painter's account in *The Palace of Pleasure* (1567) freely translated Boaistuau's handling of the legend, which was also the basis for the Brooke document of 1562, Shakespeare's source.

Brooke's key function for Shakespeare, and therefore for Gounod, was in sharpening the characters from other sources. The Nurse becomes an amoral force in the tale; Juliet's parents are etched; Juliet sleeps alone to take the potion; the riot is more developed; Mercutio's nature is embellished. Brooke also introduces the element of Fate or Fortune as a factor in the lovers' destiny. Bringing together the influences of Bandello and Boaistuau, Brooke's *Romeus and Juliet* amalgamated sources for Shakespeare. Shakespeare, however, succeeded in greatly accelerating the story, which in Brooke takes place over a period of months. In Shakespeare the action is compressed to four or five days, lending a breathless, relentless force to the tragic story. And the Bard adds greater passion to the tale by setting it in torrid mid-July.

Shakespeare's *Romeo and Juliet* is a great Renaissance document, celebrating individuality of choice and action. This is emphasized in the play by Romeo's gradual alteration, particularly in three central speeches. In the first scene of Act I ("Love is a smoke made with the fume of sighs"), Romeo speaks with the stereotypical metaphors sanctioned by the tradition of *l'amour courtois* (courtly love). In the fifth scene, however, after meeting Juliet, Romeo addresses her in the form of the sonnet ("If I profane with my unworthiest hand"), modifying the Petrarchan language of his initial appearance. His transformation to utter individuality occurs in the famous Act II, Scene 2, balcony scene ("But, soft! what light through yonder window breaks? /It is the East, and Juliet is the sun!"). The nature imagery has become totally individualized. His language, now uniquely his own, applies solely to his beloved. The contrast of light and darkness, retained by

Gounod throughout *Roméo et Juliette*, expresses this radical individualism of the lovers.

Gounod too was concerned with the development of the lovers. The libretto by Jules Barbier and Michel Carré retains the propulsion of the Shakespearean source within the five acts of the opera. Gounod, like Shakespeare, includes a prologue. Writing during the composition of the scene of Juliet's drinking the potion, Gounod remarked about the opera's structure, "The first act ends *brilliantly*, the second is *tender* and *dreamy*, the third *bold* and *animated*, with the duels and Romeo sentenced to exile; the fourth is *dramatic*, the fifth *tragic*. It is a fine progression."

Just as *Romeo and Juliet* is anchored in the three passages transforming Romeo's language of love, *Roméo et Juliette* is constructed around four love duets. The first, "Ange adorable," based on the sonnet "If I profane" from the play, is suitable in its formality for the first meeting. Act II begins with Roméo's aria "Ah! lève-toi, soleil," derived from Shakespeare's Act II, Scene 2 ("It is the East, and Juliet is the sun!/Arise, fair sun, and kill the envious moon"). Gounod's structure therefore follows Shakespeare's emphasis on the lovers' independence from stereotypical emotion. In the duet in Act II ("O nuit divine!") the lovers' separation from the world begins as they plan their wedding. As in Shakespeare, Gounod's Roméo transforms his language into Juliette herself ("Sois l'aurore"). The Act IV duet, "Nuit d'hyménée" individualizes the lovers in their language ("Le ciel rayonne en moi"). The final duet, "Console-toi, pauvre âme," evokes the lark/nightingale motif from the marriage-night episode in Shakespeare.

Gounod is very much a part of his time in this final episode, where Roméo and Juliette sing together before their death. In Shakespeare, Romeo is dead before Juliet awakens, but eighteenth- and nineteenth-century audiences would not tolerate such a scene without some farewell words exchanged by the lovers. This tradition is based on David Garrick's 1761 play-text of Shakespeare, which included the final dialogue in the tomb. After Romeo takes the poison, Juliet awakens asking, "Where am I?" Romeo exclaims, "She speaks, she lives!" The lovers discourse about their future until the poison seizes Romeo. Juliet stabs herself, as in Gounod. Gounod also follows Garrick in cutting the appearance of the fathers and their reconciliation, bringing down the curtain with Juliet's suicide.

During the nineteenth century, the legend of Romeo and Juliet became increasingly popular in music and art. Gounod's *Roméo et Juliette* is part of a continuous operatic and orchestral interest in the lovers. Treatments by forgotten composers such as Nicola Zingarelli (1796) and Nicola Vaccai (1825) might have posed no threat, but Gounod's opera was competing with Vincenzo Bellini's *I Capuleti e i Montecchi*, premiered in 1830. Its literary sources are unknown, though they may have included Bandello's novella. Felice Romani's libretto for *I Capuleti e i Montecchi* had been used for the Vaccai *Giulietta e Romeo* but was revised for Bellini's.

The differences between the Bellini and the Gounod are significant. The two leads in Bellini are a soprano and mezzo-soprano; Lorenzo is a doctor rather than a friar; Romeo has slain Capulet's son before the opera commences; Tebaldo is betrothed to Giulietta and is not slain by Romeo; no Nurse or Mercutio is included. As Bellini's title indicates, the ambience of *I Capuleti e i Montecchi* is martial and warlike. The lovers are representatives of the two houses, whose political strife (the Montagues are Ghibelline, the Capulets Guelph) is emphasized throughout. In this respect, the Bellini echoes the references in Dante's *Purgatorio* to the Montecchi and Cappelletti, which he cites in his denunciation of civil war. In Bellini the city of Verona is violent, almost anarchic. Giulietta from the beginning is filled with doom. So chaotic is the universe that the lovers are never even married.

When still a young man, Gounod had heard Hector Berlioz's dramatic symphony *Roméo et Juliette* (1839), a work Berlioz described as "neither an opera in concert form nor a cantata, but a symphony with chorus." Berlioz's work draws its inspiration from Garrick, whose version he had seen performed in 1827 by Charles Kemble's company, evoking in the music the elements of Garrick's additional final scene (Romeo's suicide, the lovers' brief dialogue, and Juliet's end). Though Garrick cut the reconciliation of the Montagues and Capulets, Berlioz includes a lengthy scene for Père Laurence, who denounces the violence of the families and compels their reconciliation, as in Shakespeare. Gounod's opera preceded by two years Tchaikovsky's fantasy-overture *Romeo and Juliet*, first heard in 1870.

Heavily revised in 1872 and in 1880, the overture begins with ecclesiastical harmonies suggesting Friar Laurence, passes to the street fight and then to the lovers and concludes with a tempestuous coda evoking their doom.

In the twentieth century, three compositions have been inspired by the legend. With *A Village Romeo and Juliet* (1907) British composer Frederick Delius drew his inspiration from the novella *Romeo und Julia auf dem Dorfe*, written by Gottfried Keller in 1856. The opera recounts the tragedy of Sali and Vreli, son and daughter of rival farmers. The lovers have a wedding only in a dream, achieving a brief union on a barge, which they intentionally sink in mutual suicide. Nothing of Italy or any Shakespearean influence appears except in the title. The Italian Riccardo Zandonai, best known for *Francesca da Rimini* (1914), composed *Giulietta e Romeo*, which received its premiere in 1921. Like the Bellini, Zandonai's opera presents a violent world. The lovers have been secretly married before the action begins. Preserving the imagery of Shakespeare, the first act moves from darkness to daylight. As in Gounod, the lovers have a brief dialogue before their death. Zandonai's uniqueness lies in his language and musical idiom. For the choral numbers he consciously uses archaisms. In the third act the chorus sings in a form derived from the Tuscan *stornello*. The lovers' language, however, is based on Venetian popular song. Zandonai goes beyond Gounod in reducing the cast to a minimum, concentrating the dramatic tension. The most recent distinguished realization of the Romeo and Juliet idea is in Sergei Prokofiev's ballet introduced in 1938. The first Soviet performance of the ballet took place in 1940, with choreography by Leonid Lavrovsky.

Visual interest in the legend of Romeo and Juliet reached its peak during the late eighteenth century and in the middle and late nineteenth, particularly in England. In the late eighteenth century the publisher John Boydell conceived the idea of a Shakespeare Gallery, which would exhibit paintings of Shakespearean scenes. The Gallery opened in May 1789 with thirty-four canvases; additions increased the total to over 150 by the time the collection was sold in 1805. Some of the most preeminent artists of the time exhibited in the Gallery. James Northcote completed (1792) a tomb scene, showing Juliet dismissing the Friar as Romeo and Paris lie slain at her feet. John Opie's *Juliet in the Trance* (1791) is based on Act IV, the presumed death of Juliet. William Miller finished a canvas of Romeo and Juliet in eighteenth-century dress for the famous touching of hands in Act I.

Two canvases from the period not completed for Boydell are particularly noteworthy. Matthew William Peters (1742-1814) depicted the suicide of Juliet ("O happy dagger"), a Shakespearean *Pietà* with Romeo lying in her lap as she raises the fatal weapon. Peters focuses on the incident that ended the play in Garrick. In 1809 the Swiss-born Henry Fuseli completed *Romeo Slaying Paris at the Bier of Juliet* from Act V. Romeo thrusts his sword at Paris as Juliet lies between them, the dynamism of Fuseli's conception enchanced by the Shakespearean contrast of darkness and light. In 1836 J.M. W. Turner exhibited *Juliet and Her Nurse*, showing Juliet gazing over the Piazza San Marco in Venice. The French artist Eugène Delacroix in 1846 showed the two lovers embracing after their wedding night as Romeo prepares to go into exile in Mantua.

The story of Romeo and Juliet became especially popular in British painting from midcentury onward. Several factors contributed to this interest. The art critic John Ruskin published his monumental study *The Stones of Venice* between 1851 and 1853, evoking the glory of Italy while chronicling its demise. Politics also renewed interest in Italy, especially the events surrounding the Risorgimento, the movement to unify Italy and free it from Austrian domination. In the early 1850s, Giuseppe Mazzini, founder of the liberation movement Giovane Italia (Young Italy), was in exile in England after the failed revolt of 1848, where he received financial support for his cause. In June 1860, when Giuseppe Garibaldi liberated Sicily, British foreign policy endorsed Italian unification. These events aroused interest again in Shakespeare's defiant lovers.

The young Pre-Raphaelite artist John Everett Millais painted *The Death of Romeo and Juliet* (c. 1848), showing the two lovers clutched in an embrace while the families rush into the tomb. In 1853 William Grant exhibited *Juliet and the Friar* from Act IV, a theme not frequently portrayed; Juliet appears cautious, the Friar aged and beneficent. Frederic Leighton, who had studied in Italy and preferred Shakespeare's Italian dramas, depicted incidents from the drama three times. The first, *The Duel Between Romeo and*

Tybalt (1850), is untraced. In 1855 Leighton exhibited *The Reconciliation of the Montagues and the Capulets over the Dead Bodies of Romeo and Juliet.* The Prince stands between Capulet on the left and Montague on the right, who points to the corpses of the lovers; Lady Capulet has thrown herself over their bodies, and Paris lies dead beside them. The rich coloring of the canvas evokes the mystery and splendor of the Italian Middle Ages. In his 1858 canvas *The Feigned Death of Juliet*, Leighton depicts Count Paris arriving for his marriage and discovering his bride "dead." Leighton distills the varied reactions of the characters around the bed, from the old Nurse to the Friar.

A particularly poignant theme that attracted artists was the parting of Romeo and Juliet after their wedding night, from Act III. The Pre-Raphaelite artist Ford Madox Brown completed a richly colored version in 1870, showing Romeo kissing Juliet passionately before he descends, as dawn breaks over the city. Brown captures the tension by the foot in the rope ladder and Romeo's extended arm. To recreate the atmosphere of Italy, Brown had borrowed photographs from his colleague Dante Gabriel Rossetti, whose father had come as a political exile from Italy in 1825. In 1884 Frank Dicksee, one of the later great Victorian painters, also depicted the lovers parting.

There had been a famous revival of the drama in 1882, which ran twenty-four weeks in London, starring Ellen Terry. Under the management of Henry Irving, this revival was the first authentic presentation of Shakespeare's text in the nineteenth century, omitting Garrick's emendations. Anna Lea Merritt painted *Juliet and Her Nurse* in 1883, illustrating Act II of this production. Though Dicksee's canvas exhibits similarities to Brown's, Dicksee interprets the scene quite differently. The colors are muted and soft, whereas Brown's are glowing and passionate. The lovers in Dicksee separate tenderly rather than frantically, and Dicksee avoids showing Romeo's foot in the ladder. The face of Juliet suggests Ellen Terry's. The canvases by Brown and Dicksee display two dramatic alternatives for the scene. In 1888 the *Graphic Gallery of Shakespeare's Heroines* was published, illustrating many of Shakespeare's women.

The legend of Romeo and Juliet became a powerful symbol in the nineteenth century for musicians and artists. The defiant love ethic of these two characters paralleled the reformist political impulse of the century and confirmed the individualism of nineteenth-century romantic self-assertion. Gounod's *Roméo et Juliette* is part of a cultural legacy including composers from Bellini to Zandonai and artists from Fuseli to Dicksee. "Never was a story of more woe/Than this of Juliet and her Romeo." As this extensive tradition demonstrates, the love depicted in *Roméo et Juliette* has become more deathless than ever.

Born of Obsession:
Strauss and *Salome*

Once, in Berlin, I went to Max Reinhardt's Little Theater to see Gertrud Eysoldt in Oscar Wilde's *Salomé*. After the performance I met Heinrich Grunfeld, who said, "My dear Strauss, surely you could make an opera of this!" I replied, "I am already composing it." The Viennese poet Anton Lindner had sent me this exquisite play and had offered to turn it into a libretto. When I agreed, he sent a few cleverly versified opening scenes, but I could not make up my mind to start composing until one day it occurred to me to set to music "How beautiful is the Princess Salome tonight" straight away. From then on, it was not difficult to purge the piece of purple passages so that it became quite a good libretto. Now, after the dance and especially the whole closing scene have been clothed in music, it is easy to say that the play "cried out for music." Yes, but one had to see it.

This is how Richard Strauss recalled the momentous evening in November 1902 when he saw a renowned performance of Oscar Wilde's *Salomé*. Dissatisfied with Lindner's attempt, Strauss decided to use the translation by Hedwig Lachmann of Wilde's 1891 drama. Having begun serious work on the score around August 1903, Strauss wrote Ernst von Schuch in September 1904, "I have completed my one-act opera *Salome* . . . in rough (it has become very fine), and hope to be able to let you have the complete score in the autumn of 1905." In May 1905 he played parts of the music for his father, Franz, who declared, "It's like having ants in your pants." In July, Strauss was able to state, "With the exception of the dance, *Salome* is being engraved in full score and vocal score." By August, he had finished the Dance of the Seven Veils.

The premiere on December 9, 1905, in Dresden was a *succès fou* but had had its problems. It was not easy to cast the heroine, described by Strauss as "the sixteen year-old princess with the voice of Isolde." The first Salome, Marie Wittich, grasping the parameters of the role, declared, "I won't do it—I'm a decent woman." Still, she went on. Strauss saw the revolution he had initiated: "I had long been criticizing the fact that operas based on Oriental and Jewish subjects lack true Oriental color and scorching sun. The needs of the moment inspired me with truly exotic harmonies, which sparkled like taffeta, particularly in the strange cadences. The wish to characterize the dramatis personae as clearly as possible led me to bitonality."

Strauss also had definite ideas about the characters, claiming that "Salome, being a virgin and an Oriental princess, must be played with the simplest and most restrained of gestures." Toward Jochanaan the composer was unsympathetic:"I didn't want to treat him too seriously. You know, Jochanaan is an imbecile. I've got no sympathy at all for that kind of man. I would have preferred above all that he would appear a bit grotesque." Equally specifically he noted, "Herodes in particular must remember, amidst the comings and goings of the hysterical crowd, that he should endeavor, Eastern parvenu though he is, to preserve his dignity and composure before his Roman guests . . . notwithstanding all momentary erotic indiscretions." The dance itself should be "as serious and controlled as possible, thoroughly restrained . . . greater movement only in the C-sharp-minor passage, and in the last two-four a rather orgiastic climax."

Though Gustav Mahler's verdict stands—"one of the greatest masterpieces of our time"—the opera is the product of centuries. The legendary princess of Judea, as yet unnamed, first appears in the Gospel of Mark (6.14-28) around 70 A.D.:

> Herod on his birthday gave a banquet for his courtiers and officers
> and the leading men of Galilee. For when Herodias' daughter came
> in and danced, she pleased Herod and his guests; and the king said

to the girl, "Ask me whatever you wish, and I will grant it." And he vowed to her, "Whatever you ask me, l will give you, even half of my kingdom." And she went out, and said to her mother, "What shall l ask?" And she said, "The head of John the baptizer." And she came in immediately with haste to the king, and asked, saying, "1 want you to give me at once the head of John the Baptist on a platter." And the king was exceedingly sorry; but because of his oaths and his guests he did not want to break his word to her. And immediately the king sent a soldier of the guard and gave orders to bring his head. He went and beheaded him in the prison, and brought his head on a platter, and gave it to the girl; and the girl gave it to her mother.

Fifteen years later, Matthew recorded (Chapter 14) a similar account, though there it is suggested that Herodias and her daughter had previously determined the request. It was Flavius Josephus (c. 37-93 A.D.), author of *The Jewish War* and *Antiquities of the Jews*, who named Herodias' daughter Salome, ironically derived from the Hebrew "shalom" (peace). Josephus makes no mention of Herodias and Salome: "Herod, who feared lest the great influence John had over the people might put it into his power and inclination to raise a rebellion . . . thought it best, by putting him to death, to prevent any mischief he might cause. Accordingly, he was sent a prisoner, because of Herod's suspicious temper, to Machaerus and was there put to death." The story of Salome, Herodias, Herod Antipas and the events of 30 A.D. became legend. If John was dead, Salome had barely begun to live.

The Salome revitalized by Wilde and Strauss personifies the nineteenth-century fixation on this enfant terrible, prompted by women's demands for independence and men's fear of their power. The first to recognize the potential destructiveness of Herodias and Salome was Heinrich Heine. In his verse narrative *Atta Troll* of 1841, Herodias appears as a spirit:

> If a devil or an angel,
> I know not. With women never knows one clearly, where the angel
> leaves off and the devil begins . . .
> ln her hands she carries ever that sad charger, with the head of
> John the Baptist, which she kisses:
> Yes, the head with fervid kisses.

Heine's perception of the connection of eroticism with sadism, masochism and murder was not lost on succeeding writers.

In 1862 a young American, Joseph Converse Heywood, published anonymously his dramatic poem *Salome, the Daughter of Herodias*, a work important to Wilde and Strauss, which Wilde reviewed on its reissue in 1888, three years before undertaking his own *Salomé*. In Heywood's version, Salome and Sextus, a Roman legionnaire, are lovers, though she reveres John the Baptist. Herodias, plotting against John for denouncing her incestuous marriage to her first husband's brother, forces Salome to request John's decapitation after her dance by threatening Sextus' death. At the conclusion, Salome encounters Jesus Christ, who absolves her of sin. Heywood so distorts history that he imagines a Roman general as Salome's father instead of Antipas' elder brother. Inspired by Heine, most startling is Heywood's scene of Herodias with the Baptist's severed head, the prototype of Wilde's ending:

Now thou art mine, I can embrace thee even,
And weave my lily fingers in thy hair,
And stroke thy temples, fondle thee, and hate.
Call thyself back to life, and List to me
While here I mock thee, spurn thee, spit on thee . . .
Come, let me press thy virtuous, scornful lips—

Heywood provided Wilde a paradigm, with its transformation of the legend, pseudo-Biblical language and vicious characterization of Herodias.

Salome's next renascence took place in France. In 1864 Stéphane Mallarmé began *Hérodiade*, a work eventually consisting of three parts—"Ouverture," "Scène" and "Cantique de Saint Jean." The central section, a dramatic scene between a nurse and Herodias, published in 1871, became a famous Symbolist touchstone, rather than defining the perversity of Salome's mother. Herodias enigmatically refers to "the white shuddering of my nakedness," "my shivering star of chastity," and "the horror of being virgin," concluding, "I await a thing unknown."

In 1877, Gustave Flaubert finished his tale *Hérodias*, which he published that April as part of the collection *Trois Contes*. Flaubert's Herodias has abandoned her first husband for Antipas because of her insatiable desire for power. Jokanaan reviles both the Queen and Herod Antipas: "Grovel in the dust, daughter of Babylon! . . . Your shame shall be discovered, your infamy shall be seen, your sobs will break your teeth! The Lord abhors the stench of your crimes! Accursed creature! Die like a bitch!"

Herodias intentionally brings her estranged daughter from Machaerus so the tetrarch will fall in love with her. There is a vividly detailed description of the girl's dance: "The nomads inured to abstinence, the Roman soldiers skilled in debauchery, the avaricious publicans, the old priests soured by controversy, all sat there with their nostrils distended, quivering with desire." At the prompting of her mother, Salome demands "with a childish air" the head of Jokanaan, which she keeps only a few minutes. Three of Jokanaan's disciples take the head to Galilee. The last line in the tale is famous: "As it was very heavy, they each carried it in turn." Flaubert's Salome does not die; in fact, history records she had two marriages.

A musical precedent for Strauss was the premiere of Jules Massenet's *Hérodiade* in 1881, based on Flaubert. In this opera, Salome loves Jean, who emphasizes that their love can be only spiritual. When the prophet is executed, Salome prepares to stab Hérodiade, only to learn that she is her mother, whereupon the girl commits suicide. *Hérodiade* prefigured the uproar generated by Strauss' *Salome* when Massenet was given a minor excommunication by the Archbishop of Lyons.

A catalyst of Wilde's *Salomé* was *À Rebours* (Against Nature) by Joris-Karl Huysmans, published in 1884, a novel called "the handbook of the perfect neurotic" and "the breviary of decadence." Its hero, Due Jean Floressas des Esseintes, is obsessed with the Salome depicted in two paintings by Moreau, the oil *Salome Dancing Before Herod* and the watercolor *The Apparition*, both exhibited in 1876. "In Gustave Moreau's work, which in conception went far beyond the data supplied by the New Testament, Des Esseintes realized at long last the weird and superhuman Salome of his dreams . . . the disquieting delirium of the dancer, the subtle grandeur of the murderess." Des Esseintes believes "She had become, as it were, the symbolic incarnation of undying Lust, the Goddess of immortal Hysteria, the accursed Beauty, . . . the monstrous Beast, indifferent, irresponsible, insensible, poisoning . . . the soiled vessel, ultimate cause of every sin and every crime." In *The Apparition*, where Salome views the suspended decapitated head, she becomes "a courtesan, petrified and hypnotized by terror... a true harlot, obedient to her passionate and cruel female temperament" with "the charms of a great venereal flower." Later in the novel, the hero luxuriates in Mallarmé's *Hérodiade* while contemplating Moreau's pictures.

Intoxicated with the paintings of Moreau, the decadence of Huysmans, the fondling of the head in Heine and Heywood, the marmoreal verses of Mallarmé, the neurosis of Flaubert and the eroticism of Massenet, Wilde wrote *Salomé*, at first called *La Decapitation de Salomé*, in French in 1891. Having begun the work one night, Wilde went to the Grand Café, exclaiming to the orchestra leader, "I am writing a play about a woman dancing with her bare feet in the blood of a man she has craved for and slain. I want you to play something in harmony with my thoughts." Primed by this stimulus, Wilde returned to his rooms in the Boulevard des Capucines and finished the play that night, its lush style modeled on the Song of Solomon. Wilde declared, "I flee from what is moral as from what is impoverished. I have the same sickness as Des Esseintes." Contrasting the perverse sensuality of Salome and the misogynistic spirituality of Jokanaan, both of them equally demented, Wilde regarded Herod as the pivotal figure in the drama. *Salomé* was published in 1893; an English version appeared in 1894, with Aubrey Beardsley's notorious illustrations.

Wilde's innovations are startling. His Herod Antipas, for example, combines the three Herods of the New Testament—adding Herod the Great, the father of Herod Antipas, and also Herod Agrippa. Wilde's Salome becomes erotically obsessed with Jokanaan, regarding the prophet as a "thin ivory statue . . . an image of silver," dwelling successively on his body, his hair and his mouth. The necrophilic Liebestod of Salome with the severed head epitomizes the century's patriarchal fears of women's sexuality, power, and dominance. Pervading the drama, the moon—symbol of both woman and madness—amalgamates these themes. In Wilde, it is Salome alone who demands the head; this time, there is no instigation from Herodias. "It is not my mother's voice that I heed. It is for my own pleasure," she declares. Finally, Wilde has Herod command, "Kill that woman!" Salome is crushed beneath the soldiers' shields—a death inspired by, but unlike, the suicide in Massenet's *Hérodiade*.

In adapting Wilde's text, Strauss excised nearly half of Wilde's ornate language. Certain minor characters—a Nubian, a young Roman called

Tigellinus—are removed. Less fortunately, Strauss cut a discussion between a Cappadocian and a soldier early in Wilde's text that indicated the fate of Salome's father, imprisoned in the cistern now holding Jokanaan: "The Tetrarch's brother, his elder brother, the first husband of Herodias the Queen, was imprisoned there for twelve years. It did not kill him. At the end of the twelve years he had to be strangled." While no historical evidence confirms this, Wilde's Salome is not only avenging herself against Jokanaan but also exacting revenge on Herod and Herodias for murdering her father. When the young Syrian Narraboth slays himself, in Wilde the enamored Page of Herodias delivers a sensitive eulogy; it is cut by Strauss to increase the brutality of the opera. To maintain his focus on the erotic tension among Herodes, Salome, and Jochanaan, Strauss omitted many passages expressing the tetrarch's anxiety about his political standing with the emperor in Rome.

Deploying nearly thirty musical motifs designating characters and situations, Strauss constructs the one-act opera around five episodes, some set off by interludes: 1. Discussion among the Page, Narraboth and soldiers about Jochanaan and Salome, both at this point absent; 2. Salome coaxing Narraboth to produce the prophet, followed by an interlude; 3. Salome and Jochanaan, with his denunciation of her and her mother; 4. Herodes, Herodias and Salome, culminating in the Dance of the Seven Veils; 5. Salome's Liebestod with the head of Jochanaan, concluding with her execution. With its superimposed incest, narcissism, sadism, masochism, murder, necrophilia, castration anxiety and proto-feminist defiance, no one has disputed Strauss' observation about his *Salome*: "It is symphony in the medium of drama, and it is psychological, like all music."

Both Strauss and Wilde knew that observers would bring to performances a consciousness of the pictorial representation of the tale. Botticelli for the San Barnaba Altarpiece depicted Salome carrying the head on a charger, while Giotto finished *The Dance of Salome* for the Peruzzi Chapel in Florence. Titian with his *Salome* of 1515 and Caravaggio with his *Salome with the Head of John the Baptist* of 1607 suggested the element of erotic attraction, explicit in Francesco del Cairo's *Herodias* of 1638. Andrea del Sarto completed frescoes of the *Arrest of the Baptist*, the *Dance of Salome*, and the *Beheading of the Baptist.* Eugène Delacroix finished a grisly *Death of St. John* in 1858, while Frederic Leighton painted a *Salome Dancing* in 1863.

During the latter half of the nineteenth century, artists became obsessed with the idea of Salome. Henri Regnault in 1870 depicted a *Salome* with a satisfied heroine holding a charger and knife. Moreau's images from 1876 catalyzed succeeding artists. Lavis Corinth's 1899 *Salome* shows the princess opening one of Jokanaan's eyes as the executioner leers. Lucien Lévy-Dhurmer's 1896 pastel *Salome Embracing the Severed Head of John the Baptist* is the most powerful necrophilic image. Edvard Munch conveyed his misogynistic attitudes through conceptions showing men smothered and dominated by long-haired women. In the twentieth century, Franz van Stuck with his 1906 *Salome* (dancing as the severed head appears) or Gustav Klimt with his 1909 *Judith II (Salome)* reified the image of woman as castrater. Strauss admitted that in Klimt's art he detected "much of my own music, especially *Salome*." The most famous illustrations, those by Aubrey Beardsley published in the first English edition in February 1894, were ingenious designs in black and white—a parodic commentary on the drama rather than an illustration of it, with their absence of shadow, their flatness, asymmetry, fetuses and hermaphrodites. Perhaps because he himself is caricatured as the Man in the Moon, a Jester and Herod, Wilde disliked Beardsley's conceptions: "They are all too Japanese, while my play is Byzantine."

The orchestral dissonances of Strauss' score indicate the tale's psychomachia between instinct and conscience, a mental war between the anarchic id (Salome) and the self-righteous superego (Jochanaan), with Herodes the besieged ego. Eschewing morality for psychology, Strauss, echoing Wilde, asserted, "In art there is never the moral or the immoral; such conceptions are incompatible with the conception of art. The artist refuses to answer the question 'Is your art moral?'" Romain Rolland wrote Strauss, "Oscar Wilde's *Salomé* is not worthy of you. You surpass your subject, but you cannot make one forget it." Like Salome with the prophet, however, Strauss did not intend to obliterate Wilde, only to execute him: a drama of the fin-de-siecle was transmuted to a vision of the *fin du monde*.

The Feared Woman:
Saint-Saëns and *Samson et Delilah*

"I was told officially that you are the composer of the symphony they played on Sunday . . . You are beyond your years. Always go forward, and remember that on Sunday, December 11, 1853, you incurred an obligation to become a great master." So wrote Charles Gounod, composer of *Faust*, to the young Camille Saint-Saëns. Born in 1835, Saint-Saëns had given his first piano recital in 1846. To a jaded listener who asked, "What music will he play when he is twenty?" his mother replied, "He will play his own." Such words proved prophetic. Saint-Saëns became one of the major composers of his age, the Second Empire under Napoleon III, then the Third Republic and the Belle Époque.

There was a ruler of another sort in Europe during the nineteenth century—cruel, perverse, sadistic, powerful, beautiful, sensual, defiant, demonic, degrading, mysterious, deceptive, unfaithful, inaccessible, instinctual, torturing, treacherous—a bearer of danger, disaster, death. This was the archetypal femme fatale.

A synthesis of male fears and anxieties, the "fatal woman" had an extensive pedigree, going back to Greek and Roman myth and history. Helen of Troy, Clytemnestra, Elektra, Phryne, Pandora, Medusa, Circe, Medea, the Sphinx, the Siren, Messalina and Cleopatra are only a few of her antecedents. Another source was the Bible, beginning with Eve and descending to Judith, Jael, Salome and Jezebel. Worthy to stand beside these was Delilah, the Philistine priestess of Dagon who destroyed the Israelite hero Samson around 1150 B.C.

Just before his death, in 1921, Saint-Saëns recorded the origin of *Samson et Dalila*. He wrote, "It was a long time ago when I first became interested in the idea . . . Sacred and serious oratorios were then very much in fashion. The City of Paris originated a prize to encourage the creation of interesting compositions of this nature, and in this manner such works as Massenet's *Marie-Magdeleine* and my own *Le Déluge* came to be written. An old music-lover and friend of mine called my attention to the subject of Samson and told me about Voltaire's libretto (1733). He even sketched the opening scene of a scenario for my purpose. Shortly after, a cousin of mine married a charming young man who soon became my intimate friend. He was an amateur poet, and I soon perceived he had real talent."

This man was Ferdinand Lemaire, whose influence was decisive. If he had not intervened, *Samson et Dalila* would have been an oratorio rather than an opera. "I asked him to devise for me the text of an oratorio on the subject of Samson. 'Why an oratorio?' he replied. 'Let's write an opera.' He soon convinced me, and while he was making a close study of the Biblical text, I started to evolve an outline of the work. I even wrote the plan of some of the scenes, so that he had only to write the lines. I do not know why, but I wrote the second act first." Saint-Saëns had found *la femme fatale* in 1867.

But the opposition he had to face with his creation proved enormous. Before the Franco-Prussian War broke out, in 1870, a private reading of the second act was given, with the painter Henri Regnault as Samson and Augusta Holmes as Dalila. Saint-Saëns recorded that the select audience "understood absolutely nothing. When I spoke of this project to theatrical people, you should have seen how they reacted! They said a Biblical subject was impossible on the stage. In the face of this general hostility, little by little I gave up my project." In 1873, after the end of the war, Saint-Saëns went to Algeria, where he completed the sketches of the music.

In 1874 a private performance of the second act took place at Croissy-sur-Seine, with Pauline Viardot, to whom Saint-Saëns dedicated the score, singing Dalila. In 1875 the composer conducted the first act at the Théâtre du Châtelet. He had complained of the reception of his work to Franz Liszt, who told him, "Finish your piece—I shall have it performed at Weimar." As a result, the world premiere took place on December 2, 1877, at the Hoftheater in Weimar. The first French performance took place in Rouen in 1890, and *Samson et Dalila* finally reached Paris at the Théâtre d'Éden in the same year, receiving a performance at the Opera only in 1892. The long resistance recalls the corresponding opposition to *Carmen*, with its femme fatale heroine.

Biblical subjects on the stage had already been established by such precedents as Méhul's *Joseph* (1807), Rossini's *Mosè* (1818) and Verdi's *Nabucco* (1842). The resistance to *Samson et Dalila* cannot be explained solely by objections to such representations. The Second Empire and the Belle Époque were marked by a new assertiveness of women, a movement that can be distinguished throughout Europe during the nineteenth century. The resulting male gynophobia led to the feared woman.

The concept of the femme fatale expresses male anxiety at female sexuality, power and domination. Religious, social, even medical factors aroused male doubts about woman's nature during the era. In *Samson et Dalila*, the Old Hebrew, a character not found in the Biblical account, sums this up when he refers to Dalila as full of "serpent's venom."

Without denying woman's significance, religious authority nevertheless asserted man's supremacy. St. Paul in First Corinthians declared, "I wish you to understand that, while every man has Christ for his head, woman's head is man . . . For man did not originally spring from woman, but woman for the sake of man." Nineteenth century opinion concurred. Max Nordau in *Degeneration* (1892) thundered, "The right of woman to assert her own personality is the inversion of the healthy and natural relation between the sexes."

Scientific opinion during the nineteenth century reinforced ideas of women as dangerous or primitive. A popular manual, Sylvanus Stall's *What a Young Man Ought to Know*, used the Samson and Delilah tale to describe spurious sexual diseases, alleging that Samson's weakness was caused by his salacious fantasies of Delilah. Orson Fowler wrote in 1875 that sexual misconduct was the "Delilah which allured" him from purity.

Writing in 1855, the physician William Acton desexualized women to remove male anxieties: "I should say that the majority of women (happily for them) are not very much troubled with sexual feelings of any kind." Anthropological doctrine held that the female brain was smaller than the male's, indicating women were from an earlier stage of human evolution. Such theories reinforced the male's preferred image of women as passive, loving, serviceable, self-effacing, brainless, asexual, compliant, submissive and subordinate—the opposite of the femme fatale.

These attitudes were challenged as the century advanced. Women began arguing for more access to education, including university-level instruction and certification. The rise of birth-control movements during the 1870s aroused male fears that women would deny their maternal roles.

Occupations such as nursing and typewriting freed women from financial dependence on males, and the law regarding property changed so that a woman no longer had to consign all possessions to her husband upon marriage. These legal, marital, educational and occupational transformations, giving women further independence, caused men to consider women as femmes fatales bent on destroying male authority and abolishing male privileges. *Samson et Dalila* presented a terrifying example of female power.

Saint-Saëns and Lemaire react to the femme fatale in two ways: by elevating the dignity of Samson, and by increasing the venality of Delilah. Their source, the Book of Judges 13-16, presents a divinely guided but extremely fallible Samson. In the Bible, Samson is a Nazirite—that is, an individual consecrated to God. Yet he is constantly attracted to the women of the Philistines, the Israelites' enemies, first marrying one, then consorting with a Philistine harlot at Gaza before finally suffering at the hands of Delilah. Even before he encounters Delilah, Samson capitulates to a woman when he tells his Philistine wife the solution to a riddle, which she then reveals to his enemies.

Samson is a *shophet* or "judge," but not in the modern sense. In the Bible this means "one who procures justice," a man of militaristic presence who defends the nation of Israel. Yet all his actions (burning the Philistines' grain, slaying Philistines with the jawbone of an ass, carrying off the gates of Gaza) are for personal rather than patriotic reasons. Even his final act is one of personal revenge, as he prays to God: "Strengthen me . . . only this once, O God, that I may be avenged upon the Philistines for one of my two eyes." In the Bible, the source of Samson's strength is God, though egoistically he believes it resides in himself, symbolized by his locks.

This flawed hero has been gradually transformed in Western culture. Flavius Josephus (c. 37-93 A.D.) in *Antiquities of the Jews* eliminates the physical connotations of the riddle, stating that Samson lodged at an inn at Gaza rather than consorting with a prostitute. Josephus declares, "It is but right to admire the man for his valor, his strength and the grandeur of his end . . . That he let himself be ensnared by a woman must be imputed to human nature, which succumbs to sins; but testimony is due to him for his surpassing excellence in all the rest." To heroize Samson further, he calls Delilah a harlot. In the Bible she is only "a woman in the valley of Sorek."

Early Christian apologists believed Samson was a prefigurement of Christ. Peter Abelard wrote a poem about Samson, conceiving of him as a tragic figure, and Boccaccio believed Delilah was the source of all Samson's trials. Milton's *Samson Agonistes* (1671) transformed the Biblical character into a Greek tragic hero, tormented internally by his guilt. Handel's *Samson* (1743), based on Milton, with Dalila as Samson's Philistine wife, further elevated his stature. In *Samson et Dalila*, Samson is heroic from the beginning, with his Act I exhortations to the Hebrews. In contrast to his Biblical counterpart, he expresses patriotic rather than personal motives for his actions. By isolating Samson in submissive humility at the beginning of Act III, and by making his final prayer an appeal to avenge God as well as himself, Lemaire and Saint-Saëns vaunt the hypermasculine heroism, valor and virtue of the male.

The insidious femme fatale, on the other hand, is constantly emphasized in the representation of Dalila. In the opera she is not merely a woman— she has become a Philistine priestess of Dagon, a religious heretic from the Hebraic perspective. Though in the Bible the episode involving Delilah is only one part of Samson's history, the opera focuses on her, increasing her fatality by increasing her prominence. In her encounter with the High Priest in Act II, Dalila is different from her Biblical proto-type in a crucial way. In the Bible, each of the Philistine princes pays her 1,100 pieces of silver to entrap Samson. In the opera she refuses the money, declaring she is dreaming of personal vengeance because she hates Samson. She is not the pawn of the Philistines Chiefs, as in the Bible. By this strategy, the Dalila of Saint-Saëns and Le maire emerges as her own agent. This creates a woman of fierce, lethal individuality, the femme fatale par excellence.

The opera also emphasizes her treachery. In the Bible, Delilah tries three times to discover the source of Samson's strength; three times he foils her. In the opera, though she mentions these three previous failures, one forgets them, because only her successful attack is depicted. Particularly striking in the opera is the fact that Samson's hair is never mentioned, and its cutting is never witnessed. This is a masterstroke: Samson's defeat becomes not only sexual but psychological. There is nothing about Dalila at all until her appearance in the sixth scene of Act I. She virtually arises from the subconscious, as an irresistible power.

Lemaire associates her with grating nasal sounds: "En vain je suis belle!/ Mon coeur plein d'amour,/Pleurant l'infidèle,/Attend son retour!" she sings in her first aria. In this evocation of spring, the season of fertility, her sensuality is already blazoned. The same emphasis appears in her second aria at the beginning of Act II: "Amour! viens aider ma faiblesse!/Verse le poison dans son sein!/Fais que, vaincu par mon adresse,/Samson soit enchaîne demain!" In her mockery of Samson in Act III, she echoes her passionate Act II aria.

Music and text reinforce each other to depict her deadly essence. In "Printemps qui commence" the use of the ascending ninth on "l'espérance" illustrates her deceptive allure, while in "Mon coeur s'ouvre" the chromatic phrases of Dalila's music contain the cliché ascending seventh ("Réponds") that reveals her fatal power and her falsity. The verse lines drive home this impression. In "Amour! viens aider" Lemaire uses octosyllabic lines, but as her wrath increases in the encounter with the High Priest, the structure changes, and with "J'ai voulu de sa force" she begins to speak in the twelve-syllable Alexandrine line immortalized in the tragedies of Racine. At this point, Lemaire endows her with monumental evil: "Et je sais qu'à cette heure, abandonnant les siens,/Il revient en ces lieux resserrer nos liens./ Pour ce dernier combat j'ai préparé mes armes:/Samson ne pourra pas *résister à mes larmes.*" The "n" consonant of the first couplet conveys her evil, while the liquid "m" and "r" consonants of the second enhance her seductiveness. The *coup de théâtre* of this technique is "Mon coeur s'ouvre," which intertwines Alexandrine and six-syllable lines, the former exposing her power, the latter her carnality.

Delilah is not only an individual femme fatale but also a mythical one. Although in the opera she is unquestionably a Philistine, in the Bible no nationality is given her, making her universal in significance. Samson's name derives from *shemesh*, meaning "one of the sun," while Delilah's name derives from *laylah*, the Hebrew word for "night." The legend is the primal mythical combat of day and night. The male is associated with the stable, rational light, the female with the unbalanced, irrational darkness.

Samson et Dalila partakes of the controversial nineteenth-century "solar theory," which contended that all myth could be traced to this elemental conflict. When Samson is in the ascendant, as in Act I, the sun appears, fully risen after the Hebrews' victory. Dalila, who refers to her ebony tresses at her first appearance, gains the ascendancy in Act II, which begins at twilight and concludes in the chaos of the stormy night of the seduction. This storm, which does not appear in the Bible, increases the sense of moral chaos associated with the femme fatale. Samson may have been a primitive "solar hero." Only when plunged into physical darkness does he succeed in seeing the spiritual light.

The impression of the femme fatale in *Samson et Dalila* is enhanced by the psychological power of the symbolic action. Freud was to identify decapitation with castration. Though in the Bible a man "shaves" Samson's seven locks, in the opera Dalila shears the hair in a symbolic beheading, darkness/night eclipsing the rays of sun/day. The blinding of Samson, another symbolic emasculation, recalls the similar blinding of Oedipus in Sophocles' tragedy. The connotations are made clear in the first scene of Act III, where Samson "grinds" at the mill, a task usually given to women. (This detail associates Samson with the Greco-Roman Hercules, who was a slave to Omphale for three years.) "Grinding" has always been a euphemism for intercourse. At the opening of Act III, therefore, the impotent Samson reenacts the rendezvous that led to his downfall.

The idea of having Delilah sever Samson's locks derives from extensive pictorial tradition. In a monochrome painting of about 1495, Andrea Mantegna depicts Delilah cutting Samson's hair in a symbolic outdoor setting. The vine twining about the tree indicates Delilah's serpentine entrapment of Samson; the grapes allude to his lust. Carved on the tree trunk is an inscription: "An evil woman is three times more wicked than the Devil." In the early sixteenth century, Francesco Morone depicted a Philistine cutting Samson's hair as Delilah cradles his head in her lap.

Rubens painted this episode around 1609, showing Samson lying on Delilah's scarlet-robed lap as a Philistine cuts his locks. Her naked bosom, and especially the presence of the old woman/procuress, signals she is a prostitute in a brothel. In the seventeenth century, the expression "Delilah's lap" meant consorting with whores. In his canvas of c. 1618-20, Gerrit van Honthorst, in contrast to Mantegna, depicts Samson and Delilah indoors, but he retains the old woman and the candle from Rubens. Van Dyck's canvas of 1621, a reversal of the Rubens, shows a man about to cut the locks as Delilah raises a cautionary finger, while in Lucas Cranach's depiction Delilah does the cutting herself. Rembrandt depicted four incidents from the story of Samson, including *Samson Betrayed by Delilah* in 1628, with the hero asleep at her breast. In 1636 Rembrandt completed the gruesome *The Blinding of Samson*.

In the nineteenth century, the theme was frequently depicted by such artists as Delacroix. In the 1821 Prix de Rome competition at the École des Beaux-Arts, the assigned subject was Samson and Delilah, and the winning canvas by Joseph-Desire Court shows the naked Samson reaching to his shorn head as the Philistines burst into Delilah's chamber. Jean-Louis-Ernest Meissonier depicted *Samson Overthrowing the Philistines* around 1845, presenting the hero in triumph rather than submission. British artists were interested in the theme, including Frederick Pickersgill in 1850, Frederic Leighton in 1859 and Solomon J. Solomon in 1887, the latter showing a jeering Delilah. Probably directly inspired by the opera version, Jean-Léon Gérôme painted the lost *Samson Turning the Millstone* around 1890. All these canvases were pictorial ideograms, the message of which was that women are evil seductresses, men their helpless victims. Since Saint-Saëns was an atheist, the story in the Old Testament was of no religious relevance to him. Instead, the legend constituted a treatise on the femme fatale.

Saint-Saëns makes one more crucial alteration from the Biblical source. In the Book of Judges, Delilah disappears from the narrative; she does not die in Samson's destruction of the Temple of Dagon. Saint-Saëns has her die to reassert male power against the femme fatale. Nevertheless, Samson's death is a suicide. In the end, the solar hero/sun is destroyed by the fatal woman/night.

Delilah did not really die. In his poem "The Wrath of Samson" in 1839, a text surely known to Saint-Saëns and Lemaire, Alfred de Vigny expressed the nineteenth century's actual belief:

> An eternal struggle, ever present and everywhere
> In the world, is waged before God's stare
> Between the goodness of Man and Woman's guile,
> For Woman's being of body and soul is vile,
> And more or less, Woman is forever DELILAH.

Romantic Rebel:
Wagner and *Tannhäuser*

The composition of *Tannhäuser* marked the struggling emergence of the real Richard Wagner. After completing the score, on April 13, 1845, he recalled his travails:

> In writing this work I was under a genuine spell; whenever I was dealing with my material, I trembled in fever. After the long interruptions that divided me from my work, I was always with one breath reimmersed in the atmosphere that enraptured me when the idea first came into my head. My whole existence was so consumed with the project that the closer I got to the end, the more consumed I became with the idea that sudden death would prevent me from finishing it. Therefore, when I had set down the last note, I rejoiced as if I had just escaped mortal danger.

Although this seemed a life-and-death struggle to Wagner, the result proved that life had just begun. The premiere of *Tannhäuser* at the Dresden Hofoper on October 19, 1845, so indicated, even to one not remembered for Wagnerolatry:

> *Tannhäuser* is not a composition in which I could find pleasure merely by understanding how nicely this or that had been accomplished. It was, rather, a musical experience, carrying the listener irresistibly with it, in such a way that what occurred in the orchestra and on the stage became part of his own life. I am of the firm opinion that it is the finest thing achieved in grand opera in at least twelve years.

Eduard Hanslick, later in life satirized as Beckmesser in *Die Meistersinger*, went on to wonder:

> Is German opera entirely bereft? Is there no one else? We must look for a man who has already accomplished enough to justify founding one's hopes upon him, but not so much that we can expect nothing further. I think we have such a man. He is Richard Wagner. If there is anyone among contemporary German composers from whom we can expect something distinguished in grand opera, it is he. Richard Wagner, I am convinced, is the greatest dramatic talent among all contemporary composers.

Wagner himself had had premonitions that he was at a turning point, for on December 18, 1844, he had written Ernst Kietz that he believed the work would be a "great revolution; I feel that I have made giant strides towards my ideal." As Hanslick recognized, part of this revolution was the welding of musical and dramatic elements that makes *Tannhäuser* a pivotal work with a tense signature. Wagner creates it from the polarities that defined his own existence—chaste love and sensual desire, paganism and Christianity, grand opera and music drama, France and Germany, radical art and conservative society, medieval conformity and Renaissance individualism. Wagner's revolution was to evolve an opera about the "Greatest of Centuries," the thirteenth, which incorporated the contradictions of a civilization in transition.

The tensions that caused this revolution are evident in the genesis of *Tannhäuser*. Returning home to Germany from Paris in April 1842, Wagner had a revelation:

> A genuine ray of light was granted me by encountering the Wartburg. I was uncommonly moved by the sight of the castle on the hill. A more distant ridge I at once labeled the Horselberg, and thus, while driving through the valley, I constructed the setting for the third act of *Tannhäuser*. It was very significant that now for the first time, on the journey from Paris, I crossed the German Rhine with its legendary associations, so it seemed a prophetic occurrence, foreboding, that I should see before me the Wartburg, so rich in history and myth.

Later that month Wagner finished a prose draft of the opera called—as it would be for three years—*Der Venusberg*. By April 1843 the text was complete, and two years later the score was complete. The revolutionary importance of *Tannhäuser* is indicated by the fact that twice more, in 1847 and in 1861, Wagner revised the opera. These two revisions are startling evidence of the polarities within *Tannhäuser*, since in 1847 Wagner emphasized the medieval Christian element and in 1861 the pagan Venusberg.

These revisions aimed to make the opera a *Gesamtkunstwerk*, a "total work of art." In his 1849 essay "On the Performance of *Tannhäuser*," calling the opera a "dramatic composition," Wagner declared, "Its only chance of making its effect lies purely in that cohesion between the dramatic action and the music." In the 1845 version of Act III there was no re appearance of Venus and no bier of Elisabeth, but in 1847 Wagner added both. For Paris in 1861 Wagner composed the Venusberg bacchanal, which reflected the intervening composition of *Die Walküre* and *Tristan und Isolde*. Wagner's changes in the first scene—a more impassioned Venus, with an extended conflict between her and Tannhäuser—suggest he was balancing the effect of the Christian element in the 1847 revisions of the final scene.

This polarization within *Tannhäuser* originates in Wagner's literary sources, an opposition apparent in the complete title of the opera, *Tannhäuser und der Sängerkrieg auf Wartburg* (Tannhäuser and the Song Contest of the Wartburg). Wagner had to link two distinct legends, one pagan about Venus and Tannhäuser, the other Christian about the Song Contest. Wagner first encountered the legends in his uncle's library, where he read Ludwig Tieck's "The Faithful Eckart and the Tannenhäuser" (1799) and E.T.A. Hoffmann's "The Contest of the Singers," from *The Serapion Brothers* (1819). During his last month in Paris, 1842, Wagner found new references in the *Deutsche Sagen* (1816-18) of the brothers Grimm, which included separate tales of Tannhäuser and the Hörselberg and of the *Sängerkrieg*, but with no relation between them. Other sources preserved the distinction, including Josef von Eichendorff's "Marmorbild" (1819) about the Venus palace and Heinrich Heine's poem "Der Tannhäuser—eine Legende" (1836). It was only in Ludwig Bechstein's Stories of *Eisenach and of the Wartburg* (1835) that Wagner may have found a linking reference to Tannhäuser being welcomed by the Landgraf of Thuringia at the Wartburg.

The sources concerning only Tannhäuser are key documents of nineteenth-century German romantic consciousness. In Tieck's story, Friedrich von Wolfsburg encounters his long-lost friend, here named Tannenhäuser, who tells him he murdered his beloved Emma's fiancé. Ignoring the warning of Eckart, who guarded the Venusberg, he stayed there for an unknown number of years. Friedrich, however, tells Tannenhäuser his story is a delusion, since he himself married Emma. When Tannenhäuser fails to gain absolution from the pope, he returns and murders Emma. Having been kissed in his sleep by Tannenhäuser, Friedrich goes mad and is lost in the Venusberg. Tieck's Tannenhäuser is in fact a deranged demon, as he tells Friedrich: "Believe me, Wolfsburg, many a man has, at his birth, an Evil Spirit linked to him, that vexes him through life, and never lets him rest, till he has reached his black destination. So has it been with me; my whole existence has been but a continuing birth pain, and my awakening will be in Hell."

Tieck's tale contains no dialogue between the poet and Venus, which constitutes the first part of Heine's "Der Tannhäuser." In its second section, Tannhäuser and Pope Urban converse, with the pope telling him nothing can save him from "the devil called Venus." Beyond the help of the church, Tannhäuser in Heine is self-condemned and unredeemable, possessed by an *amour fatale*. As a force in the Young German movement, Heine elevated Hellenic delight in sensual love over the ascetic Nazarene school of Christianity, an idea appearing in Wagner's second opera, *Das Liebesverbot*, also of 1836. In fact Wagner had found in Heine the plot of another self-obsessed hero, the Flying Dutchman.

The Young German movement would instinctively revere the historical Tannhäuser as a model. Born around 1205 in either Bavaria or Salzburg, the younger son of a minor noble family, he became a minnesinger—one of a group of lyric poets flourishing from about 1170 who praised chivalrous love in forms like the winter or spring song, the *Tagelied* or dawn song and the *Wechsel* or dialogue between a lover and his lady. An adherent of Friedrich II of Austria, Tannhäuser participated in the Crusade of 1228 and probably the Cyprian War of 1231, after which he wandered through Europe, establishing contact with the French *amour courtois*. Sixteen poems by the historical Tannhäuser have survived, seven *Leich* (songs with irregular lines), six minnesongs (including two spring songs and two winter songs) and three *Spruch* cycles (usually monostrophic). One encounter he recalls:

> There was no court society
> in the blooming clover there but we.
> She did as I thought good
> and what a lady should . . .
> I caused her very pleasant pain.
> I'd like to do it all again . . .
> The memory will never fade
> of us two lovers in the glade.

With the death of his patron Friedrich in 1246, Tannhäuser roamed a poor minstrel. "Choice food of a morning, pretty women and good wine/ and taking baths two times a week, all make my wealth depart," he wrote. Though he died around 1266, the stories about him did not: Hermann von Sachsenheim in his verse novel *Der Mörin* (1453) recounted the presence of Tannhäuser at the Venusberg, an association recurring in Sebastian Brant's *Hoffgesindt Veneris* (1517). The Mastersingers of the sixteenth century so admired Tannhäuser that they named a distinct *Ton* after him.

The source of these accounts is ballad, the *Tannhäuserlied*, well known during the fifteenth century but not printed until 1515 in Nuremberg. In the *Evagatorium* (1483) the Franciscan monk Felix Faber alludes to this poem:

> There is told a song about him, which is openly sung by the people throughout Germany, about a certain noble Swabian, whom they call Danhuser, from the Danhusen villa near Dünckelspüchel. They represent him at the time as having lived with Venus on the mountain and, led by penitence, he confessed himself to the pope. Denied absolution, he returned into the mountain and has never reappeared. He is living in lust, as they say, until the day of Judgment.

References in the *Tannhäuserlied* to Urban IV, pope from 1261 to 1264, plus the poet's known adherence to the Hohenstaufen party and its antipapal element, date the work around 1270, only a few years after the death of Tannhäuser. Composed of twenty-six four-line stanzas, half the poem presents Tannhäuser's dialogue with Venus, requesting his freedom three times, as in Wagner's Act I. This is followed by sixteen lines of dialogue between the poet and the pope, who against all doctrine denies him absolution. Tannhäuser leaves Rome:

> He went forth from the city's gate in grief and sick at heart.
> "Maria, mother, Holy Maid, from you I now must part."
> He journeyed to the mountain then to stay eternally.
> "I'll go to see my lady sweet where God would have me be.

In the poem, no one intervenes to prevent Tannhäuser from returning to the Venusberg, and it is he who addresses the Virgin—not Elisabeth, who in the opera prays for her lover. There is a suggestion that Tannhäuser is predestined to return to the Venusberg, an idea used by Tieck. The strangest element of the *Tannhäuserlied* is its final stanza:

> But he was in the mountain there
> with Venus as before,
> and so the Pope, Urban the Fourth,
> was lost forevermore.

After the staff blooms, it appears it is not Tannhäuser who is condemned but the pope, because of his intolerance.

Prominent among elements of the *Tannhäuserlied* are two important motifs. The first, the supernatural sojourn, has a legendary history as far back as the exploits of Ulysses with Calypso and Circe in the *Odyssey*; the tale of King Numa and the goddess Egeria; the Celtic legend of Morgan le Fay; the story of Arthur in Avalon with Argante; and the account of Thomas the Rhymer's stay with the Queen of Elfland. The other motif, the blossoming staff, arises from the designation of the Virgin as "the flowering rod of Aaron," symbolizing forgiveness, also from *acta sanctorum* or saints' lives (especially St. Joseph and St. Christopher) and from stories such as those of Tristram and Iseult.

The presence of the sojourn and the staff suggest that much of the story existed before being connected with Tannhäuser. Tannhäuser's name, literally "forest dweller," might have led him to be associated with the Mountain of Venus. After its printing in 1515, the account in *Tannhäuserlied* was widely circulated. Hans Sachs made Tannhäuser the subject of his "Das Hoffgesindt Veneris" in 1517.

The contrasting element of *Tannhäuser*, the song contest at the Wartburg, arises from a probably historical encounter in 1208 during the reign of Landgraf Hermann of Thuringia (1190-1217). The *Wartburgkrieg* or *Der Sängerkrieg auf Wartburg*, the account of this contest, is an anonymous fragmentary dramatic poem composed between 1233 and 1287. The six participants include all Wagner's poets except one: in place of Tannhäuser, Heinrich von Ofterdingen appears in all the chronicles. The subject of this contest was not the essence of love, as in the opera, but the virtues of princes. Coming from Austria, Ofterdingen praised Duke Freidrich II of Austria over Landgraf Hermann, for which he was sentenced to death. He was saved only by Landgräfin Sophie, who covered him with her cloak.

Reading the *Sängerkrieg* was crucial not only to *Tannhäuser* but to subsequent Wagner operas. Wagner's irritation at the poetic style of such works led him to compose *Die Meistersinger* as a critique of the stagnation of German verse. Further, it was this poem that led Wagner to explore the Lohengrin legend.

In the nineteenth century, several key accounts of the song contest appeared. Wagner may have known Friedrich de Ia Motte-Fouqué's "Der Sängerkrieg auf der Wartburg" (1828), and it was the novel *Heinrich von Ofterdingen* (1802) by Novalis that renewed interest in German medievalism. Wagner knew *Legends and Legendary Cycles of Thuringia* (1835-37), containing stories of Tannhäuser and St. Elisabeth as well as a reference linking Tannhäuser to the Wartburg. In his monograph *The Contest of the Wartburg* (1838), the scholar C.T.L. Lucas identified Tannhäuser with the renegade Ofterdingen. While there is no proof for such an association, it was momentous for Wagner. In the opera, both Wolfram and Walther address Tannhäuser as "Heinrich."

One of Wagner's most important nineteenth-century sources was E.T.A. Hoffmann's story "The Contest of the Singers" (1819). From this Wagner was able to develop Act II, aspects of Elisabeth's character and details of the second scene of Act I.

For the middle-aged Sophie of the *Sängerkrieg* Hoffmann substituted a young and beautiful widow, Mathilde von Falkenstein, loved by both Wolfram and Heinrich, who in Hoffmann as in Wagner are close friends. For Act II, Wagner derives Elisabeth's character from Mathilde in Hoffmann;

for Act III, to develop her saintly function, he goes to the historical model of St. Elisabeth of Hungary (1207-31), Landgraf Hermann's daughter-in-law, who had married his son Ludwig IV. Wagner's Elisabeth therefore derives her rescue function from the *Sängerkrieg*, her amorous role from Hoffmann, and her saintly nature from history.

Elisabeth must be seen as part of the crucial tension of pagan with Christian in *Tannhäuser*. The two scenes of Act I oppose the ethics of the Hörselberg to those of the Christian Wartburg. This opposition is fully realized in Act II with the appearance of Elisabeth, whose Nazarene pure love is contrasted with the Young German Hellenism of the worship of Venus, the classical conflict between *eros pan demos* (profane love) and *eros uranos* (heavenly love). Patterned after the Greek myth of Alcestis, who died to release her husband from death, Elisabeth is one of many women in the Wagner canon, including Senta, Isolde, and Brünnhilde, who redeem through love. The appearance of both Venus and the bier of Elisabeth in the final scene of Act III shows the irresolution of this opposition in *Tannhäuser*, which rests on the definition of "Love."

In Act II the Christian chastity of Wolfram's "Blick ich umher" competes with the pagan sensuality of Tannhäuser's "Dir, Göttin der Liebe." In Act II, Wagner again draws on history, for behind the minnesingers of German medievalism was the French *amour courtois*, known to Tannhäuser. Courtly love achieved its apex during the life of Marie de Champagne (1145-98), daughter of Eleanor of Aquitaine, and was codified in *The Art of Courtly Love* by her chaplain André in 1174. Courtly love was adulterous, because marrying for love was rare and, in the days of complex alliances, nearly impossible. One of its maxims was "Marriage is no real excuse for not loving." In the eyes of its adherents, courtly love was ennobling, since its fidelity originated in personal integrity rather than social or religious coercion. In the eyes of the Church, however, courtly love was unquestionably sinful. Wagner's own relationships with women made the conflict a vivid one for him.

In the medieval world, *l'amour courtois* was the first great individualistic opposition to ecclesiastical authority, leading to the Renaissance. In *Opera and Drama*, Wagner recognized this transition: "Searching the history of the world, since the decay of Grecian art, for an artistic period of which we may justly feel proud, we find that period in the so-called Renaissance, a name we give to the termination of the Middle Ages and the commencement of a new era. Here the inner man is struggling, with a giant's force, to utter himself."

Rejecting the dogmatism of the Middle Ages and striving for the liberation of the Renaissance, Tannhäuser stands between two worlds. His apostasy in turning to Hellenism, his espousal of love by individual inclination and his use of song for secular purposes enforce the transitional nature of his position. The Rome narrative "Inbrunst im Herzen" expresses the anguish of two existential conceptions, the social and the individual, mirrored in the juxtaposition of the music of Venus with that of Elisabeth.

Tannhäuser is also one of the greatest nineteenth-century romantic rebels, in revolt against artistic as well as religious authority. Tannhäuser's frustration with outmoded artistic attitudes mirrors Wagner's own antagonism to the opera of his day (embodied in Meyerbeer), the "artist of the future" battling an uncomprehending academy. Wagner hoped *Tannhäuser* "would be capable of winning me the hearts of my German fellow countrymen," but *Die Meistersinger* presented the besieged artist again in Walther von Stolzing.

The disturbed nature of *Tannhäuser* concerned Wagner all his life. Cosima noted in her diary, October 19, 1881, "As far as *Lohengrin* is concerned, R. says he is completely satisfied with it, but in *Tannhäuser* he would criticize some still-remaining traces of operatic tradition." A year later, Cosima recorded another sign of doubt: "R. says he would like to stage *Tannhäuser*, which he regards as a consummate drama, but then again not, since he feels that musically some things are insufficiently expressed."

In his essay "Richard Wagner and *Tannhäuser* in Paris," Baudelaire observed, Tannhäuser represents the struggle between two principles that have chosen the human heart as their battleground: the flesh and the spirit, hell and heaven, Satan and God." The conflict between the Venusberg and the Wartburg, the Renaissance and the medieval, for Wagner comprised a revolutionary transitional moment.

Wagner in *Tannhäuser* is in fact his own emerging Renaissance man, "struggling to utter himself." It is as inevitable as it is final that Wagner's last written words before his death were "Love—Tragedy."

Snows of Yesteryear:
Massenet and *Thäis*

In medieval Paris a rogue poet, clutching his shivering body with numb fingers, nevertheless kindled poetic fire when he invoked the names of "Ladies of Time Lost":

Tell me, in what country
Is Flora, the lovely Roman?
Where is Hipparchia, where is Thaïs,
One as beautiful as the other?
Echo singing along river and stream,
She whose beauty was more than human?
But—where are the snows of yesteryear?

Centuries later, those names produce shivers still, not from cold but from fervor. Speaking for generations, Francois Villon blazed at the name of Thaïs.

He was not alone. Jules Massenet's *Thaïs* represented the apex of an age-long interest in this legendary lady, from ancient Greece to the film with Mary Garden in 1918. Anatole France's *Thaïs*, which had appeared in 1889, inspired the librettist Louis Gallet to exhort Massenet to compose his opera: Villon's fire was burning yet.

Two courtesans, one Greek and one Egyptian, shared the famous name Thaïs. The Greek Thaïs, accompanying Alexander the Great to Asia in 331 B.C., drove him to burn Persepolis. In John Dryden's *Alexander's Feast* (1697), this action prompted comparison with the beauteous Helen, who literally and figuratively burned the city of Troy:

> Thaïs led the way
> To light him to his prey,
> And, like another Helen, fir'd another Troy.

Two references in Roman literature enhanced her fame: Thaïs became the prototypical harlot in Terence's comedy *The Eunuch* (161 B.C.), clever, conspiring, tolerant; the poet Martial, in the first century A.D., devoted a stinging epigram to her looks, ruined by her profession. The Egyptian Thaïs, appearing in a Syriac text from the seventh century, became famous around 970 A.D. when a Benedictine nun, Hrosvitha, recounted the conversion of Thaïs by Paphnutius in a "miracle" play. In 1839, Charles Magnin translated her plays, and Anatole France saw marionette performances of them in 1888 while he was working on *Thaïs*.

In fact, Anatole France had been preoccupied with Thaïs even earlier. In 1867 he wrote a poem, "La Legende de Sainte Thaïs," about Thaïs and Paphnutius. (Only in the libretto by Gallet did Paphnutius become "Athanaël.") The editor of the *Revue des Deux Mondes*, where the novel appeared in three installments during 1889, changed the title from *Paphnuce* to *Thaïs*. While Anatole France had enjoyed previous popularity with *The Crime of Sylvester Bonnard* in 1881, *Thaïs* created a sensation: its "immorality" and its overwhelming irony devastated *fin de-siècle* Paris.

Both the novel and the opera *Thaïs* must be seen in the context of two problems disturbing nineteenth-century France, the great concern for courtesans and the loss of faith resulting from Darwinism. In the French novel, a long tradition, going back to Prévost's *Manon Lescaut* (1731), concerned the courtesan or prostitute. In the nineteenth century, however, it became an obsession. Constant's *Adolphe*, Balzac's *Splendors* and *Miseries of Courtesans*, Musset's *Confessions of a Child of the Century*, Mürger's *Vie de Bohème*, Dumas' *Camille*, Daudet's *Sapho* and Zola's *Nana* remain famous: the courtesan was a symptom of nineteenth-century *mal du siècle*, which Massenet himself was to explore in *Manon* (1884) and *Sapho* (1897), based on two of these novels. Simultaneously, religious discord becomes mirrored in art, particularly in opera, such as Meyerbeer's *Prophète*, Halévy's *Juive*, Gounod's *Faust* and above all Wagner's *Tannhäuser*, *Lohengrin* and *Parsifal*.

Wagner's work is especially concerned with the conflict of paganism with Christianity which figures so pervasively in *Thaïs*. Anatole France's novel and Massenet's opera represent the merging of the themes of the harlot and of religious skepticism.

E. M. Forster regarded Anatole France's *Thaïs* as a model of novelistic form, conceived as the Greek letter chi, X, with one character ascending morally, the other precipitously declining. The transformation of the courtesan into the saintly nun indeed suggests Massenet's 1873 oratorio *Marie-Magdeleine*, for which Gallet had written the text. The novel *Thaïs*, set in the fourth century A.D., is divided into three parts, which roughly correspond to the divisions Gallet and Massenet retained in the opera. From the very opening paragraphs, extreme skepticism is evident: for instance, of the monks in the Thebaid desert it is said, "The odor of their virtues rose up to heaven" or that "their benevolence was sometimes terrible." These irons are only the beginning.

Massenet and Gallet followed the first part of the novel closely, reproducing these ironies by several devices. One of the most important is Massenet's constant use of broken rhythm. In the first scene, for example, one moves from the steadiness of the Cenobites' chanting to the disturbance of Athanaël's entrance to the seductiveness of his vision of Thaïs dancing in the theater of Alexandria, presented in such a musical idiom as to be quite alive despite all his masochistic asceticism. What was his real motive for revisiting Alexandria? This ignorance of himself becomes his downfall. In the libretto, Gallet retained some of France's choicest ironies, especially the fact that Nicias calls Athanaël his "condisciple" when they meet in the debauched city. Unlike the first part of the novel, where Athanaël (Paphnutius) sees Thaïs only in visions and in the theater, in the opera he meets Thaïs in its first act. Her query at the conclusion of Act I, "What wretched folly drives you to avoid your destiny?" is weighted with the irony of Anatole France. Athanaël's reply, "I shall defeat hell by triumphing over you," is fraught with disaster: is he really saving her, or only using her to try to save himself?

Though Act II of Massenet's opera corresponds with part two of the novel, much of Thaïs' prior history is eliminated by Gallet. As a young girl, Thaïs, daughter of innkeepers, is encouraged to become a Christian. Her "faith," however, is much enforced by the erotic language used to describe religious experience: "But Jesus in heaven will count her among his brides." Unfortunately a procuress, Moeroë, entices Thaïs, despite her baptism, into prostitution and debauchery. Gallet makes no reference to this childhood baptism, which in the novel supplies a credible basis for Thaïs' conversion at the end. The libretto, moreover, deemphasizes the extremely erotic language Athanaël uses in the novel upon meeting this courtesan, a clear suggestion that his supposed "spiritual" motivation is delusory: "I love you, Thaïs! I love you more than my life and more than myself. I have left my precious desert for you, and with my lips, sworn to silence, I have spoken profane words for you." Such sacred love proves to be the most profane. In fact, in the novel the famous mirror episode takes place before Thaïs meets Athanaël, indicating he is not the cause but at best the catalyst of her conversion.

The famous Méditation is substituted for an extremely important episode in the novel, a philosophic symposium or banquet, during which most of the major ideologies of the world are belittled: political allegiance, Christianity, Stoicism are shown to be obsessional lies, false explanations for an inexplicable world. Nicias, who most represents Anatole France's own ideas, observes, "I simply do not see a great difference between the all and the void." At the conclusion of the banquet, the material used in Act II, Scene 2, of the opera commences: Thaïs' house is torched while Nicias, by scattering gold, prevents the enraged crowd from killing Athanaël. (Here Massenet and France recall the Greek myth of prostitution, Zeus visiting Danae in a shower of gold.) The libretto omits one of the most ironic comments on Thaïs' departure, Nicias' final remark, "Pluto ravished Proserpina, and Thaïs has chosen to follow my uncivilized friend out into the desert." Here the morbidity of Athanaël's quest, its life-denying impulse and its sexual connotation are summarized. The second part of the novel concludes with what became the oasis episode, added after the premiere of the opera (Act III, Scene 1), with the duet "Baigne d'eau mes mains et mes lèvres."

Gallet made his greatest cuts in the third part of the novel, which details the horrifying torments suffered by the monk in his attempt to forget Thaïs, his nightmarish visions of jackals and his decision to plant himself on a phallic column in the desert to avoid temptation. Though Gallet condensed these to the second scene of the third act, the death of Thaïs is completely faithful to the novel. The Cenobite monk is now tortured: "I was a fool not to possess Thaïs while there was still time! . . . God and heaven, all are nothing." In the end, Athanaël "had become so hideous that, passing his hand over his face, he could feel its ugliness."

Anatole France's tale is a *roman à thèse*, a novel of ideas, whose complexity is produced by its devastating irony. Indeed, one of the earliest interpreters of Athanaël, Maurice Renaud, achieved his famed characterization by study of the novel. During the banquet symposium, Callicrates the poet speaks not only of Alexandria but of nineteenth-century Europe when he declares, "I blush to be living in a time without glory." This idea is explained by Hermodorus, the priest of Serapis: "We recognize the positive signs of a world nearly fallen into ignorance and barbarism. We have been chosen to watch civilization in its death throes."

In the opera this mood is suggested by Thaïs' early words to Nicias: "I am Thaïs the frail idol, come to sit for the last time at your flower-bedecked table." She tells him, "But for tonight, be merry. Let the blessed hours pass in bloom, and let us ask from this night nothing more than a little intoxication and divine forgetfulness (*divin oubli*)." Much of this sounds like Fitzgerald's translation of the *Rubaiyat*, even like the longing for oblivion in Wagner's *Tristan und Isolde*. *Thaïs* is the swan song of a dying age, a dead faith and lost illusions. The debacle of the Franco-Prussian War thus remained debilitating a generation later. As if to add to this despair, the confluence of Darwin's *Origin of Species* with Ludwig Feuerbach's *Essence of Christianity*, which stated Christ was not divine, produced a traumatic loss of religious belief in Massenet's era. Twenty years later, this age was destroyed in the fires of World War I.

The nineteenth-century interest in the courtesan finds its summation in another revolution, that caused by Freudian psychology. In 1910 Freud investigated what he called "love for a prostitute," of which the relationship of Thaïs, Athanaël and Nicias constitutes an astounding dossier. In this attraction to a prostitute, Freud distinguished four necessities—that the woman be attached, that she be of questionable virtue, that she be valued, and that she seem "redeemable." Each of these four conditions produces a reaction—rivalry, jealousy, compulsion and "rescue"—each of which finds ample illustration in Massenet's opera. Nicias ensures the first condition, Thaïs' past the second, Athanaël's dreams the third, his longing to save Thaïs the fourth. In analyzing "debasement in love," in fact, Freud concluded that Christian asceticism actually made the psychical value of such a love all the greater. It is no exaggeration to say that the legend of Thaïs is the key to Freud's theory.

Massenet's achievement rests in the fact that the libretto and the music of *Thaïs* retain many of these significances. Gallet, who had previously supplied texts for *Marie-Magdeleine* (1873), *Eve* (1875), *Le Roi de Lahore* (1877) and *Le Cid* (1885) , devised a *poésie mélique*, a system of free verse that transcends prose by its correspondences of sounds. The influence of Anatole France's sensuous, insinuating style is obvious if one compares the mirror passages from the novel and from the libretto, which share many of the same sonorities. In addition, Gallet's use of the dash is a great ironic device, for the dash is the most ambiguous of punctuation marks, showing a connection without defining it, exactly corresponding to the tone of the novel.

Was Thaïs ever in need of rescue? Was her faith a greater delusion than her prostitution, especially considering her adviser? Was Athanaël following the dictates of severe psychic disorder rather than religious conviction? The name Athanaël, which Gallet devised, derives from Athanasius, an early Bishop of Alexandria, and from Nathaniel, the guileless disciple. Gallet went so far as to include the fig tree under which Jesus first saw Nathaniel as the scene of the death of Thaïs. The irony remains: the fig tree, by which Adam and Eve covered themselves, in medieval thinking became a symbol of lust.

This ironic uncertainty and despair Massenet reflected by one of his musical signatures, broken rhythm, and by a constant juxtaposition of conflicting musical styles, producing a sensuous tension that remains his alone, the very reflection of Anatole France's questioning frame of mind. Within a scene, or between scenes, Massenet undercuts one mood by an orchestral interlude completely at variance with it. In the first scene, for example, the Cenobites depart to rest ("Prions que les noirs démons de l'abîme") with a calm chant, rapidly succeeded by the harps accompanying Athanaël's vision of Thaïs' lascivious dances, succeeded by the stern tones of his desire to rescue her ("J'ai compris l'enseignement de l'ombre"). In the second scene, Athanaël's virile denunciation of Alexandria leads to the seductive ministrations of Crobyle and Myrtale.

Such is the nature of the Méditation between the two scenes of Act II or the equally stunning interlude between the second and third scenes of the final act. Here the storm outside, signifying the tempest of Athanaël's mind, gradually transforms into the Méditation, which leads to the prayers of Albine and her nuns at the deathbed of Thaïs. Nowhere is the juxtaposition of sacred and profane love more perfectly reflected. By rhythm and by flexible phrasing, Massenet found the equivalent of Gallet's *poésie mélique* and Anatole France's tense ironies.

The transformation of novel into opera reveals the extraordinary flexibility of Massenet's musical idiom, capable of revealing the Middle Eastern influence of *Hérodiade*, the heroism of *Le Cid*, the sentiment of *Manon*, the exoticism of *Esclarmonde*, the pathos of *Werthe*r. Anatole France himself, though irritated with Gallet for the cuts he made, wrote to Massenet, "I am happy and proud to have supplied you with the theme on which you have developed phrases of the highest inspiration." More than in any other opera, Villon's dead ladies survived the snows of yesteryear in a vision whose beauty is more than human—*Thaïs*.

Eternity's Exile:
Wagner and *The Flying Dutchman*

In *A Communication to My Friends* (1851), Richard Wagner emphasized the elemental nature of the figure that was to be for him both personal paradigm and universal archetype:

> The figure of the Flying Dutchman is a mythical creation of the People: a primal trait of human nature speaks out from it with heart-enthralling force. This trait, in its most universal meaning, is the longing after rest from amid the storms of life. In the blithe world of Greece we meet with it in the wanderings of Ulysses and his longing for home, house, hearth and wife . . . The Christian, without a home on earth, embodied this trait in the figure of the Wandering Jew: for that wanderer, forever doomed to a long-since outlived life . . . Death was the sole remaining goal of all his strivings; his only hope, the laying down of being.

Each of these three outcasts has offended superpowers—the Dutchman by swearing a rash oath at the Cape of Good Hope, for which he was punished by the devil; Ulysses for desecrating the sacred shrines at Troy; the Wandering Jew (Ahasuerus) condemned to exile until the Second Coming for spurning Christ on his way to crucifixion. When *Der Fliegende Holländer* had its premiere on January 2, 1843, in Dresden, it encapsulated the most powerful of romantic characters, the hero as outcast. Examples appear in Goethe's Werther, Byron's Harold and Manfred, and in Hugo's Hernani. Most particularly it recalled Coleridge's *Rime of the Ancyent*

Marinere (1798), where motifs of exile, ocean and expiation coalesce.

Wagner's interpretation, however, transcends specific prototypes to assume the status of a new ideology, that of the alien redeemed through sacrificial love, the essence of his belief after 1843:

> The Dutchman . . . may gain this redemption . . . at the hands of—a *woman* who, of very love, shall sacrifice herself for him. The yearning for death thus spurs him on to seek this Woman . . . the quintessence of womankind; and yet the still unmanifest, the longed-for, the dreamed-of, the infinitely womanly Woman—let me express it in one phrase: *the woman of the future.*

Senta's sacrifice is the originating model of Elisabeth in *Tannhäuser*, Isolde in *Tristan und Isolde* and Brünnhilde in the *Ring*, whose failed opposites are Elsa in *Lohengrin* and Kundry in *Parsifal*. The Dutchman's weltschmerz, an incurable dissatisfaction with this world, finds its paradoxical antidote in a redemptive love whose essence is self-destruction.

Wagner was aware that his opera recorded his own personal turmoil as well as the true beginning of his professional life:

> This was that Flying Dutchman who arose so often from the swamps and billows of my life and drew me to him with such resistless might . . . From here begins my career as a *poet,* and my farewell to the mere concocter of opera texts . . . I was driven to strike out for myself as an artist, a path as yet not pointed me by any outward experience.

Wagner here is reborn as the nineteenth century's greatest mythmaker, as he reconfigures preceding archetypes to create a new mythic identity. He transforms exile into exaltation.

In his *Autobiographical Sketch* (1842) Wagner asserted that the sailors aboard the *Thetis*, on which he sailed to London, had "recounted" the story of the Flying Dutchman to him: "The Flying Dutchman, whose intimate acquaintance I had made at sea, occupied my imagination constantly." He then adds: "In addition, I came across H. [Heinrich] Heine's remarkable version of this legend in one part of his *Salon.*" Wagner completed the prose sketch of the tale during the spring of 1840, writing the libretto in May 1841 at Meudon, near Paris. He completed the orchestration in autumn 1841,but the work did not receive its premiere until 1843, in a three-act format—not the one-act opera he originally had envisioned.

Wagner's immediate source was Heine's *Memoirs of Herr von Schnabelewopski*, written in 1831 and published in the *Salon* in 1834. The narrator records his attendance at a play in Amsterdam based on the legend of the Dutchman. Heine records the tale of "the captain, a Holländer, who once swore by all the devils that he would get around a certain mountain . . . though he should sail till the Day of Judgment. The devil took him at his word, therefore he must sail forever, until set free by a woman's truth." Heine reports the drama as being set in Scotland, where the Dutchman encounters a nobleman whose home has a portrait of the Dutchman, at which the daughter, Katherine, "often looks with strange sorrow."

Although the Dutchman/bridegroom initially pretends to repudiate the legend, Katherine grasps that the man in the portrait and her bridegroom are the same. Heine continues: "The bride regards him with deep earnestness, casting glances meanwhile at the portrait. It seems as if she has penetrated his secret; and when he asks: 'Katherine, wilt thou be true to me?' she answers: 'True till death.' " Attracted by a woman's laugh, Heine's narrator leaves to make love to her, returning for the final scene, which is close to the finale of Wagner's opera:

> When I reentered the theater, I came in time to see the last scene of the play, where the wife of the Flying Dutchman on a high cliff wrings her hands in despair while her unhappy husband is seen on the deck of his unearthly ship, tossing on the waves. He loves her and will leave her, lest she be lost with him, and he tells her all his dreadful destiny, and the cruel curse which hangs above his head. But she cries aloud, "I was ever true to thee, and I know how lo be ever true unto death!" Saying this, she throws herself into the waves. The Flying Dutchman is saved, and we see the ghostly ship slowly sink into the sea.

In the *Memoirs* Heine contrasts the story of Katherine's fidelity with the narrator's dalliance with a "Dutch blonde" in the theater gallery, undercutting the legendary fidelity of the tale with an account of contemporary infidelity. Heine concludes this part by noting, "The moral of the story is that women should never marry a Flying Dutchman, while we men may learn from it that one can, through women, go down and perish—under favorable circumstances!" This "moral" accords with the narrator's skepticism and mockery.

Wagner seized on Heine's crucial innovation in the tale—that a woman's love and fidelity may be redemptive—and forged his own version. For the composer, Heine is the radical artistic innovator he would wish himself to be, and the Dutchman—alienated but daring—embodies the aggressive if doomed self-assertion cherished by the romantics.

A key letter from 1837 indicates that Heine, like Wagner, identified with this estranged dimension:

> Alas, I have lived for a long while in strange lands, and it often seems to me that in my fabulous homesickness I am like the Flying Dutchman and his shipmates, who are constantly tossed on the cold waves . . . I trust . . . the Flying Dutchman's fate will not be mine: to wit, his letters were usually addressed to persons at home who had died long since! Alas, how many loved ones have gone, while my ship of life was being driven here and there by the worst storms.

Heine's identification with the Dutchman here evokes two English sources of the legend. In May 1821, the tale "Vanderdecken's Message Home; or, The Tenacity of Natural Affection" was published anonymously in *Blackwood's Magazine*. It recounts how sailors from Vanderdecken's crew try to leave letters on a British ship. These sailors resist taking the letters, reputed to sink any vessel that accepts them. The Dutch sailors leave them on the deck, but a wind blast hurls them out to sea, and the British eventually make safe passage home. The British captain at first treats the account of the Dutchman, discussed by his sailors, as a joke, until he is advised by the chaplain to be more cautious.

The *Blackwood's* story contains the key elements of the legend in an especially detailed account of the curse. The Dutch sailors are quoted longing for Amsterdam in the very language used in Heine's letter, which makes it almost a certainty he knew the *Blackwood's* version. "Vanderdecken's Message Home" contains no mention of redemption through a woman's fidelity, which is Heine's innovation; but this version certainly was known to the author of the other English source, Edward Fitzball's *The Flying Dutchman; or, The Phantom Ship: a Nautical Drama* of 1827.

It is possible that the play recorded in Heine's text is in fact Fitzball's drama. There can be no doubt, however, that Fitzball knew the *Blackwood's* account, since the sailor Tom Willis in the latter reappears as a character in the 1827 play. Fitzball's drama is a variant of the extremely popular nautical melodramas that appeared on the British stage in the early part of the nineteenth century, distant ancestors of Gilbert and Sullivan's *H.M.S. Pinafore* (1878) and *The Pirates of Penzance* (1880).

In Fitzball's drama, Vanderdecken is held in subjection by the submarine sorceress Rockalda. Every 100 years, Vanderdecken is commanded by Rockalda, "Go seek a bride to share thy stormy fate." Vanderdecken is famous in the history of melodrama for being a miming part, since Rockalda enjoins him to remain silent when on earth. The heroine, Lestelle Vanhelm, is betrothed by her guardian, Captain Peppercoal, against her will to Peter von Bummell, even though she loves William Mowdrey. Lestelle and her saucy maid, Lucy, discuss the Dutchman, and the drama abounds in paintings—of his ship, of Vanderdecken himself, even of Lestelle as a shepherdess. Like Wagner's Senta, Lestelle sings a song, taught to her by her mother, including the lines "I'll hold thee fast to my virgin heart,/And my bosom shall pillow thy head."

At the end of Act II, Vanderdecken abducts Lestelle as the sailors on the phantom ship sing an "Invisible Chorus." In the final scene, Vanderdecken and Mowdrey have a duel, during which Vanderdecken speaks, which forces him to return to the deep:

> I have spoken! The spell which admits my stay on earth is destroyed with my silence. I must be gone to the phantom ship again . . . Malediction! malediction! You triumph. But I go to my revenge. Tremble, tremble! The rushing waves which rise to welcome the return of Vanderdecken shall bury ye deep, deep in their unfathomed darkness. Burst, stormy clouds, and overwhelm them!

Just before being engulfed, Mowdrey and Lestelle are saved by his clever servant, who sails a cutter to his rescue, after which British flags are unfurled. Such scenes in post-Napoleonic Britain roused the audience to patriotic frenzy.

In Fitzball, the Dutchman never finds release. Fitzball's drama, however, does deploy characters serving the same function as in Wagner. Peppercoal suggests Daland; Lestelle, Senta; Von Bummell, Erik; Vanderdecken and Mowdrey combine to become Wagner's Dutchman.

Since Fitzball was at the height of his fame in the 1820s and '30s, it is possible that Wagner may have heard of this melodrama when he arrived in London after his own harrowing voyage in 1839. The ghostly chorus, the arrival of the Dutchman's ship ("with crimson fire"), the paintings, the song about the Dutchman and his disappearance "amidst thunder and flames of red fire," the sailors' repeated "Yo! ho!" and the appearance of Vanderdecken rising "from the sea in blue fire" indicate that Wagner's *Holländer* is an amalgam, brilliantly transformed, of standard motifs from nautical melodrama.

To distinguish his opera from melodrama, Wagner left specific notes about the characters. "The actor [of the Dutchman] must never let himself be betrayed into exaggerated stridings to and fro: a certain terrible repose [is] in his outward demeanor." Of Senta, Wagner wrote in 1852-53, "Let not the *dreamy* side of her nature be conceived in the sense of a modem, sickly sentimentality."

The exile Wagner constructs from the Dutchman legend is not merely a man suffering from romantic weltschmerz. This Vanderdecken is not only socially, maritally, sexually and professionally alienated, he is existentially so. Existence itself is inexplicable, contradictory and unknowable. Thus the world of *Der Fliegende Holländer* is a nexus of paradoxes, right from the overture, which aligns the horns (Dutch man-torment) with the woodwinds (Senta redemption). The opera pits seamen (Dutchman, Daland) against hunters (Erik), helmsman's wheel against spinning wheel, materialists referring to gold (Daland, Mary) against non-materialists (Erik, Senta), the spirit world (Dutchman, Senta) against the mundane (Mary, Erik), fidelity (Senta to Dutchman) against infidelity (Senta to Erik), anarchic individualism (Senta, Dutchman) against structured community (Mary, Erik), man (Erik) against woman (Senta), man (Erik) against man (Daland), believer (Senta) against skeptic (Erik), defiance of devil (Dutchman) against defiance of Christ (Wandering Jew), portrait (Dutchman) against actuality (Dutchman), portrait (Dutchman) against ballad (Senta on Dutchman), image against language, storm against tranquility, the exiled against the linked.

The opposition of sea against land means that everyone and everything is on the shore—that is, *on the brink*, decentered. This is the state of Wagner at the period of *Holländer*: "That opera [*Rienzi*] once finished,

I stood entirely outside the territory of my recent past"—that is, *Rienzi* against *Holländer*. This same state of liminality torments the Dutchman, at sea but compelled to land, exiled but coerced to fuse.

In his monologue "Die Frist ist um," the Dutchman recounts one suicidal attempt after another in his quest for death. He is the modern hero, condemned not to death but to life. His only consolation is that he will die at last, by default, on Judgment Day. This attitude was not far from Wagner's thoughts, as this letter of 1835 records:

> My life?!—Almighty God, can there be a more wretched, more miserable life! I am alone here in this town, alone, deserted as if dead: not a soul, not a thing that arouses the tiniest spark of interest in me; everything for me is cold and empty!

Der Fliegende Holländer deconstructs its own redemptive premise. In it, salvation can be attained only by self-destruction. To call it self-sacrifice screens the scenario of suicide essential to its substance. In February 1853, Wagner wrote to Liszt apropos of *Holländer*, "This melancholy hero is never out of my head," adding, "For me there is no salvation but *death*." In their transfiguration at the end, Senta and the Dutchman escape *from*, not *to*. The condition of exile itself persists.

Exotic Seas:
Bizet and *The Pearl Fishers*

"YOU'RE AN IDIOT—HERE IS MY CARD." So runs a famous—perhaps false—anecdote of the challenge the young Georges Bizet issued to a critic who disliked Wagner's music. Fortunately no duel occurred, but the fiery temperament that led Bizet to challenge the mediocrity of French music of his time is at the root of his first great operatic success, *The Pearl Fishers*, which premiered September 30, 1863, at Paris's Theatre-Lyrique. Although famous today for the immortal *Carmen* (1875), Bizet had made his name—and staked his claim at age twenty-four—with his exotic tale of lovers in Ceylon.

Not that Bizet was a neophyte to music. In 1848, aged 10, he had been admitted to the Conservatoire, where the following year he won first prize for solfeggio. At age 19, he won the coveted Prix de Rome, which brought him to Italy, where the lure of the exotic soon became evident. As part of his obligation as a prize-winner, he composed an ode-symphony entitled *Vasco da Gama*, based on the adventures of the Portuguese navigator who had made the first voyage from Europe around Africa to India in 1498; already the region of Ceylon (present-day Sri Lanka) had been confirmed in Bizet's mind as quintessentially exotic.

French opera, particularly during the nineteenth century, was marked by a penchant for remote locales and strange customs, but in fact this tradition goes as far back as Rameau's *Les Indes Galantes* of 1735. In particular, several works by the composer Félicien David were marked by such exoticism, especially his ode-symphony *Le Désert* (1841) and his opera *Lalla-Roukh* (1862), both credited with introducing Oriental melodies into French music. Following Bizet's *Pearl Fishers*, composers as diverse as Meyerbeer with *L'Africaine* (1865), Massenet with *Le Roi de Lahore* (1877) and Delibes with *Lakmé* (1883) raided distant lands to import and exploit strange musical effects on the stage.

Interest in foreign lands, however, was not merely superficial. The nineteenth century was a period of extraordinary French colonial expansion. The protectorate over Annam in 1874, the development of the Congo in 1884, the treaty with China in 1892, the Indochinese Union in 1887, the annexation of the Ivory Coast in 1892 and of Madagascar in 1896, and the establishment of French West Africa in 1895 all reflect French colonial ambitions. It is not strange that the operatic stage reflected these policies, for the diversity of cultures was becoming more manifest by the minute.

The situation of Bizet's *Pearl Fishers*, however, is even more unusual than such events might indicate. The setting for the opera had originally been Mexico rather than Ceylon, and here the opera intersects decisively with French history. The French undertook an expedition to Mexico in 1861, and French troops remained after subjugating part of the country. In July 1863, with French support, a group of exiled Mexicans established an imperial government for the country, offering the throne to Maximilian, the brother of Franz Joseph, Emperor of Austria.

In 1864, Maximilian was proclaimed Emperor of Mexico, after which, with French assistance, he routed the statesman and nationalist Benito Juárez. The French Emperor Napoleon III, however, at the behest of the United States, withdrew his support for Maximilian, who was eventually conquered by Juárez and executed in 1867. There can be no doubt that *The Pearl Fishers* is part of both colonial and musical history, given the year of its premiere. Even so, to exploit the lure of the exotic (and perhaps to camouflage the politics, which were quickly becoming too hot to handle) the locale of the opera was shifted from Mexico to Ceylon.

In 1862, Leon Carvalho, the Director of the Théâtre Lyrique, offered Bizet the libretto of *The Pearl Fishers*, written by Michel Carré and Eugène

Cormon (pseudonym for Pierre-Étienne Piestre). By early 1863, Bizet had completed the score. A letter Bizet wrote to his friend Paul Lacombe illuminates the reason for his attraction to the exotic subject of the opera. "I am an eclectic. I lived in Italy for three years and there adopted . . . the temperament of some of its composers. Furthemore, my sensual nature lets itself be gripped by that music, which is at once facile, lazy, amorous, lascivious, and passionate."

The composer Gounod, who acted as Bizet's mentor, advised him: "Don't pay any attention to any known successes. *Be very much yourself . . .* A first original work is always a *Duel*; a second becomes a *Battle*; a third is a *Victory*, not always apparent, but certainly in reality and in truth. Have faith *in your own emotion*, that it is a success and a *promise.*"

Gounod's advice was necessary, for the tale of a virgin priestess who violates her vows for love had already been created by Spontini in *La Vestale* (1807) and Bellini in *Norma* (1831), with mythical precedent in the legend of Hero and Leander.

Incredibly, the libretto was still not finished a few days before the premiere. When the librettists could not decide on a conclusion. Carvalho is reported to have said: "Throw it in the fire," a desperate suggestion taken literally, as Zurga sets fire on the pearl fishers' camp. Referring to his libretto, Cormon reportedly remarked after the premiere, "If we had realized Bizet's talent we should never have given him that infamous bear." Damned since its premiere, does the libretto deserve this assessment?

In fact, it does not. The libretto is not bad. But it is codified, according to the formula of the piece *bien faite* or "well-made play," standard for the time, which mandated that a drama be structured in five acts. These are clearly evident in *The Pearl Fishers*: 1. Exposition and background (Act I, scenes 1-5); 2. Hero and rival conflict (Act I, scenes 6-8); 3. More reversals, with the hero reaching his *peripeteia* or point of lowest fortune (Act II); 4. The *scène à faire* (obligatory scene), a crisis, with the hero rising above his rival (Act III, part one, when Zurga recognizes the necklace and realizes he must spare Leïla); and 5. Resolution and denouement, with the hero and heroine gaining the upper hand (Act III, part two, with the escape of Nadir and Leïla). This tightness of connection is reinforced by the first and last acts being mirror images of each other, as Act I moves from sunrise to darkness and Act III from night to dawn.

Throughout *The Pearl Fishers*, Bizet deploys a number of strategies to emphasize its exoticism. A variety of instruments preserves this foreign, mysterious aura throughout the opera. Note, for example, the bassoon in Nadir's "Des savanes et des forêts" in Act I; the tambourine accompaniment to the opening chorus of Act II ("L'ombre de cend des cieux"); and particularly the oboe and harp for Nadir's serenade "De mon amie" in the same act with its hallucinatory 12/8 rhythm. This serenade is even more suggestive by being sung off-stage.

Furthermore, throughout the opera, Bizet uses the theme of the tenor/baritone duet from Act I ("Au fond du temple saint") as a leitmotif to link parts of the score for dramatic effect: when Zurga recognizes Leïla at the end of Act II; when Leïla removes the necklace token at the end of part one of Ace III; and of course at the opera's conclusion, where it emphasizes Zurga's sacrifice for his friend and his paid obligation to Leïla, who had once rescued him and whom he now liberates.

Many elements of the tale emphasize its romanticism and exoticism. Leïla's name suggests the Hebrew word *layla* ("night"), particularly appropriate because of her remoteness as a priestess and the constant references to her being veiled; she is woman constructed as mysterious, foreign, elusive and possibly unknowable. The veil also suggests her disturbing sexuality, the focus of conflict for the two men.

The tenor's name, Nadir, evokes another romantic clement, the lowest point, the nadir or depth, of experience, possibly disastrous but always intense, challenging and unnerving. To the romantic sensibility, such immersion in the depths and the loss of self become paradoxically the highest experience and realization of the self. It is no accident that a hero named Nadir sings at the conclusion of the opera that "heaven itself will guide our steps." The lowest point from the rational perspective (note the constant violation of oaths throughout the opera) is the highest from the romantic.

This paradoxical and enigmatic romanticism coalesces in Nadir's serenade "De mon amie" in Act II, where he describes his beloved as like a flower in the depths of a silent lake, where despite the waves he can perceive her eyes. In the second stanza, she is the crystal in the darkened abyss, that is, the light of darkness, the romantic's light *as* darkness, evocative of Leïla's name. Nothing conveys this more convincingly than the alternating major and minor key of this air, reinforced by the harp. As Nadir sings, it is the *pur* (clear) in the *obscur.*" Leïla *is* the pearl, concealed in the depths, veiled in darkness but thereby the light of greatest price.

The Pearl Fishers played for eighteen performances in 1863 and did not reappear until 1886, eleven years after Bizet's death. The critics, while acknowledging the young composer's debt to Gounod, David, Verdi and Meyerbeer, were forced to recognize Bizet's talent. "There were neither fishermen in the libretto nor pearls in the music," recorded Benjamin Jouvin in *Figaro*, but he was compelled to acknowledge the "great assurance in the way Bizet deals with the orchestration and mass vocal effects." To Berlioz, it went beyond being a *succès d'estime*.

In the final critical essay he wrote for the *Journal des Dèbats*, Berlioz wrote of *The Pearl Fishers*: "The score of this opera had a real success . . . It includes a considerable number of beautiful, expressive pieces full of fire and rich coloring. There is no overture but an introduction sung and danced with great verve and spirit . . . The score of *The Pearl Fishers* does M. Bizet the greatest honor, and he will have to be recognized as a composer in spite of his rare talent as pianist."

Bizet's affinity with Berlioz's standards is reflected in an essay Bizet wrote *for La Revue Nationale et Étrangère* in 1867, where he noted: "There are only two kinds of music—good and bad . . . The artist has neither name nor nationality. He is inspired or he is not: he has genius or talent or he has not." Undoubtedly recalling his experience with *The Pearl Fishers*, Bizet added: "Music! What a splendid art, but a dreary profession!"

During the composition of *The Pearl Fishers*, Gounod had advised the young composer: "You regret that the laws do not permit the assassination of certain musicians? But they certainly do permit and the divine laws *order* it . . . Beethoven—there was a grand assassin! Try to be in the camp of the assassins; there is no middle way between that and the camp of the victims." True to his own critical standards, with *The Pearl Fishers* Bizet launched his career as the assassin of mediocre French composers like Halévy and Meyerbeer, as Berlioz recognized. With another exotic weapon, *Carmen*, he was to finish the job.

The German Carmen:
D'Albert and *Tiefland*

The world premiere of Eugen d'Albert's *Tiefland* at the New German Theater in Prague on November 15, 1903, saw the emergence of an opera destined to be famous throughout Europe and above all in Germany. Composed with lightning speed from July 1902 to July 1903, *Tiefland* after its premiere was reworked from a three-act to a two-act version during 1904, which was first staged at Magdebourg in June 1905. The success of the revised version was so great that in October 1907, when the work was presented in Berlin, it had a run of 400 performances.

What were the reasons for this extraordinary triumph? The key to *Tiefland* rests on its synthesis of two elements, both crucial to the nineteenth century: *espagnolisme*, or the vogue for all things Spanish; and *verismo*, or realism, the movement inaugurated in Italy in 1890 with the first performance of Pietro Mascagni's *Cavalleria Rusticana*. With its location in the Pyrenees, *Tiefland*, whose name can be translated as "The Lowlands," brilliantly joined the interest in Spain to the revolutionary operatic movement initiated by Mascagni and advanced by Leoncavallo, Puccini and Giordano.

Behind it all is the great model of Georges Bizet's *Carmen* of 1875. *Tiefland* is before anything else the German *Carmen*.

One of the distinguishing marks of nineteenth-century Europe was the preoccupation with things Spanish, which one might label Hispanism. At the beginning of the century, Spain appeared so exotic and remote that

Alexandre Dumas declared: "Africa begins at the Pyrenees." The involvement of British and French armies in the Peninsular War of 1808-1813, however, was the event that brought Spain to European consciousness. Under Wellington and Napoleon, thousands of soldiers became acquainted with the Iberian peninsula, while their generals plundered Spanish paintings to give the French and British public their first engagement with Spanish artistic achievements.

These events inspired historians and writers throughout the world to begin chronicling this strange country. Washington Irving spent three years in Spain beginning in 1826, the outcome of which was his *History of Christopher Columbus* (1828), his *Chronicle of the Conquest of Granada* (1829) and his immortal *The Alhambra* (1832). In France, Théophile Gautier published his *Voyage en Espagne* in 1845, while the French Romantic dramatist Victor Hugo exploited Spanish exoticism in his dramas *Hernani* (1830) and *Ruy Blas* (1838). George Ticknor's *History of Spanish Literature* (1849) recorded the achievements of Spanish writers for British and American readers.

There was one work, however, which more than any other distilled the essence of Spain for the nineteenth century—Prosper Mérimée's *Carmen* of 1845. Mérimée first journeyed to Spain in 1830, and this experience led to his great short novel, recording the exploits of the gypsy femme fatale Carmen with her lover Don José. Mérimée's text consolidated many motifs relevant to the Spanish obsession: the stark and harsh landscape, the gypsies, the men of the bull fights, the brigands, the passion and the violence, much of which was retained in Bizet's operatic *Carmen*.

Operas set in Spain, however, had prepared the way for *Carmen* and for *Tiefland*. One thinks of Beethoven's *Fidelio* (1805), Rossini's *The Barber Seville* (1816), Donizetti's *La Favorita* (1840), and at least four works by Verdi (*Ernani*, 1844; *Il Trovatore*, 1853; *La Forza del Destino*, 1862; and *Don Carlos*, 1867)—not to mention, last but not lease, Wagner's *Parsifal* of 1882. *Tiefland* echoes many of these works. In its rejection of the tyranny of Sebastiano, the mill-owner/capitalist exploiter of his workers, *Tiefland* evokes *Fidelio*; in its suffering heroine Marta one can trace the Leonoras of *Favorita*, *Trovatore* and *Forza*; and in its shepherd hero Pedro, the innocence and idealism of Wagner's holy fool Parsifal.

These echoes, however, are linked to the paradigm established by *Carmen*, which *Tiefland* consciously but subtly evokes. The setting in Spain automatically lends the work an element of the exotic, while the plight of Marta, the victim of an erotically obsessed male, Sebastiano, suggests the similar situation of Carmen confronting Don José. The sexual triangle of Marta/Pedro/Sebastiano in *Tiefland* parallels that of Carmen/Don José/Escamillo in outline. The strong emphasis on honor is common to both *Carmen* and *Tiefland*, while the famous episode of Marta's dance to the guitar in *Tiefland* recalls the performance of Carmen in Bizet's Act II. Marta is surrounded by female associates just as is Carmen in the opera, and the hostility of Don José and Escamillo anticipates that between Pedro and Sebastiano. Furthermore, as dissimilar as Marta and Carmen are in character, both long for freedom from the constraints imposed on them by tyrannous males.

D'Albert is careful to incorporate these parallels without stressing them, for *Tiefland* also strives to distinguish itself from *Carmen*. For example, no Roma appear in *Tiefland*; Marta does not embrace the sexual freedom of Carmen; and in the end, unlike Carmen, Marta survives to find a new life in the mountains with Pedro who, unlike Don José, lives to be the heroic rescuer of his beloved. In its revised version, *Tiefland* exhibits the flashing intensity of works in the veristic tradition rather than the extended form of *Carmen*.

Even with these differences, however, *Tiefland* unquestionably evokes the tradition of *espagnolisme* during the nineteenth century, subtly engaging Beethoven, Donizetti, Verdi and Bizet. D'Albert's genius was in taking the Catalan drama *Terra baixa* (The Lowlands) by Angel Guimerà and welding it to the tradition of Spanish subject opera.

In this process, d'Albert found an invaluable method of construction in the other key tradition contributing to *Tiefland*—verismo. Here, the composer had a range of distinguished examples before him, including Mascagni's *Cavalleria Rusticana*, Leoncavallo's *Pagliacci* (1892), Puccini's *La Bohème* (1896) and *Tosca* (1901), Giordano's Andrea Chenier (1896), and Massenet's *La Navarraise* (1894). The setting of *La Navarraise* in the Basque provinces of the Pyrenees specifically anticipates the locale of *Tiefland*.

Verismo or realism takes its origin from the French literary movement known as naturalism, summarized in Émile Zola's manifesto *The Experimental Novel*, in which he argued that writers must study man in society like scientists—coolly, objectively, clinically. In Zola this took the form of concentrating on the lower classes rather than the nobility, as with the laundress of *L'Assommoir* (1877) or the courtesan of *Nana* (1880). In Italy, Zola's ideas influenced the work of Giovanni Verga, who published a collection of stories, *Vita dei Campi* (Life in the Fields) in 1880, one of which was the "Cavalleria Rusticana" that inspired Mascagni's opera. Verga aspired to study characters he called "i vinti" or the vanquished, people of lowly estate ground down by life, such as Sicilian peasants, impoverished farmers and other outcasts.

Verismo in opera meant that the characters would be from "ordinary life" rather than from mythology or royalty. As with the seamstress Mimi of *La Bohème*, the poor traveling players of *Pagliacci* or the abandoned "fallen" Santuzza of *Cavalleria Rusticana*, so in *Tiefland* d'Albert concentrates on the plight of Marta, an orphaned girl whose poverty leads to her seduction by the authoritarian and brutal mill-owner Sebastiano. Just as Verga's peasants suffer at the hands of landlords, so too do the workers under Sebastiano, one of whom, Moruccio, rebels against this economic exploitation.

Tiefland exhibits its veristic inheritance in other dimensions. The triangulated love affair of Marta/Pedro/Sebastiano evokes similar situations with Nedda/Canio/Silvio of *Pagliacci*, Lola/Turiddu/Alfio of *Cavalleria Rusticana*, or, in loftier circles, Tosca/Cavaradossi/Scarpia of *Tosca*, while strikingly anticipating the Giorgetta/Luigi/Michele of Puccini's *Il Tabarro* of 1918. Elements of local color infiltrate veristic opera to give it a strong sense of location, as with the guitar music of Sebastiano's "Tanzlied" or the horns of the prelude connoting the Pyrenees. The time of the action, as in many verismo works, is "the present."

It goes without saying that verismo is often marked by violent episodes: Turiddu is slain by Alfio at the conclusion of *Cavalleria*, Michele slays Luigi in *Tabarro*, Canio kills Nedda and Silvio in *Pagliacci*, while all three principals are destroyed in *Tosca*. In *Tiefland*, when Pedro strangles Sebastiano at the end, veristic violence is affirmed. As in his treatment of the *Carmen* model, however, d'Albert confronts the veristic code with a subtle difference—in *Tiefland* the lovers Marta and Pedro *live* at the end.

In constructing his opera, d'Albert also drew on strong symbolic precedents. For example, in the name of his characters he evokes the quality of his patron saint, the rock on which Christ would build his church. Note Pedro's piety as evinced by his prayers in the opening scene. His passage from loyalty to repudiation to loyalty in his relationship with Marta alludes to the disciple Peter's similar movement from loyalty to denial to loyalty in his affiliation with Jesus.

As a shepherd, Pedro suggests the Good Shepherd, who saves one of the flock—Marta—who has been lost. Marta in her serving of food to Pedro and attention to domesticity suggests her biblical prototype (Martha), who served Jesus the Passover supper at Bethany. According to some legends, Martha influenced the conversion of Mary Magdalene, so d'Albert's heroine combines the domestic with the fallen woman.

D'Albert also develops the symbolism of both mountain and wolf. Traditionally, the mountain stands for constancy, firmness, idealism, aspiration and repudiation of material greed. The title *Tiefland* or the "lowlands" therefore alludes to a symbolic geography: the lowland is marked by greed, exploitation, suffering, hypocrisy, violence, materialism, dishonesty and moral anarchy. As such, it contrasts with the pastoral rectitude of the mountain embodied in Pedro, the Good Shepherd who protects his flock.

At the end of Act I, through his famous "Wolfserzählung" or narration of his fight with the wolf, Pedro reveals himself as the rock or shelter (Schutz) he will be labeled by Marta in Act II. The bloody coin with which Sebastiano rewards him for killing the wolf shows the corruption of the lowland world invading the idealized mountainous stronghold. The wolf, traditionally the symbol of evil, rapaciousness, lust, craftiness and cruelty, connotes Sebastiano himself, as Pedro declares after killing him: "The wolf is dead, and I have killed him."

By its very title, *Tiefland* evokes the long tradition of pastoral in European culture. Alexander Pope's definition of pastoral (in his *Discourse on Pastoral* of 1704)—"an imitation of the action of a shepherd or one considered under that character"—precisely defines the nature of *Tiefland*. Pastoral juxtaposes two worlds, the simple country life of the shepherd (here the highlands) and the disturbed world of commerce/city (the lowlands). At its conclusion, *Tiefland* emphatically endorses the ethical values of the pastoral world and rejects those of the urban milieu. Pedro exults in his final words that he will depart "Away up in my mountains/Away to light and freedom!"

In doing so, he espouses the ethical system of pastoral: contentment with little, freedom from economic constraints, avoidance of greedy ambition, the preference for contemplation rather than action, and above all contentment, that is, the equating of necessity with desire. The several references to Pedro and his slinging of a stone evoke the biblical David who slew Goliath. Pedro, after slaying his Goliath Sebastiano, becomes a later David, the shepherd/king of his mountain realm.

D'Albert's *Tiefland* remains the one indisputable masterpiece of German verismo. The key to this endurance is its amazing synthesis of pastoral, verismo and *espagnolisme*: the German *Carmen*, yes, but absolutely unique.

All My Soul:
Massenet and *Werther*

"I scarcely had the book in my hands than I was eager to read it, so we went into one of those immense beer halls that are everywhere in Germany. We sat down and ordered two enormous bocks. It is needless to tell what I endured in that thick, foul air, laden with the bitter odor of beer. But I could not stop reading those burning letters, full of the most intense passion." So wrote Massenet in his *Recollections* about the summer of 1886. The "burning letters" were those of Goethe's *Die Leiden des Jungen Werthers* (*The Sorrows of Young Werther*), which had shocked not only Germany but the world when it appeared in 1774. Massenet's publisher, Georges Hartmann, achieved a major coup: Massenet had wanted to write a *La Bohème* based on Henri Mürger's novel, but his shrewd advisor had other plans. When Hartmann and Massenet went to Bayreuth for *Parsifal* in 1886, Hartmann led Massenet to Wetzlar, to the very house where Goethe had created *Young Werther*. Pulling the book from his pocket at this strategic moment, Hartmann gave Massenet the text that led to one of his greatest operas.

The effect of that turbulent reading remained. Massenet noted, "Such delirious, exotic passion brought tears to my eyes. What a moving scene, what a passionate picture that ought to make! It was *Werther*, my third act." A century after the appearance of *Young Werther* in Germany, its legacy was reborn—in France.

It is one of the peculiarities of opera history that the works of Johann Wolfgang von Goethe have achieved immortality through foreign, not German, composers. From his *Faust* (1808) derived Berlioz's *Damnation de Faust* (1846) Gounod's *Faust* (1859) and Busoni's *Doktor Faust* (1925). From *Wilhelm Meister's Apprenticeship* (1795) came *Mignon* (1866) by Ambroise Thomas, a strong early supporter of Massenet who secured the libretto for the latter's first opera, *La Grand'tante* (1867). Through *Mignon* Massenet had his first glimpse of Goethe. That glimpse later became a vision.

Massenet's initial reaction to Goethe's novel in 1886 practically duplicates the hysterical response to the novel when it was published in 1774. The events it chronicles have their origin in May 1772, when Goethe, at the vulnerable age of twenty-two, came as a young lawyer to the Supreme Court in Wetzlar. Scarcely a few weeks had passed before he became overwhelmed through a fateful meeting on June 9 at a dance in the small village of Volpertshausen. There he met Charlotte Buff and fell instantly in love with her. He did not know, however, that she had been betrothed for over a year to Johann Christian Kestner, secretary to one of the embassies at Wetzlar. Goethe's discovery of this engagement was traumatic.

In his *Autobiography*, Goethe left graphic accounts of Charlotte Buff and Kestner when he first knew them. His praise of Charlotte was the origin of the woman in both *Young Werther* and in Massenet's *Werther*: "She belonged to those who, if they do not inspire ardent passion, are nevertheless formed to create a general feeling of pleasure. A figure lightly built and neatly formed; a pure, healthy temperament, with a glad activity of life resulting from it; an unembarrassed management of the necessities of the day—all these were given her." Of Kestner, who became Massenet's Albert and whom Goethe called the Bridegroom, he claimed, "He distinguished himself by a calm, agreeable deportment, clearness of views, definiteness both in speaking and in acting." Of himself, whom Goethe called the Newcomer, the account was more devastating: "He quietly went his way but was soon so drawn in and riveted that he no longer knew himself." By September, Goethe's state was so desperate at realizing Charlotte loved Kestner that he left Wetzlar.

Goethe, however, maintained an intense correspondence with Kestner and Charlotte, which proved prophetic. In the fall of 1772, Goethe learned from Kestner that their friend Karl Wilhelm Jerusalem had, on October 30, committed suicide. Jerusalem, whom Goethe had known as a student at Leipzig, had become a secretary at Wetzlar, where he fell hopelessly in love with the wife of a colleague. In his *Autobiography*, Goethe recalled Jerusalem in a famous outfit: "His dress was that introduced in Lower Germany in imitation of the English—a blue frock coat, waistcoat and breeches of yellow leather, and boots with brown tops." Of Jerusalem's temperament, Goethe observed, "He lived for himself and his own sentiments." Kestner's account of Jerusalem's death supplied many of the details of Werther's suicide in *Young Werther*. As if Goethe's state of mind were not sufficiently distressed, Kestner married Charlotte in April 1773. In a supremely masochistic gesture, Goethe ordered their wedding rings.

Jerusalem's death, Goethe wrote, "stirred me to passionate emotion, with all the fire that leaves no distinction between the poetical and the actual. I completely isolated myself. Under such circumstances, I wrote *Werther* in four weeks, without any scheme of the whole, or previous work on any part. I had written almost unconsciously, as if in a trance." On September 29, 1774, the work appeared in Leipzig. To understand Massenet's reaction to *Young Werther*, it is crucial to grasp the Germany that it stunned.

"When I was eighteen, Germany was only eighteen itself—a man could do something," declared Goethe in old age. The 1770s in Germany are characterized as the period of *Sturm und Drang*, "storm and stress," a time of extreme reaction to the Enlightenment or *Aufklärung*. Whereas the Enlightenment had praised reason and discipline, writers of the *Sturm und Drang* glorified feeling, independence and individualism. "We wanted to live, not learn" became their credo. Under the influence of Johann Herder, the German philosopher; Samuel Richardson, the author of *Clarissa*; and Jean-Jacques Rousseau, creator of *The New Heloise* and the famous *Confessions*, Goethe became an impassioned advocate of emotionalism, primitivism, revolt against authority and rapturous adoration of nature. The reaction to the book was extraordinary. Goethe remembered, "The effect of this book was great, nay immense, and chiefly because it exactly hit the temper of the times. For as it requires but a little match to blow up an immense mine, so the explosion that followed my book was mighty, from the circumstance that the youthful world had already undermined itself; the shock was great, because all extravagant demands, unsatisfied passions and imaginary wrongs were suddenly brought to an eruption." This was the mood of *Weltschmerz*, or discontented "weariness of life." Thomas Carlyle accurately described the situation: "*Werther* is but the cry of that dim, rooted pain under which all thoughtful men of a certain age were languishing; it paints the misery, it passionately utters the complaint, and heart and voice all over Europe respond to it." The causes of *Weltschmerz* were not far to seek. The Industrial Revolution began to despoil nature and then demean the individual. Doubt assailed religion. The individual lost his or her way in a world of change. Goethe wrote that he was surprised when people believed that "the moral of *Young Werther* was to be imitated, and that at any rate one ought to shoot oneself," but such in fact began to happen after the appearance of the novel. Men and women disillusioned with the world and themselves committed suicide with the text of *Young Werther* open to chapter and verse. In England in 1784 a woman committed suicide with a copy of *Werther* under her pillow. When her death became known, this detail was emphasized "in order, if possible, to defeat the evil tendencies of that pernicious work." In a brief poem appended to the second printing, Goethe has Werther's ghost say, "Be a man, and do not follow me."

Massenet's reaction to reading *Young Werther*, however, is directly in line with what Goethe began to realize as he grew older. To his secretary, J. P. Eckermann, Goethe confided: "If one examines it closely, the much talked-of Age of Werther, it is true, does not belong to the course of world culture, but rather to the life process of every individual who, with a free and innate sense of nature, seeks to find himself and adapt to the restrictive forms of a world grown old. Thwarted happiness, hampered activity, ungratified desires—these are not the infirmities of a particular period but of every single human being."

How closely Massenet identified with the protagonist of Goethe's novel is evident from the fact that *Werther* is one of his few operas with a male central character. When he returned from Germany, Massenet set intensely to work after receiving the libretto from Edouard Blau and Paul Milliet, with assistance from the ever watchful Hartman. Massenet had virtually original territory, for only Rodolphe Kreutzer, with *Charlotte et Werther* in 1792, had used the material for an opera.

This was a happy time for Massenet: "I was now all life and happiness. I was wrapped up in work and in an almost feverish activity. It was a task I wanted to do, but into which I had to put if possible the song of those moving, lively passions." Since *Young Werther* is a *Bildungsroman* or "novel of growth," Massenet had to depict this passionate evolution in a highly compressed structure. Hoping for a premiere in 1887 at the Opéra Comique, he orchestrated the work in less than six months. How engrossed he was with *Werther* is evident from his *Recollections*: "Four works above all others in my long career gave me such joy in the doing that I freely describe it as exquisite: *Marie-Magdeleine, Werther, Sapho* and *Thérèse*." Such joy, however, was mixed with Massenet's awareness, strikingly similar to Goethe's own experience, that "Into *Werther* I put all my soul and artistic conscience."

The libretto is among the finest derived from a literary masterpiece. Stanislavsky, rehearsing a performance of *Werther* in Moscow, went so far as to claim the drama of the opera was "invented by Goethe *and* Massenet," an exceptional tribute: "Goethe has given you the words, Massenet the rhythm."

An epistolary novel, *Young Werther* is divided into two parts. In the first, composed of letters to Werther's friend Wilhelm and a few to Charlotte, Goethe reveals his protagonist clearly: his attraction to nature, his Rousseauistic praise of children and rural life, his sense of alienation, his melancholy, his undisciplined passion and his feeling of imprisonment by society. If Part I of *Young Werther* involves the rural values and qualities of Oliver Goldsmith's *Deserted Village* and *Vicar of Wakefield*, Part II derives more from the "Graveyard School" of eighteenth-century English poetry, including Edward Young's "Night Thoughts," Robert Blair's "The Grave," Thomas Warton's "Pleasures of Melancholy" and Thomas Gray's famed "Elegy Written in a Country Churchyard." These poems, with their

Weltschmerz and disillusionment, had a peculiar appeal not only for Goethe but for Massenet's world, the Belle Epoque, since France was experiencing a terrible *fin de siècle* crisis following the disastrous Franco-Prussian War of 1870 and the dehumanization of modern industrialism.

In Massenet's *Werther*, Act I directly invokes the first part of Goethe's novel. Scarcely a single detail is accidental: the fountain that is part of the setting is a crucial *Sturm und Drang* symbol of overflowing self-expression and freedom; the garden is an image of free natural beauty as opposed to urban corruption. The introduction of the children evokes the Rousseauistic qualities of the "Noble Savage" and education by nature expressed in *Emile*. It is no accident that Werther appears onstage with a peasant or that he sings "Je ne sais si je veille" in front of the fountain. This aria is a direct adaptation of many expressions in *Young Werther*: "Many a man before me has felt that life is but a dream, and this feeling attends me constantly. I turn back upon myself and find a world!" The letter of May 10 contains the same images as the aria—a cascading brook, the rays of the sun and particularly the "impenetrable darkness" and half-light cherished by the *Sturm und Drang*. Likewise, Charlotte's devotion to the children derives from the rural virtue worshiped by Rousseau.

In Act I a striking philosophic clash results from the placement of Albert's aria ("Elie m'aime") just before the famous Clair de Lune ("Il faut nous séparer") at the return of Charlotte and Werther from the dance. In contrast to Albert, Werther here uses expressions like "mon être" and "mon âme" derived from the hallmark word of the *Sturm und Drang*, "Seele"— "soul" or "being." Based directly on the novel, Charlotte's long description of her mother ("Mes enfants . . . vous avez dit vrai!/Si vous l'aviez connue!") wonderfully contrasts her unselfishness with Werther's self-indulgence. Her query "Pourquoi tout est-il périssable?" indicates the influence of the "Graveyard" poets. When Werther learns she is betrothed, his reaction is typical *Sturm und Drang*: "Moi, j'en mourrai, Charlotte!" One crucial element Massenet changed to accord with Goethe's, not Werther's, life: in the novel Werther knows Charlotte is betrothed before he sees her; in actuality and in the opera, he learns this only after he is disastrously in love.

The atmosphere of *Young Werther* and the *Sturm und Drang* penetrates

Act II of Werther, perfectly anticipated by the impassioned crescendo of "Douce extase!" from Act I. Particularly important in the second act is Werther's Désolation, "Un autre est son époux!" Here the mood of *Weltschmerz/fin de siècle* is evident in Werther's despair at the insufficiency of existence. For the first time, Massenet universalizes the issues of *Werther*: the futility of Werther's love for Charlotte symbolizes his despondency at existence itself. Capturing the essence of Goethe's novel, Werther's reactions "J'ai peur de blasphémer!" and "Tout man corps en frissonne, et tout man être en pleure!" derive from the novel's letters of August 21 and November 15, detailing Werther's alienation from God and religion. In *Young Werther*, in the letter of November 30, Werther cries, "God in Heaven! Have You so decreed men's fate that they are happy only before they attain the state of reason? Wretched Man!" This same letter supplies the famous image of the Prodigal Son during Werther's consideration of suicide in "Lorsque l'enfant revient d'un voyage."

The greatest changes Massenet effected from Goethe's *Young Werther* appear in Acts III and IV of *Werther*. Though in the novel Charlotte asks Werther to remain away until Christmas Eve, a detail Massenet retains, in the novel he returns on December 21, so distraught he is unable to accede to her request. In the novel Goethe creates the character of an Editor who assembles Werther's papers to reconstruct the suicide, a function Massenet in a brilliant decision gives to Charlotte, who collects Werther's letters in her famous scene ("Qui m'aurait dit/Ces lettres!") Here it is clear that Massenet's Charlotte loves Werther, whereas in Goethe there is great sisterly concern but never sexual love. In this single respect Massenet's Werther, unlike Goethe's, is more fortunate, since he receives love from Charlotte before his death. By changing the date of Werther's death from Goethe's December 22 to Christmas Eve, Massenet also alters one of Goethe's intentions, to have Werther die on the longest night of the year.

The crucial episode leading to the Lied d'Ossian ("Pourquoi me réveiller?") is taken directly from the novel as recounted by the Editor. Massenet uses only the final selection, "Why do you wake me?" of Goethe's extensive quotations from James Macpherson's *Poems of Ossian* (1763). Massenet's condensation produces an intensity the novel fails to achieve, especially by evoking the conflict between waking and dreaming from Act I. Goethe's Werther writes that his death will be a protest and an exultation: "What does it mean that Albert is your husband?" he writes to Charlotte. "Husband? That is something for this world—and for this world it is a sin that I love you. Sin? Very well! And I am punishing myself for it—I have tasted this sin in all it heavenly bliss. I am going ahead, going to my Father. I will complain to Him." As in the novel, Massenet's Werther then requests the pistols with a note about this "long journey," following the paradigm of the Prodigal Son returning to his father.

Act IV is almost entirely Massenet's creation. In Goethe, Charlotte never attends the dying Werther; it is Albert who goes with the doctor to find the dead Werther, "fully dressed, wearing his boots, his blue coat and yellow vest." Massenet supplies some final solace for his Werther when Charlotte in Act IV confesses her love, giving him a dying kiss as the children's Christmas song ("Jésus vient de naître!") harshly contrasts Christ's birth and Werther's death to emphasize Werther's exclusion and alienation. Werther's final words in the opera, about his burial near the linden trees and the passing of the priest, come directly from the last letter he sends Charlotte in Goethe's *Young Werther*. In the novel one learns of Charlotte's fate only the enigmatic fact that "Lotte's life was feared to be in danger." The two final sentences of the novel are stark: "Workmen carried him. No clergyman accompanied him." Whatever Goethe's disclaimer, Werther's suicide in the context of *Sturm und Drang* came to stand for an ultimate act of defiance, revolt and individualism.

At the end of their respective centuries, both Massenet and Goethe seized the universal feeling of malaise. About *Young Werther* Goethe remarked, "I fed him with my own blood," and to the end of his days he could not reread it. "It is a mass of explosives, and I am distressed when I look at it. I dread lest I should once more experience the pathological state that produced it." Still, Werther's name (Wert=worth) implies he is valued, even honorable, in his defiant individualism.

Massenet's opera was to be strangely connected with Goethe's own life as the result of such *Sturm und Drang*: on the same evening as the Vienna premiere of *Werther*, a grandson of Charlotte's, George Kestner, committed suicide. Furthermore, when *Werther* was first performed in Leipzig, the title role was sung by a tenor named Buff, a grandnephew of Goethe's Charlotte. Massenet had done as he said: "Into *Werther* I put all my soul."

Glossary

A Cappella (Italian (It) "in chapel style")—vocal music without instrumental accompaniment.

Aria (It)—a solo song; melodic composition for solo voice with instrumental accompaniment, generally elaborate and complete enough in itself that it can be excerpted from the opera of which it is part and performed separately.

Aria Cantabile (It)—a quiet, flowing, lyrical aria expressing tenderness or pathos. aria di bravura—a difficult aria showing a display of vocal virtuosity or technical prowess. arietta—a short aria or song in more or less simple style.

Baritone, Barytone (French (Fr)), **Baritono** (It)—the male voice between bass and tenor, with a compass between low G and G two octaves above. A low baritone is sometimes called a bass baritone.

Bass, Basse (Fr), **Basso** (It)—the lowest male voice, with a compass between low E and the E or F two octaves above. Basso profondo is the deepest bass voice. Basso buffo is a bass comedian.

Bel Canto (It) "beautiful song")—term applied to the traditional Italian manner of cultivating and using the voice, and to the operas where this technique is required. In bel canto primary consideration is the beauty of vocal tone; dramatic concepts are secondary.

Buffo (It)—male singer who takes comic parts in opera.

Bravo (It)—shout of approval meaning "well done!" Brava may be used if the performer is a female, or bravi if intended for more than one artist, but bravo as an exclamation is appropriate for all occasions.

Bravissimo (It)—"bravo" in the highest degree; singularly outstanding.

Brindisi (It)—a drinking song.

Cabaletta (It)—the short final section, usually more rapid, of an aria.

Cadenza (It)—in opera, the florid, ornamental passage immediately preceding the final cadence—often left to the skill or caprice of the performer.

Cantilena (It/Spanish (Sp))—smooth, lyrical melody. May be an entire aria or just a phrase.

Canzona (Sp), **Canzone** (It)—a song with a melodious folk-like quality.

Cavatina (It), **Cavatine** (Fr)—smooth, melodious air distinguishable from the normal aria by its simplicity.

Chest tone, Chest voice—the lowest sound in the range of the voice, which differs from the clear tone quality of the opposing "head voice." In a contralto these often sound mannish and different in quality from the notes above.

Chorus, Core (It), **Choeur** (Fr)—company of singers who do not sing solos but perform concerted vocal numbers. Chorister is an individual member of the chorus; chorus master is the director and leader of the chorus.

Coloratura (It)—vocal music in the head register which is ornamental so that several notes are sung for each syllable of the text. Coloratura soprano is a high, clear soprano with vocal capabilities often exceeding high C, and ability to produce the coloratura ornamentation.

Comprimario (It)—singer who supports lead singers or performs character roles.

Contralto or Alto (It)—lowest of the three types of female voice, the others being soprano and mezzo-soprano. Voice extends from the F or G below middle C upwards for two octaves.

Corps de Ballet (Fr)—the company of dancers who perform ballet and pantomime sequences in opera.

Ensemble—vocal number requiring more than one performer.

Entr'acte—orchestral music played between the acts of an opera. finale—the conclusion, usually elaborate, at the close of an act.

Grand Opera—usually, a serious opera with no spoken dialogue; more broadly, any opera sung and produced in the "grand manner".

Head Voice—the upper register of the voice, with clearer quality, as opposed to the chest voice.

Heldentenor (German (Ger))—a dramatic tenor (see tenor), typical in Wagnerian opera.

Intermezzo (It)—originally the musical part of a dramatic entertainment introduced between the acts of operas. In the 19th century, "intermezzo" came to be used to designate an instrumental work between opera acts, often with completely new and different musical material.

Leitmotiv (Ger), Leading Motive—a theme of recognizable melodic or rhythmic identity first used in connection with certain character or incident and which returns time and again with a reminiscence of the original association.

Libretto (It "booklet")—the text of an opera; the book in which the text is written.

Librettist—writer of a libretto.

Melodrama—in opera, a scene in which the actor recites his part while the orchestra comments on the situation.

Mezzo-Soprano (It)—the second of the three female voices, lower than soprano and higher than contralto.

Opera—Rousseau's definition: "A dramatic and lyric spectacle in which one endeavors to combine all the graces of the fine arts in the representation of a passionate action, with the intention of arousing interest and creating illusion by means of pleasant sensations."

Opera Buffa (It), **Opera Bouffe** (Fr)—farcical comedy opera; what we call comic opera. Italian style has dry recitative, French has spoken dialogue.

Opera Comique (Fr)—any opera, even serious operas, with spoken dialogue rather than any sung recitative.

Opera Seria (It)—opera with a serious theme, where all dialogue is recitative, and the ensembles usually elaborate.

Operetta—a small, light opera similar to opera buffa with spoken text. Approaches musical comedy or vaudeville and does not have the elaborate score of the true light opera.

Overture, Ouverture (Fr), **Overtura** (It)—the elaborate prelude to an opera, often making use of thematic material from the body of the opera.

Pastorale, Pastourelle (Fr)—sequence within opera, or short entertainment of a rustic nature or subject.

Phrasing—the act or art of delivering music with due regard to its melody and rhythmic punctuation, relation, and contrast.

Portamento (It)—a singer's legato (smooth, unbroken) style and technique.

Prima Donna (It)—"leading lady" in opera; the chief soprano.

Quartet, Quartetto (It)—composition for four singers.

Quintet, Quintetto (It)—composition for five singers.

Recitative, Recitativo (It)—musical declamation recitation; "sung dialogue" as opposed to the strict melody of aria and ensemble. There is secco ("dry") recitative, in which the singer is accompanied only by occasional chords to keep the key; and accompanied recitative or recitative stromentato, in which the rhythm follows a more definite pattern and the accompaniment fuller and more complete.

Scenario (It)—a preliminary sketch of the scenes and main points of libretto.

Scenic Designer/Set Designer—the artist who designs the scenery and who thereby visually interprets the emphases of the opera, working in collaboration with the stage director, and consulting with lighting and costume designers to produce a visually effective entirety. He oversees the construction of the sets, the collocation of properties, and the movements necessary to alter sets between acts or scenes.

Sextet, Sestetto (It)—composition for six singers.

Singspiel (Ger)—German opera with spoken dialogue alternating with arias and ensembles.

Soprano—the highest kind of human voice, typically the highest female voice. Dramatic soprano is the more powerful, heavier soprano, while lyric soprano is the lighter, more flexible voice.

Sotto Voce (It)—in an undertone; quietly; an aside.

Soubrette (Fr)—an opera comedienne, calling for a fresh, light soprano voice.

Stage Director, Regista (It)—the professional who oversees the dramatic presentation of an opera, turning concert into theater. He must interpret the demands of the opera libretto and arrange for the principals, chorus and supers to move or declaim in an effective, relevant manner.

Supernumeraries, Comparsi (It)—"supers" for short—costumed individuals in opera who do not sing but perform some needed function to the drama such as creating the appearance of multitudes or engaging in some stage activity such as portage of properties, bearing of weapons or assisting the principals in mechanical tasks.

Technical Director—director whose function is to oversee or provide a liaison between the designers (scenic, lighting, etc.) and stage director on the one hand, and the stage management responsible for execution of their creative ideas on the other.

Tenor, Tenore (It)—the highest natural adult male voice. The Dramatic Tenor is a robust, powerful tenor with "heroic" quality, while the Lyric Tenor is the lighter, more facile tenor.

Terzetto (It)—same as trio; that is, a composition for three singers.

Tessitura (It)—the general "lie" of a song or phrase; its average pitch.

Tutti (It "all")—all the principals and chorus together; the entire company.

Vibrato (It)—vocal trembling of a note, consisting of slight variations in pitch.

Zarzuela (Sp)—a form of Spanish opera with spoken dialogue among set arias and ensembles. The genero chico is the one act comic zarzuela, while the zarzuela grande may have two or three acts and be either comic or serious. Example, Breton's *La Dolores*.

Operas by Composer

Franco Alfano (1875-1954)
Risurrezione

Georges Bizet (1838-1875)
Carmen
The Pearl Fishers

Eugen d'Albert 1864-1932)
Tiefland

Gaetano Donizetti (1797-1848)
Lucia di Lammermoor

W.S. Gilbert (1836-1911)
Arthur Sullivan (1842-1900)
Patience

Umberto Giordano (1867-1948)
Andrea Chénier

Charles Gounod (1818-1893)
Roméo et Juliette

Ruggero Leoncavallo (1857-1919)
Pagliacci

Pietro Mascagni (1863-1945)
Cavalleria Rusticana

Jules Massenet (1842-1912)
Don Quichotte
Thaïs
Werther

Wolfgang Amadeus Mozart
(1756-1791)
Cosi fan Tutte
Don Giovanni

Francis Poulenc (1899-1963)
Dialogues des Carmelite

Giacomo Puccini (1858-1924)
Il Tabarro
La Bohème
Madama Butterfly

Camille Saint-Saëns (1835-1921)
Samson et Delilah

Richard Strauss (1864-1949)
Ariadne auf Naxos
Elektra
Salome

Pyotr Ilyich Tchaikovsky
(1840-1893)
Eugene Onegin
Pique Dame

Giuseppe Verdi (1813-1901)
Aïda
Hernani
La Traviata
Macbeth
Rigoletto

Richard Wagner (1813-1883)
Lohengrin
Parsifal
Tannhäuser
The Flying Dutchman

Riccardo Zandonai (1883-1944)
Francesca de Rimin

Acknowledgements

With his background of study in Classics and Victorian literature, interest in art history, gender, and cinema, as well as a contagious enthusiasm for the art form, Joseph Kestner brought a varied interdisciplinary and unique approach to his writings on opera. After his sudden death, it seemed important to gather together these writings to publish and preserve them for fellow opera lovers and students.

This book would not have been possible without the help and guidance of many friends and associates. I want to express my gratitude to Dr. Joseph Willis for encouraging me to find a publisher; Rachel G. Caldwell for help organizing materials; Russell Renfrow for invaluable technical assistance; Dr. Robert Spoo and Dr.Carol Kealiher for their advice and kind words.

Thanks to *Opera News*, *The Washington Opera*, *Houston Grand Opera*, and *The Dallas Opera Magazine* for providing the original homes for these essays.

Unending gratitude to publisher extraordinaire Shawn Crawford, for his original approach, creative ideas, kind guidance and infinite patience.

Anna Norberg

The Calliope Group would like to thank Julia Crawford and Nick Alexandrov for their considerable editorial assistance. A special thanks to Anna Norberg for trusting Calliope with this project.

CPSIA information can be obtained
at www.ICGtesting.com
Printed in the USA
LVHW100742251022
731430LV00004B/47